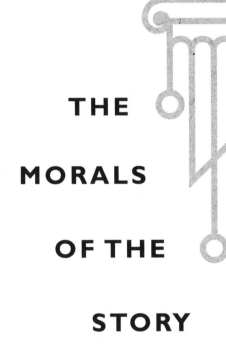

# THE
# MORALS
# OF THE
## GOOD NEWS
## ABOUT A
## GOOD GOD
# STORY

## DAVID BAGGETT AND
## MARYBETH BAGGETT

## IVP Academic
An imprint of InterVarsity Press
Downers Grove, Illinois

*InterVarsity Press*
*P.O. Box 1400, Downers Grove, IL 60515-1426*
*ivpress.com*
*email@ivpress.com*

*InterVarsity Press® is the book-publishing division of InterVarsity Christian Fellowship/USA®, a movement of students and faculty active on campus at hundreds of universities, colleges, and schools of nursing in the United States of America, and a member movement of the International Fellowship of Evangelical Students. For information about local and regional activities, visit intervarsity.org.*

*While any stories in this book are true, some names and identifying information may have been changed to protect the privacy of individuals.*

*Cover design: David Fassett*
*Interior design: Daniel van Loon*
*Images: speckled background: © GOLDsquirrel / iStock / Getty Images*
      *Greek column: © sumkinn / iStock / Getty Images Plus*

*ISBN 978-0-8308-5207-9 (print)*
*ISBN 978-0-8308-8649-4 (digital)*

*Printed in the United States of America* ♾

*InterVarsity Press is committed to ecological stewardship and to the conservation of natural resources in all our operations. This book was printed using sustainably sourced paper.*

**Library of Congress Cataloging-in-Publication Data**

*A catalog record for this book is available from the Library of Congress.*

| **P** | 23 | 22 | 21 | 20 | 19 | 18 | 17 | 16 | 15 | 14 | 13 | 12 | 11 | 10 | 9 | 8 | 7 | 6 | 5 | 4 | 3 | 2 | 1 |
|---|---|---|---|---|---|---|---|---|---|---|---|---|---|---|---|---|---|---|---|---|---|---|---|
| **Y** | 38 | 37 | 36 | 35 | 34 | 33 | 32 | 31 | 30 | 29 | 28 | 27 | 26 | 25 | 24 | 23 | 22 | 21 | 20 | 19 | 18 | | |

TO JAN AND WILLIAM LANE CRAIG

*Mere* morality *is not the end of life. You were made for something quite different from that. . . . The people who keep on asking if they can't lead a decent life without Christ, don't know what life is about; if they did they would know that "a decent life" is mere machinery compared with the thing we men are really made for. Morality is indispensable: but the Divine Life, which gives itself to us and which calls us to be gods, intends for us something in which morality will be swallowed up.*

C. S. LEWIS, *GOD IN THE DOCK*

# CONTENTS

# THE PLAYERS

It is our pleasure to thank various people who made this book possible. Some go without saying, of course: we'd be out of publishing luck save for Johannes Gutenberg, for example, and nonexistent without our great grandparents, and so on. But you'll understand that for convenience's sake, we've had to narrow down the list a bit.

At the risk of inflating his ego, we start with Jerry Walls. What follows is our attempt to distill quite a bit of material from two books that I (Dave) wrote with Jerry, *Good God* and *God and Cosmos*. His influence is felt on every page of this book, though he gave us his blessing to launch this project on our own. It would be impossible in a few words to communicate the depth of our indebtedness to this dear brother and friend, teacher and collaborator.

Many thanks to the editorial and production team at IVP Academic, who believed in this project from the start and gave it a chance to see the light of day, particularly David McNutt. Thanks as well to the two thoughtful, conscientious reviewers whose comments were invaluable in the revision process. They spared us from several oversights and infelicities and reminded us of a number of important points to bear in mind.

Thanks to all the contributors to MoralApologetics.com, who have enriched us by your wisdom and perspicacity, and to our colleagues and university administration for friendship, encouragement, and support. There is something of you all that fills this volume.

Special thanks to another old professor, Joe Dongell, whose insights on the biblical motif of life as an overarching theme helped shape part of our analysis. He is, God bless him, the one who first taught me (Dave)

New Testament Greek in his Asbury office around 1990, and we were excited to hear him at Eaton Rapids Camp Meeting (Michigan) in 2016. It was delightful to see him, all these years later, continuing to be such a blessing to others by his diligent study of Scripture.

We owe a special debt of gratitude to a kindred spirit, Corey Latta, for useful feedback on a portion of an early draft. It's our sincere hope that one day we will live in closer proximity to him so we can celebrate Festivus together. We have every intention of pinning him in a remarkable feat of strength and then to air our many grievances. In his name we recently made a contribution to The Human Fund: "Money for People." May we suggest that everyone do the same? Giddyup!

Deepest appreciation to Elton Higgs, fabulous friend and professor and mentor extraordinaire, for reading the entire manuscript and offering numerous helpful and perspicacious editing suggestions. He also, it should be recorded for posterity, vetted our jokes, putting the veritable kibosh on various and sundry ones. Much to our readers' chagrin, we stubbornly clung with more than a modicum of rapacious obstinacy to a few of our favorites—usually the most patently absurd.

Finally, the book is warmly dedicated to William Lane Craig and his wife, Jan, for their inspiration and faithful efforts in the work of ministry and courageous outreach.

# THE PLAYBILL

# OUR FOCUS AND
# INTENDED AUDIENCE

THIS BOOK ISN'T FOR EVERYONE. Dead people, for example. But it's for everyone else. Except zombies.

This extended essay is about moral arguments that God exists. Arguments of this stripe trace back to Plato, with contributions from Augustine, Aquinas, Immanuel Kant, C. S. Lewis, and many others besides. And so, now that the amateurs are done with it, we figured that it's high time for the professionals to clear this thing up once and for all.

Just kidding.

We intend to offer a rational defense of the faith. Ours will be an effort to identify, scrutinize, and defend a number of considerations that arguably weigh in favor of God's existence. By "God"[1] we will mean something very specific: the trinitarian God of the Bible. This means that this book will also be theological. Although this will be our ultimate destination, much of the book can be read with profit without initially assuming the biblical God. Our argument rarely appeals to biblical teaching; rather, we will be working primarily in the realm of what's called natural theology. This means that we will heavily rely on general revelation, what God has revealed about himself through nature and the human condition. General revelation contrasts with special revelation, such as the deliverances of the Bible. Limiting ourselves in this way, we

---

[1]Readers might be tempted to read something unintended into our quotation marks. We "assure" you that we would "never" employ "extraneous" scare "quotes."

obviously can't refer to all the features of New Testament theology. But if the God of the Bible makes the best sense of the moral picture that emerges, then the argument can provide reason to take such a depiction of God seriously. At certain points, too, we will show how elements of biblical theology can bolster the case we're building.

Enough about us; now we want to talk about *you*. What value does this book have for our readers? Who's our intended audience? First off, the book is (unapologetically) about apologetics. The term *apologetics* etymologically derives from the Greek ἀπολογία (transliterated *apologia*). To do apologetics is to speak in defense of something; to do moral apologetics in particular is to offer arguments based on morality for the existence of something, such as freedom or immortality. In the case of this book, moral apologetics will be specifically used to defend the existence of God, as presented in both classical monotheism (the belief that there is only one God) and Judeo-Christian Scripture.

Apologetics of various kinds sport a venerable history. One of the earliest and most significant uses of the term appears in Plato's *Apology*— the defense speech of Socrates during his trial. Apologetics has also been an important and honored practice from the earliest days of Christianity. Paul used the term in his trial speech to Festus and Agrippa when he said, "I am to make my defense" (Acts 26:2). Justin Martyr's two *Apologies* before an emperor and the Roman Senate further normalized the practice. William Lane Craig argues that apologetics today can still serve important purposes, including (1) shaping culture, (2) strengthening believers, and (3) evangelizing nonbelievers.[2] Doug Groothius in his *Christian Apologetics* anticipates and answers various objections to apologetics. He adduces no less than nine objections to natural theology and offers a refutation of each.[3]

Even still, apologetics does have its contemporary critics. Paul Moser, echoing the likes of Karl Barth, highlights some of the hubris,

---

[2]William Lane Craig, *Reasonable Faith: Christian Truth and Apologetics*, 3rd ed. (Wheaton, IL: Crossway, 2008), 15-23.
[3]Douglas Groothuis, *Christian Apologetics: A Comprehensive Case for Biblical Faith* (Downers Grove, IL: InterVarsity Press, 2011), 174-84.

overreaching, poor argumentation, and misguided efforts of certain professional or lay apologists in what he likes informally to call the "apologetics-industrial complex." Although Moser concedes that there are good arguments for the truth of theism and Christianity, he is nevertheless concerned with the ways in which they are often deployed today. Moser is a terrific philosopher, and his warnings are worth reading and occasionally humorous, but at least some of them leave us unpersuaded. Thus the book you hold in your hands.

Since the book is about apologetics, it also qualifies as a book about evangelism. To evangelize is to proclaim the good news of salvation, the historical message of Christianity. Apologetics can and often should play a part in that proclamation. Fulfilling the Great Commission (Mt 28:18-20) is a vital part of every Christian's calling in this world, and it's not a task to be taken lightly. On the other hand, neither should the charge to evangelize be seen as onerous. It is our hope that this book will take away some of the scariness and awkwardness often associated, fairly or not, with evangelism.[4]

Evangelism can come in different varieties, and apologetics is just one dimension of the task. If only for purposes of "seed planting," rational arguments in support of Christian doctrine are important resources to avail ourselves of. Ultimately, of course, evangelism is about sharing the good news of the gospel, encouraging and exhorting people to enter into a life-transforming relationship with God. But all sorts of questions potentially arise in these engagements: Who is God? Is there reason to think God exists? Does God love us? Is it rational to believe in God? These

---

[4]A substantive book on evangelism is William Abraham's seminal *The Logic of Evangelism*. Abraham sees with crystal clarity the need to connect evangelism with sturdy theology. "Reflection on evangelism forces us to wrestle with what the essence of Christianity is and with such topics as conversion, faith, and repentance; it leads us to come to terms with the nature of the kingdom of God and the place of the kingdom in the ministry of Jesus; it leads us to think deeply about the nature of baptism and of Christian initiation; it encourages us to explore the relation between the intellect and the emotions in Christian commitment; it draws us to examine how far the faith of the early centuries can be expressed in the modern world; it makes us tackle anew the nature of apologetics; it makes us focus on how far, if at all, theistic proposals are amenable to rational persuasion." See *The Logic of Evangelism* (Grand Rapids: Eerdmans, 1989), 11. We also recommend Mark R. Teasdale's *Evangelism for Non-Evangelists: Sharing the Gospel Authentically* (Downers Grove, IL: IVP Academic, 2016).

questions can't be responsibly ignored. Contending with such questions does not at all preclude the other aspects of evangelism of which Moser appropriately and powerfully writes.[5]

It's true that mere belief that God exists is hardly all that God wants from us—even the devils believe that (Jas 2:19)! Even still, the use of materials beyond those from personal experience or Scripture is appropriate to evangelism and apologetics. Indeed, Scripture itself seems to suggest the same. In Lystra, for example, Paul appeals to nature (Acts 14:8-14). In Romans 1:20 he writes that unbelievers are *anapologētous*—without excuse, defense, or apology—for rejecting the revelation of God in creation. Scripture itself appeals to general or natural revelation—distinct from revealed or special revelation—as evidentially significant.

In further consideration of Moser's critiques, however, the moral apologetics angle of this book invites a few interpretations. The first we have already mentioned: a moral argument for God's existence. But there's another, namely, doing apologetics *in a moral way.* This is a happy coincidence, since apologetics should certainly be done in a way that's respectful and bridge building.

Sometimes what makes effective sharing of the gospel difficult is the resistance people feel based on previous unpleasant experiences they may have had with heavy-handed, dogmatic, pedantic, self-righteous believers. David Horner distinguishes between two tasks in the apologetic and evangelistic endeavor: *credibility* and *plausibility*.[6] Making theism and Christianity credible involves giving reasons to think them true, whereas making them plausible helps people to think of them as *possibly* true. If someone, for whatever reason, doesn't think Christianity is even possibly true, then no number of credible reasons to believe will have much effect.

---

[5]See Paul Moser's "Death, Dying, and the Hiddenness of God," in *The Philosophy of Religion Reader*, ed. Chad Meister (London: Routledge, 2008), 613-24; and "Cognitive Idolatry and Divine Hiding," in *Divine Hiddenness*, ed. D. Howard-Snyder and Paul Moser (New York: Cambridge University Press, 2002), 120-48. Also see Paul Moser, *The Elusive God: Recovering Religious Epistemology* (Cambridge: Cambridge University Press, 2008). For an older source, see J. L. Schellenberg, *Divine Hiddenness and Human Reason* (Ithaca, NY: Cornell University Press, 1993).

[6]David Horner, "Too Good Not to Be True: A Call to Moral Apologetics as a Mode of Civil Discourse," *Moral Apologetics*, July 29, 2015, http://moralapologetics.com/too-good-not-to-be-true-a-call-to-moral-apologetics-as-a-mode-of-civil-discourse/.

Usually the forte of apologists is enhancing credibility, but some listeners with bad attitudes toward Christians may find Christianity implausible, not even possibly true. This is where doing apologetics in the right way—with kindness, gentleness, winsomeness—can help render the gospel plausible. It can also vividly remind us that Christianity is not merely a set of propositions to espouse but a transformed life to be lived. Horner argues that "although there is important work for moral apologetics to do at the levels of both credibility and plausibility, the need for making plausible the Christian worldview morally is particularly exigent at this time: softening the moral soil so that the seeds of the gospel may be able to penetrate."[7]

Most of the work this book will do pertains more to credibility, but remembering the dual meaning of moral apologetics can help apply Horner's point. Moral apologetics is as much about *winning people* as it is about *winning arguments*. The truth of humanity's moral situation matters, but we cannot pursue that by denying the dignity of others. We must be committed to upholding both.

Our contemporary moment highlights the challenge and the importance of handling disagreements well. The recent tension-filled election, for example, reminds us of the need to be tentative and provisional in presenting our argument in this book. In our estimation, too many rabid political partisans on both sides of the aisle went far beyond sharing their own convictions and why they held them. Their commitment to the truth and to promoting the conclusions they'd drawn often disrespected those who saw things differently. They tried to indict those with whom they disagreed, denying their discussion partners the mental freedom to think for themselves. In the process they aimed to function as the conscience of others. No matter the topic under discussion, such an approach is bound to backfire, to deepen divisions, and to create enemies rather than win others over. There is a better way.

One of the first steps, we think, is to keep fully in view the humanity of those we're engaging. Supreme Court justices Antonin Scalia and Ruth Bader Ginsburg offer a colorful example of how respect for the humanity

---

[7] Ibid.

of another can close the most gaping ideological divides. Ginsburg and Scalia's interpretations of jurisprudence and the Constitution often stood at odds, if not in diametric opposition. Yet, personally, they were the dearest of friends. On Scalia's recent death, Ginsburg offered this moving tribute: "He was, indeed, a magnificent [piano] performer. It was my great good fortune to have known him as working colleague and treasured friend."[8] For Ginsburg, Scalia's personhood came before his ideology, a model we would do well to emulate.

During my (Dave's) time at Wayne State, a heavily secular academic environment, I had staunch worldview disagreements with many of my colleagues and professors. Making my way through the program with my faith intact was challenging, but what helped was to recognize the shared endeavor we were undertaking and to see my interactions with those around me as a quest for cooperation, not confrontation. Personal collaborations and friendships with those I disagreed with prevented me from turning them into caricatures or demonizing their positions.

I remember one professor in particular, William Stine, for whom I house-sat quite often as we became friends. This personal interaction in no way obscured our real differences in belief, and much of Stine's influence on me was wielded in the throes of disagreement. In the midst of our protracted battle of ideas, I went to meet Dr. Stine one day as he was letting out a class. Knowing he loved the cleverly choreographed mini-drama, I was waiting outside, sitting cross-legged on the floor. As he came out into the hall, I immediately launched into a rhetorically rich passage from William James about Josiah Royce, whose philosophical ideas James vociferously rejected even while he retained a warm friendship with Royce. "You are still the centre of my gaze, the pole of my mental magnet. When I compose my Gifford lectures mentally, 'tis with the design exclusively of overthrowing your system, and ruining your peace. I lead a parasitic life upon you, for my highest flight of ambitious ideality is to become your conqueror, and go down into history as such."[9]

[8]Dara Lind, "Read Justice Ginsburg's Moving Tribute to Her 'Best Buddy' Justice Scalia," *Vox*, February 14, 2016, www.vox.com/2016/2/14/10990156/scalia-ginsburg-friends.
[9]William James, *The Letters of William James*, ed. Henry James (Boston: Atlantic Monthly, 1920), 2:135-36. This is in a letter from James to Royce dated Sept. 26, 1900.

To which Dr. Stine, in his inimitably and intentionally bombastic fashion, immediately replied, without so much as a moment's hesitation, "I would think that one reclining in the position of the Buddha would be more pacific."

Nobody we meet is ordinary. Every person contains an infinity of dignity and value, of depth and mystery. We all know this intuitively, but it's often easy, or at least tempting, to forget when disagreements are pronounced. But reducing others to the sum of their convictions is to make them smaller than they are, which should be carefully avoided, especially in our arguments about the truth.

I (Dave) have had the opportunity to try to get this right with a friend named John Shook, a smart and outspoken atheist. We met in Buffalo some years ago for a debate on God and morality. I did it with some fear and trembling because he had already debated with William Lane Craig. That night at the University at Buffalo we disagreed on most things— except how bad the decision was to cancel *Firefly* after thirteen episodes. We each walked away from the event with our basic convictions intact, but I also walked away respecting him. He's a good guy and cares about the truth, and I knew I wanted him to be a friend. We've stayed in touch and done some podcasts together. We've even discussed collaborating on a book. We still don't see eye to eye. Our discussion continues, but we agree on a lot of important things, and we see ourselves on a common pilgrimage. He's a friend and kindred spirit.

Rather than preaching to the proverbial choir, apologetics and evangelism involve conversations like this with those who see the world differently. Such conversation is one of life's great delights. Its value doesn't reside solely in convincing someone of something. The discussions and the relationships they build are valuable in themselves. It's important that we all learn how to talk with those of differing views. Even in evangelism, the learning is often two-way. It's not all proclamation. Apologetics and evangelism, at their best, often require getting to know each other better, asking lots of questions, attentive listening, and transparent sharing. For this reason, we hope that at least half the readers of this book will be nonbelievers and skeptics. If readers think us wrong, tell us so, winsomely we'd prefer. But do us honor by pointing out where you think we've gone astray.

In truth, we all have friends (and likely family) who disagree with us on matters big and small. Learning the art of how to navigate and discuss those differences is important. We hope this book can help readers in evangelistic efforts by giving them resources for productive, irenic conversations. We also aspire to equip readers who believe in moral reality to apprehend and apply its relevance to important questions about life and its meaning.

Moral arguments for God's existence exhibit a number of characteristics that can prove helpful to generating discussions, fortifying friendships, and building bridges. They serve as a useful means to engage in dialogue, establish rapport, and find common ground with others. Despite significant worldview differences, people across the ideological aisle from one another can often find that they agree more than they disagree about many things, from human rights to the need to fight injustices to the importance of feeding the hungry. Even among contemporary evolutionary moral psychologists, a trend is afoot that identifies quite a bit of shared ground about humanity's psychological nature, including a sense of right and wrong. Moral arguments can use these shared convictions to generate a conversation that isn't about accusation or invective, that doesn't raise people's hackles or put them on the defensive, but rather spurs a fertile and engaging exchange of ideas.

What also helps is that the moral argument can be cast at all sorts of levels—from the technical to the simple, directed to the young and to the old. The arguments are also not one-dimensional, appealing only to the intellect. Although some of the questions and puzzles that arise along the way are fascinating to consider, the arguments aren't a purely cognitive affair. They can also tug at the heartstrings, yet without manipulating the emotions. Many people are already deeply convinced that there is something appropriate about certain emotional responses. About a year ago we saw an image of some ISIS members literally roasting four men alive over a burning fire. Most people need no argument to be persuaded that such abominable treachery is wrong and that it should elicit from us emotions of horror and disgust. It should evoke a commitment to fight and work to prevent such instances of unspeakable cruelty. People simply should not be treated that way, and seeing it happen stirs deeply convicted feelings of disapproval, and rightly so.

David Hume was considered shocking for many reasons, one of which was his idea that, when we see these atrocities, the only evil that's able to be observed finds its seat in our emotional responses. We *feel* like something evil is taking place. The reality, he argues, is that there isn't anything outside us that's genuinely evil. Instead, it is our subjective perception of the event that accounts for our convictions there's something evil going on.[10] Then again, Hume adds, human hardwiring and social programming being what they are, such skepticism bears little impact on our everyday life. There are enough shared moral agreements and common customs of moral processing to make "feeling appalled" at such atrocities the ongoing order of the day. The result is a kinder, gentler skepticism.

Hume's analysis does indeed show that nothing follows necessarily from our aversive emotional responses. And some people, having studied a bit of philosophy or frequented coffee houses or the blogosphere enough, are aware of and impressed by arguments for various diluted ethical analyses. As a result, they may be little moved by the horror they feel when they hear of an atrocity. Even if their skin crawls and they have to look away, they refuse to let their moral indignation be the last word or to take such a response as revealing anything significant about the world. Rather than assuming their response tracks reality, they are more inclined to explain away their response as insignificant or misleading. Perhaps it's a culturally conditioned response reflective of nothing, they might suggest. Nothing more than an evolutionary byproduct, a biologically determined output.

---

[10]Our aversive emotional responses are enough to account for our sense of evil—no reference to any actual moral truth required. We can and should be skeptical of anything truly evil in the external world, on such a view.

Although we will have a bit to say about them, this book isn't primarily designed to change the minds of moral skeptics. Plenty of writers have discussed them at great length.[11] This book is more directed at the decided majority who still think that torturing children for fun (to give one example of a commonly held moral fact) is obviously and objectively wrong. Or that throwing babies into the air to catch them on the ends of spears in front of their mothers' eyes is morally perverse, and likewise with slowly roasting people to death. This is the group we will be most concerned with here. Most people, thank heavens, still find themselves in this category.

Friedrich Nietzsche (probably rightly) predicted that it would take time for the implications of atheism to sink in, and that gradually, after religious convictions waned, so too would the commitment to objective morality. Moral claims are just metaphors mistaken for objective reality. He prognosticated with prescience that, as modernity came of age, the twentieth century would be the bloodiest in history.[12] If he was right, then it would explain why so many secular thinkers still retain their moral convictions, convinced that taking God out of the equation makes no difference at all. They may be wrong, but if this is part of what explains the moral tenacity of secularists, it at least gives us common ground to cultivate, allowing for a reasoned discussion about the foundation for moral truths.

There's quite a bit more to this business of ethics and morality than the casual observer is aware of. It will do good to ponder it, to mine it, to unearth some of its riches, its challenges and distinctive qualities. The many-sided wonder of moral truth is, on reflection, a remarkable thing, well worth our time to explore more fully. To think it garden-variety, banal, or uninteresting is a mistake. Only its illegitimate domestication blinds us to its splendor. In fact, we think it can serve as a powerful clue to the nature of reality and human meaning.

---

[11]David Enoch's *Taking Morality Seriously: A Defense of Robust Realism* (Oxford: Oxford University Press, 2011) is a notable example.

[12]Friedrich Nietzsche, *The Portable Nietzsche*, ed. Walter Kaufman (New York: Penguin Books, 1968), 46-47. Also see Frederick Copleston, *A History of Philosophy* (New York: Doubleday, 1963), 7:405-6.

## THE SHAPE AND SEQUENCE OF OUR ARGUMENT

As we get under way, perhaps it will be useful to give a quick preview of coming attractions. The book is laid out in three parts, bookended by a spotlight and an encore, with an intermission in the middle. The spotlight will take us to Athens, the birthplace of Western philosophy. There Socrates offered his *Apology*, and we will note a few interesting twists in that ancient dialogue. More importantly, we will consider another early Socratic dialogue set near the end of his life, namely, the *Euthyphro*. It will prove a treasure trove of insight, especially when we examine it alongside Saint Paul's address at Mars Hill (Acts 17), also in Athens, about five hundred years after the golden days of Socrates, Plato, and Aristotle. The numerous resonances between the two texts will prove illuminating to our whole study from a variety of perspectives. Significantly, the most salient and glaring point of *disanalogy* between them will be especially telling.

Act One sets the stage for the cumulative moral argument of the book—with some of the more technical points relegated to footnotes. The first chapter will deal with the question of God's identity, for not all gods are created equal. The *Euthyphro* will have shown that the gods of the Greek pantheon are indeed vulnerable to all manner of moral critiques. The God proclaimed by Paul is altogether different. Recognition of this fact has helped contribute to a resurgence of interest in moral apologetics. Pick up most ethics textbooks still written today, and theistic ethics usually gets handily dismissed in a few paragraphs, usually because of "Plato's preemptive riposte," as Rebecca Newberger Goldstein calls it.[13] The famous "Euthyphro dilemma" asks this question: Is something moral because God wills it, or does God will something because it's moral?

This dilemma is thought by many to be the nail in the coffin of theistic ethics. Having spent the necessary time distinguishing Paul's God from Euthyphro's gods will enable us to meet this challenge, at least in a preliminary fashion. This can clear the way for moral arguments of various

---

[13]Rebecca Newberger Goldstein, *Plato at the Googleplex: Why Philosophy Won't Go Away* (New York: Pantheon, 2014), 306-7.

stripes to be introduced and interrogated. The point and purpose of such arguments will also merit brief exploration. It will be especially important as we go along for us to distinguish between the truly core concepts involved, on the one hand, and specific, more peripheral theories, on the other, that might or might not be the best way to capture the core insights and commitments.

The second chapter deals with the other half of the equation, namely, what is morality? Why are its alleged facts so obstinate, so compelling, so mysterious? What are those facts, and where did they come from? Although it won't detain us for long, we'll ask why it is that some people, far from struck by its force and beauty, are altogether skeptical about morality. Again, moral arguments don't have a ghost of a chance to sway those wholly skeptical of morality, but most people don't consistently hold to such skepticism. They still retain belief in human rights, in human dignity, in moral obligations. They still think justice is important and that people should be treated with respect, in a strong sense of *should*. If asked, they tend to think they possess at least some moral knowledge. If honest, they admit that they tend to fall short of the moral standards they think exist. And many of them still think that, somehow, devotion to the moral cause is right, even if they can't explain exactly why. That's just a smattering of the interesting features of morality that need fleshing out and careful consideration. This chapter will endeavor to sketch out such salient features of morality and broach the question of what best explains them.

A word on this issue of "explanation." Some are averse to such language in this context, thinking it overly beholden to treating a non-scientific question as a scientific one. Despite this, the particular approach of this book will be to show that theism best explains various moral phenomena. Our choice to do so is not an example of our stubbornness, but just one way among others to go about the task. It's important to stress, though, that this method is not sacrosanct. Some might prefer a logically tighter approach, while others would prefer a looser approach. This very issue itself is negotiable, not a part of the core. Someone wishing to cash the argument out differently could and is invited to do so, perhaps with profit.[14]

In fact, the last chapters of Act One, chapters three and four, offer a range of historical variants of the moral argument doing just that. This historical overview illustrates the richness and possibilities of moral apologetics and reveals what is core and central and what's more peripheral and negotiable. These past moral arguments either defend God's existence or critique a secular or naturalistic understanding of reality (or both). In short compass these chapters will canvass about twenty significant figures from the history of philosophy who have constructed one version or another of a moral argument. It isn't meant as anything like a comprehensive evaluative critique of such proposals. Here the intent is merely to provide readers a taste of what's been offered, in order to acquaint them a bit with this rich history and enable them to sense some of the scope and strategy of the proposals. That said, readers can take those chapters or leave them behind or for another time depending on their interest. Like olives or opera, some will love them, some will hate them.

Before diving into Act Two, which constructively, incrementally builds the cumulative moral case, an intermission takes time to answer various objections that came out of the Euthyphro episode in Athens. Various Euthyphro-inspired objections to theistic ethics (of various stripes) are still brandished in the public square. But a series of seven distinctions, consistently employed, can be useful to strip such objections of their perceived potency. Before building the positive case for theism, this defensive maneuver is a necessary preliminary, at least for proponents of divine command theory (a specific theistic ethical theory that we will explain in due course). Again, however, what is core is the dependence of morality on God, not divine command theory. The latter is just one

---

[14]For example, someone could argue that the probability of moral data $x$ on theism is not low but on naturalism *is* low (unexpected, surprising), so $x$ supports theism over naturalism. Perhaps $x$ doesn't make theism or Christianity more likely true than false, but at least more likely than it would otherwise be. Various aspects of morality could be plugged in for $x$. This would allow people such as Richard Swinburne, and those who may not think that God exactly *explains* objective moral principles, still to run a moral argument.

effort to flesh out what a part of that dependence *may* look like. It's not designed to suggest that someone can't feel the force of the moral argument without subscribing to divine command theory. Theistic accounts of morality, like rutabagas and roller coasters, come in all sizes and shapes.

Act Two then sets out our moral case for theism. It is a "best explanation" approach, which attempts by principled means to choose the best overall explanation for particular phenomena. To argue that theism provides the best explanation of various dimensions of morality, it's necessary to specify those dimensions, what their distinctive features are, the challenges besetting secular and naturalistic theories of various kinds to explain those features, and how theism (and Christianity) can provide a robust explanation.

Chapter five, which begins Act Two, deals with issues of moral goodness—most particularly, in light of our concern with morality and *meaning*, issues of distinctive human value and dignity. Chapter six treats moral obligations, arguing that theism provides the deeper account of their reality and authority. Chapter seven takes on the issue of moral knowledge, the arena of philosophy called moral epistemology. And chapters eight and nine pertain to two dimensions of moral faith (relying on Immanuel Kant's work): moral transformation and the connection between virtue and joy.

Act Three puts all of these pieces together in an effort to reveal the cumulative strength of the whole case, to show the power of theism and Christianity to explain this assortment of moral realities in a compelling and coherent way. The encore will then take us back to Athens one more time, to witness a more recent occurrence there that involved quite a noted apologist indeed.

We wish to make one more preliminary point: in a number of respects this book can be thought of as a companion to C. S. Lewis's marvelous novel *Till We Have Faces*, perhaps his greatest novel of all, even by his own reckoning. Readers unacquainted with the book are encouraged to sell all they have, if need be, and purchase it immediately. We have time. We will wait. You won't regret it. We will draw numerous examples from the novel for illustrative purposes. Readers who haven't yet read the novel can still read this book with profit, but we do encourage you to read the novel without delay (and repent in sackcloth and ashes for waiting so long).

As we close this introduction and begin our journey exploring these ideas together, we want to express how honored and humbled we are that you have chosen to join us. We will not take that privilege lightly. We hope that you find us fair and congenial guides to this conversation. We don't pretend to have settled the questions this material raises, or to be able to offer an argument that will convince every reader. We do, though, hope to offer a number of considerations that we have personally found compelling. Some of you might already agree, some will disagree. Perhaps some of you will come to agree, while others will retain reservations.

We admit that the questions under consideration are difficult, and the task of answering them is bound to raise new questions. We don't aim to close the questions but to invite you on a shared quest. You may or may not find what persuades us persuasive to you, and reasonable people sometimes disagree. We only hope that you will find your time with us well spent.

## TALK BACK

1. David Horner identifies the two tasks of the apologetic and evangelistic endeavor as (1) making Christianity credible and (2) making it plausible. In what ways can the credibility of the message presented be affected (positively or negatively) by the form of the message or delivery style of the messenger? What are some biblical models for integrating the message and the means of delivery?

2. How can we take to heart the central claims of the gospel we are presenting such that it shapes our own hearts, attitudes, and behaviors toward others?

3. What are some ways in which you have handled disagreements well or poorly? What are some fundamental principles to keep in

mind when engaging with another person who has an intellectual or emotional commitment to another way of thinking? Do you believe it's possible (or desirable) to form friendships with those with different faith convictions from you?

# SOCRATES AND PAUL IN ATHENS

*The unexamined life is not worth living.*

SOCRATES, IN PLATO'S *APOLOGY*

THE FIRST TIME I (Dave) attended the annual Wheaton philosophy conference, I asked my mom if she wanted to go with me. Always up for an adventure, she jumped at the chance, and so we hit the road and headed from the suburbs of Detroit to the outskirts of Chicago.

I'd never seen the campus of Notre Dame before, which was located along the way, so we stopped in. As it happened, we arrived just as a football game was letting out. We parked, and my mom decided to stay in the car while I went off to explore Touchdown Jesus and the Golden Dome.

When I got back to the car a short while later, she had a big plateful of food. "Where did you get that?" I asked her. "It was the craziest thing," she replied with amazement. "I went over to that concession stand and asked for a hot dog. They said they didn't have one, but they were so nice. They gave me this big plate of food. When I got out my purse to pay, they said they didn't want any money, and that if I come back next week, they'll have a hot dog."

---

This chapter is lightly adapted from an article by David Baggett, published at MoralApologetics .com: "Paul and Socrates: What Athens Has to Do with Jerusalem," *Moral Apologetics*, September 30, 2015, http://moralapologetics.com/paul-and-socrates-what-athens-has-to-do-with-jerusalem/.

Then, with a genuinely curious expression she added, "What I don't understand is how they can make it as a business if they don't charge anyone."

And that's the story of my mom crashing a tailgate party at Notre Dame.

Party crashers stand out: they can be disruptive, unsettling, and challenging to the status quo. But as shown by both Socrates and the apostle Paul, party crashers *par excellence*, sometimes the status quo needs to be shaken up. Or as Dr. Horrible might say, "The status isn't quo."[1]

Separated by time but linked in space, ground zero for these two epic figures was Athens, the intellectual cradle of the Western world, the birthplace of philosophy. Pre-Socratics such as Thales and Heraclitus hailing from Ionia were a rousing warm-up act. Socrates and his student Plato, and Plato's student Aristotle, were the main actors in bringing philosophy to life. Athens, at the edge of the fabled Aegean, was center stage.

Both Socrates and Paul mixed things up quite a bit and questioned prevailing assumptions. Each had important ideas to share, and what we intend to do here is highlight a number of parallels between them—the commonalities and comparisons are conspicuous. Both engaged in radically unorthodox discourse in the ancient philosophical center of Athens. They were alike in their willingness to challenge accepted ideas. In doing so, both were required to answer to critics, and they answered in unexpected ways. Both appealed to a superior authority, while realizing and asserting a deep mystery connected with moral concerns.

The punch line, however, is even more poignant: a difference between them that resides at the heart of the message of this book. Despite resonances, their understandings of reality diverged, and Paul's is the more profound perspective.

In the case of Paul, who was always ready to proclaim the gospel, his speech before the Areopagus (Acts 17) took place at Mars Hill, carved into the rocky hillside containing at its zenith the Acropolis—prominently featuring the Parthenon and other temples and shrines—and overlooking the agora, the marketplace, farther down. In that marketplace, Socrates, in whose lifetime the Parthenon was completed, tried out his ideas,

---

[1]Also, "The world is a mess, and I just need to rule it." *Dr. Horrible's Sing-Along Blog*, directed by Joss Whedon (Los Angeles: Mutant Enemy Productions, 2008).

engaging people in conversation and needling them with questions. These probing queries made him none too popular, and he became quite the pesky gadfly in the Athenian ointment.

The apostle Paul, too, nearly five centuries later, took to the streets of the agora—"when in Athens . . ." The Areopagus was the name for both the Athenian council and the meeting place of the council. It was also known as Mars Hill because it was where Ares, the son of Zeus, was thought to have been tried for having killed his cousin, the son of Poseidon. When the Romans co-opted the Greek pantheon of gods, Zeus became Jupiter; Artemis, Diana; and Ares, Mars, the Roman god of war. Thus Mars Hill.

The setting of the dialogue *Euthyphro* by Plato is the porch of King Archon, one of nine Athenian magistrates whose quasi-religious functions included presiding over cases involving impiety and homicide. Socrates is there to inquire further into accusations, levied against him by Meletus, of corrupting the youth, denying the existence of the old gods, and inventing new ones. While waiting, Socrates encounters Euthyphro, who is there to charge his father with the murder of one of his workers.

Paul and Socrates had started in the agora, but both found themselves in trouble, answerable to reigning Greek authorities, for a surprising number of overlapping reasons. Paul was on his second missionary journey when he stopped at Athens, whereas Socrates, who had spent his whole life in Athens, was nearing the end of his earthly pilgrimage, an end not unrelated to his appearance at Archon's porch. Socrates had gained a following, especially among the young men of Athens. The core of his followers, including his star student and biographer extraordinaire, Plato, was loyal. Paul, too, while at Athens, garnered a following—in the sense of converts to the faith he was proclaiming. This happened in most of the places he went, Athens no exception. The two examples of new "followers" Acts 17 adduces are Dionysius the Areopagite and a woman named Damaris, "and others with them" who go unnamed.

In addition to gaining enthusiastic followers and new adherents, both Paul and Socrates also generated quite a bit of opposition. This is hardly surprising, since each of them made points that challenged prevailing convictions, including longstanding views and customs considered largely sacrosanct. A couple of agitators they were, and opposition was something to which they had both grown accustomed. Again, in the immediate context, each is challenged to defend his ideas. Socrates is accused by Meletus (and Anytus and Lycon, we find out in the *Apology*) of corrupting the youth and impiety regarding the gods, and he will soon face those charges in court. Euthyphro initially thinks that Socrates has nothing to worry about regarding such charges. In retrospect, Euthyphro isn't the most trustworthy or insightful adviser in this matter.

Paul is brought before the Areopagus after arguing in the synagogue with the Jews and God-fearing Gentiles and with those who happen to be in the marketplace every day. The open-air strategy was a bit new for Paul, who more typically preached, proclaimed, and dialogued in the synagogue. His venturing into the agora provides a clear parallel with Socrates, whose common practice this was—while teaching for no charge, unlike the Sophists, who taught rhetoric for a fee. Euthyphro's first question to Socrates in *Euthyphro* is why he'd left the Lyceum, a public meeting place in a grove of trees in classical Athens. In Athens both Paul and Socrates were very public philosophers indeed. Paul had a first-rate philosophical mind. His ability at Mars Hill to engage in informed and insightful discourse with the reigning philosophies of his day provides evidence of this.

A summons before the Areopagus was the protocol when someone wished to introduce new gods to be revered and worshiped, and this is what the Athenians think Paul is doing. The new gods they take Paul to be proclaiming are Jesus and Anastasis—*resurrection*. Since the category of resurrection was so foreign to Greek ears, they naturally take his reference to it—transliterated *anastasis*—as a reference to a new goddess. Now Jesus and Anastasis need to be defended—their existence, their credentials, their benefits.

The protocol for introducing new deities required Paul to address the Areopagus, so his ostensible purpose is to answer questions posed to him. Specifically, who are these new gods, and why do they deserve a place among the gods recognized in Athens? Some of the philosophers present,

Stoics and Epicureans, have impugned the quality and caliber of Paul's proclamations, accusing him of babbling, cobbling together bits and pieces of a variety of worldviews and religious perspectives. If such is the case, his new ideas will hardly be worthy of recognition, but rather of categorical exclusion if not downright derision. No pressure!

Socrates also did something thought problematically "new." In his career he had made it clear that he was following what he took to be a divine directive, an inner voice that he assumed had come from God. It led him to inquire more fully into the revelation from the Oracle of Delphi that there was no one in Athens wiser than he. Socrates had been incredulous of this, because he claimed to be ignorant of nearly everything. To disprove the thesis that he was the wisest, he sought wisdom from others. He discovered through a process of searching questions that others were just as ignorant as he.

The only difference he could find was that, while they claimed to be wise and were actually ignorant, he disavowed having wisdom himself. In this sense, he finally concluded, perhaps the oracle was right. He was the wisest after all for knowing of his own ignorance, unlike others. Socrates saw ignorance as the laudably humble path trod by the judicious. If the evidence wasn't there or wasn't strong enough for a view, he remained skeptical about it, carefully apportioning belief to the evidence.

Introducing the *Apology*, Edith Hamilton and Huntington Cairns write about Socrates in these rhetorically glowing terms: "Great spiritual leaders and great saints adorn the pages of history, but Socrates is not like any of them. He is, indeed, the servant of the divine power, living in complete obedience to God; yet he always views the world of men with a bit of humor, a touch of irony."[2]

To what are they referring when they write of Socrates as the "servant of the divine power" and "living in complete obedience to God"? The

---

[2]"He spends his life in the effort to kindle into a flame the spark of good in every man, but when he fails, when he comes up against blind obstinacy or stupid conceit or the indifference of egotism, or when he draws down on himself bitter enmity, then along with his regret—because he cares for everyone—is mingled a little amusement, a feeling, as it were, of rueful sympathy, as if he said to himself, 'What silly children we are.'" *Plato: The Collected Dialogues*, ed. Edith Hamilton and Huntington Cairns (Princeton, NJ: Princeton University Press, 1961), 3.

dialogue itself provides the answer concerning this Socratic innovation. Despite his skepticism about the Greek pantheon of human-made gods, references to the divine recur time and again. Throughout the pages of the dialogue, Socrates expresses his submission to the will and command of God. Facing charges of impiety, he leaves his outcome in the hands of providence, recognizing that his highest goal is to serve God and search out his truth and commands. He sees his philosophical mission—of teaching and exhortation—as being in direct service to God.[3]

Socrates' interaction with Euthyphro is part and parcel of this mission. When Socrates, however ingenuously, offers to become Euthyphro's disciple, it is perhaps in part motivated to underscore something ironic. The master takes on the posture of the student: think Einstein enrolling in tenth-grade physics. Euthyphro is there at court not defending himself but pressing charges against his own father. While awaiting directions as to how to proceed, the father had the slave tossed into a ditch and allowed him to die from hunger and exposure. Athenian custom dictates that Euthyphro assign primacy of loyalty to his father over the life of the slave. His revisionism in suing his father for wrongdoing is a real departure from normal customs.

Socrates' own innovations, though, in heeding what he thought was a divine mandate while being skeptical of the capricious, finite, and feuding deities of the Greek pantheon, are the reason he is in trouble. With some justification, Socrates' gesture toward taking the younger and confident Euthyphro as his mentor—relegating himself to the role of protégé—accentuates the irony that Euthyphro's radical departure from custom is unquestioned while Socrates' own innovations are cast

---

[3]"However, let that turn out as God wills. I must obey the law and make my defense" (19a); "real wisdom is the property of God" (23b); "That is why I still go about seeking and searching in obedience to the divine command" (23b); "when God appointed me, as I supposed and believed, to the duty of leading the philosophical life, examining myself and others" (28e); "I owe a greater obedience to God than to you, and so long as I draw breath and have my faculties, I shall never stop practicing philosophy and exhorting you and elucidating the truth for everyone that I meet" (29d); "I shall reprove him for neglecting what is of supreme importance, and giving his attention to trivialities. . . . This, I do assure you is what my God commands, and it is my belief that no greater good has ever befallen you in this city than my service to my God" (30a). See as well 30d, 30e, 31d, 33c, and 42a.

as objectionably problematic. The Socratic subtext is that this state of affairs betrays a real inconsistency that ought to be rectified. The time is out of joint indeed.

This is an interesting point of both comparison and contrast with Paul. Paul believed in the importance of evidence, too. What he considered the most significant evidential factor to consider will be discussed momentarily, but his view concerning ignorance was quite a bit less sanguine than that of Socrates. Ignorance was no badge of honor for Paul. An altar to an unknown god was less a destination than a good start. Paul explicitly says, "The times of ignorance God overlooked, but now he commands all men everywhere to repent" (Acts 17:30). Paul thought that, with the resurrection, a vitally important truth about God had been revealed, the surprising piece whose appearance makes possible the puzzle's solution. Theology was no exercise of blind faith or empty conjecture but definitive truth now made clear. Among what had been revealed was something the philosophers in Paul's audience would have found anathema: that there was a judgment to come. The world will be judged in righteousness, by a man whose credentials have been established.

On this issue of judgment for wrongdoing, incidentally, Paul echoes a theme that both Socrates and Euthyphro seemed to agree on entirely, namely, that a wrongdoer deserves punishment. The shared nature of this belief might suggest that this insight is part of what some might call "general revelation." In *Summa contra Gentiles* Aquinas writes that the knowledge of God that is accessible independent of specific revelation pertains to (1) what may be asserted of God in himself, (2) what may be asserted about the procession of the creatures of God, and (3) about the ordination of the creatures toward God as their ends. A particularly poignant piece of natural theology is morality itself.

There is something morally instinctive, deeply intuitive, wildly instructive, and patently obvious about the idea that justice demands wrongs be addressed. The failure to effect such a remedy leaves an injustice in place and not properly fixed, which amounts to an irrational feature of reality. In one sense or another, human beings are morally accountable for their actions. The famous Boyle Lectures of Samuel

Clarke deal, in this order, with the existence of God, the attributes of God as Creator and moral governor of the world, and the certainty of a "state of rewards and punishments." These are truths assumed to be capable of formal demonstration.

Instead of questioning assumptions about moral justice, Socrates gave them his wholehearted endorsement. His claim of ignorance didn't include claims about moral responsibility. He never disavowed the category of moral accountability. He acknowledged the difficulty on occasion of identifying which actions are instances of wrongdoing; for example, he was much less confident than Euthyphro that Euthyphro's suing of his own father was morally right. Rather, he entertained grave doubts about its piety or holiness.

An actually impious or unholy action, however, was an action he thought merited punishment for the wrongdoer. This is clear, among other points in the dialogue, when Socrates discusses the alleged enmities and contentions among the gods. He says concerning the gods that they don't venture to argue that the guilty are to be unpunished. Like between Euthyphro and Socrates, there is both agreement and disagreement among the gods. They disagree on whether particular instances of alleged wrongdoing are actual ones. They agree, though, that genuine examples of wrongdoing deserve punishment.

Paul's later assertion, then, that there is righteous judgment to come corresponds with at least a dimension of Socrates' convictions, for Socrates agreed that justice demands punishment for wrongdoing. This is a rather intuitive conviction for most. Few today can hear of atrocities committed by members of the Islamic State such as roasting people alive or public beheadings without feeling a strong conviction that justice demands such horrors be judged.[4] After witnessing unspeakable and horrific injustices perpetrated on innocent people in his homeland, Miroslav Volf wrote, "Though I used to complain about the indecency of the idea of God's wrath, I came to think that I would have to rebel against a God

---

[4]Inexplicably some seem rather more exercised by relatively trivial indignities, a failure of the moral imagination reminiscent of C. S. Lewis's judgment of "men without chests." This is the title of a chapter in his *The Abolition of Man*.

who wasn't wrathful at the sight of the world's evil. God isn't wrathful in spite of being love. God is wrathful because God is love."[5]

Of course Socrates didn't have Paul's rich theology, but the parallel in pointing to the moral appropriateness of judgment and punishment for wrongdoing is conspicuous. Socrates wasn't responsible for fully anticipating all the details of additional special revelation to come. By Paul's context, in the fullness of time, the hour of ignorance was over. Socrates pointed to the lack of evidence for the Athenian gods. Paul agreed, but Paul was the new gadfly, extending the point in a positive direction. The evidence for the right theology was now available. The finite, fallible gods were dead. The God who is the ground of being, the Creator and sustainer of the universe, the God in whom there is no shadow of turning, is alive and well.

Others, such as Mark S. McLeod-Harrison, have pointed out germane overlaps and salient similarities between Paul and Socrates.[6] Some early Christian apologists identified resonances between Socrates and Jesus, in fact. Others have noted the similar structure of Paul's address at Mars Hill and that of Socrates in the *Apology*: dialogue, accusation, explanation. As previously mentioned, Socrates and Paul were both profoundly skeptical of the gods worshiped all around them. Socrates had heard the myths of the gods inherited from playwrights and poets, legends and lore.

Homer and Hesiod had fired the Greek imagination, populating it with an array of capricious and contentious gods. This reinforced a view of the world according to which fate is the ultimate determinant. Socrates sought a better way, a world of reason, regulated by structure, a cosmos rather than a chaos. For him the legends strained credulity. They revealed a world full of fallible gods filled with foibles, gods pretty clearly made in the image of men. He admitted that he found such legends hard to believe, whereas Euthyphro credulously embraced all the stories with

[5]Miroslav Volf, *Free of Charge: Giving and Forgiving in a Culture Stripped of Grace* (Grand Rapids: Zondervan, 2006), 138-39.

[6]Mark S. McLeod-Harrison, "Socrates and St. Paul: Can Christian Apologetics Be Public Philosophy?," *Essays in Philosophy* 15, no. 1 (January 2014), http://commons.pacificu.edu/cgi/viewcontent.cgi?article=1493&context=eip.

nothing but the most wooden literalness, despite their inherent tensions, conflicting claims, and warring gods. Deity, for Socrates, if it exists at all, must be free of such imperfections and flaws. None of the Greek gods, with their violence and squabbles and petty selfishness, met those criteria.

Paul of course would have concurred, and his Jewishness alone would no doubt suffice to have made him grieved and distressed at all the idolatry in Athens. The most axiomatic Jewish conviction was that there is one God alone. This is why each day Jews would repeat the Shema, taken from Deuteronomy 6:4: "Hear, O Israel: The Lord our God is one Lord."

The mentality of the Athenians seemed to be one of "covering bases." After all, devotion and payments of homage to the gods was the surefire way to secure divine blessing on the city. So they must have figured it was better to be safe than sorry. Worshiping the full panoply of gods, the full pantheon of deities, could maximize the likelihood of securing desired blessings. Euthyphro, similarly, had thought that a religious orientation called for such credulity. There was little fear of holding wrong beliefs among those who had adopted (what we can call) the Homeric spirit. It was rather a picture of an expansive range of beliefs in order to be on the safe side. No matter that these beliefs were often at odds. Affirming them all, there was less chance that some capricious god or goddess would withhold blessing.

Paul's contrasting approach was rather in the Socratic spirit. It wasn't about covering one's bases or being safe. Rather, it was a matter of caring about the truth. And Paul was adamantly committed to the truth that one God exists, not a plethora, not a panoply, not a pantheon, but one God. And rather than arguing that this one God deserved a place among the temples and shrines in Athens, Paul's point was radically subversive. He startled his audience.

This one God was the only true God, and all the other alleged gods and goddesses were a sham, unreal, nonexistent, powerless, mere idols. Moreover, this God was the Creator and sustainer of all, and hardly able to be contained within a temple, booth, or building. He was the God of all creation, and whatever the cosmology of Paul's audience, they knew the world was a big place. This God was bigger and greater still, and not afflicted with the limitations or weaknesses or flaws of the gods of Athenian lore. As much as Socrates, Paul was skeptical both of the legends and of the Homeric spirit, which privileged an ambitious range of beliefs to cover one's bases over a serious examination of where the evidence points.

This leads to an important insight of contemporary relevance. Although cooperation, dialogue, and shared missions between those of divergent religious traditions is surely a worthwhile goal, there remain irremediable theological differences that can't simply be ignored, as if they were easily eliminable or unimportant. Those core convictions are at the heart of each group's essential identities. Paul refused to set aside as trivial their worldview differences. It was a focus exactly on those differences that led to his faithful and uncompromising proclamation. Ignoring the differences—even when they show diametrically opposite convictions—is to privilege a Homeric spirit. Retaining the proper place for objective truth claims that matter and for which we're responsible is to privilege the Socratic spirit. Paul is a paradigmatic example of the latter.

Perhaps most fundamentally, Paul and Socrates agreed that people ought to be skeptical of the right things and convinced by the right things. Where evidence is lacking, suspension of belief is appropriate. Socrates was skeptical of the pantheon of old gods and the traditional myths, and he should have been. Paul was likewise convinced that the gods worshiped in Athens were mere idols.

Nevertheless, Socrates hearkened to what he considered a reliable divine voice emanating from a source other than the traditional gods, whose imperfections and contentions were legend. It was a voice that dissuaded him from courses of action he considered, and a voice that made him think he was on a divine mission for which he would be held responsible.

> When Gentiles who have not the law do by nature what the law requires, they are a law to themselves, even though they do not have the law. They show that what the law requires is written on their hearts, while their conscience also bears witness and their conflicting thoughts accuse or perhaps excuse them on that day when, according to my gospel, God judges the secrets of men by Christ Jesus. (Rom 2:14-16)

Paul, too, had received a special and personal divine revelation—of Christ. Interestingly enough, his appeal to others was not based on that personal experience but on the resurrection itself, which provided evidence for everyone. God "has fixed a day on which he will judge the world in righteousness by a man whom he has appointed, and of this he has given *assurance to all men* by raising him from the dead" (Acts 17:31, emphasis added). With a Jewish audience Paul made the case for the necessity of the resurrection from the Scriptures.

In the heart of Athens, he instead used Gentile and Stoic poets to make connections before pointing to the resurrection, often deploying the words and categories of those writers for his own purposes of proclamation. Like Socrates, Paul was skeptical of the pantheon of gods but equally insistent that his listeners be sensitive to the evidence. As foreign as reference to a resurrection was, this was the pivotal event to show that the God of whom he spoke was real. Paul started where his audience was but took them to where he knew they needed to go. It would have been profoundly unloving to do otherwise, to leave them in their ignorance and not confront the inconsistencies in their thought.

I (Dave) am embarrassed to admit that I once purchased a Christmas gift for a girlfriend altogether in haste, and it was all too obvious. At the time I justified myself by insisting I wasn't captive to a consumerist culture. The real explanation was more likely indolence. Sadly for me, gift giving for this young lady meant a great deal. It may have been one of her love languages, and suffice it to say that she wasn't loving my careless choice. So I figured I'd appeal to a helpful canard to salvage a sorry situation. "But it's the thought that counts," I offered hopefully, thinking that this would, well, cover my bases.

"Exactly! It's the thought that counts! *There was no thought!*"

So, yes, sometimes we need to do more than cover our bases. The struggle to understand the import of right and wrong and good and evil is one of those times we may need to give it more thought. The hour of ignorance is over, Paul would tell us, for the truth has been made manifest. We must be willing to follow the evidence where it leads. There is a reckoning to come—even more daunting than that Christmas of mine.

## TALK BACK

1. Read Acts 17:16-34 and take note of Paul's approach, both inter-personal and rhetorical. What are the underlying convictions of his audience? How does he address those and move the discussion forward? What can we learn from him about graciously yet truth-fully challenging prevailing paradigms?

2. In this spotlight, we claim that theology is no exercise of blind faith or empty conjecture but definitive truth now made clear. How does this understanding of theology correspond with your conceptions? What kind of claim should truth have on us once it's discovered? For what reasons might people resist accepting or ap-propriating a truth?

3. This chapter closes with a reflection on the Homeric spirit and the Socratic spirit, where the Homeric spirit embraces a pantheon of gods and allows for a multiplicity of possible—often conflicting—truths, and the Socratic spirit seeks after *the truth*. Where do you see our contemporary culture falling in this continuum? What pockets of culture embrace the Homeric spirit, and how? What seems to lie behind these preferences, and how should we think about them?

# SETTING
# THE STAGE

A ct One sets the stage by discussing the resurgence of moral apologetics, the operative conception of God in the book, various stubborn (downright recalcitrant) moral facts in need of explanation, and, in chapters three and four, a brief history of moral arguments for God's existence. The first two chapters are crucial in setting the stage for Act Two. Chapters three and four highlight an array of possible moral arguments, acquaint readers with the richness of this underreported history, and contextualize the argument of this book in a long, ongoing discussion.

Sometimes philosophers fall prey to being a bit ahistorical, so the third and fourth chapters, in particular, are aimed at preventing such a pitfall here. The history of the moral argument is incredibly rich. Even if we ignore the precursors to Kant, just consider the brainpower represented by a group that includes John Henry Newman, Clement Dore, Henry Sidgwick, William Sorley, Hastings Rashdall, A. E. Taylor, C. S. Lewis, Austin Farrer, and H. P. Owen. Many of these were Oxford dons, and several were invited to give the prestigious Gifford Lectures, in which the topic of the moral argument often came up.

Clement Webb (1865–1954), for example, taught at Oxford. The apex of his scholarly career is often thought to be his Gifford Lectures, which were later published in two volumes. The second of those volumes is the book that H. P. Owen points to in the third chapter of his own book on the moral argument for Christian theism: For the argument from the moral law to a divine Lawgiver, Owen directs readers to Webb's *Divine Personality and Human Life*. Owen also makes mention of the fact that Webb in turn acknowledges his debt to James Martineau.[1]

Webb and Lewis overlapped at Oxford and, in a letter dated November 30, 1942, Lewis thanks Delmar Banner for a painting of Webb, "one of the best modern portraits I have seen for a long time." Webb was a philosopher and theologian, educated at Westminster and Christ Church, Oxford, where he took a First in *Literae Humaniores* in 1888. He was a Fellow of Magdalen College, 1889–1922, first Oriel Professor of Philosophy of the Christian Religion, 1920–1930, and a Fellow of Oriel College, Oxford, 1922–1930. Banner painted his portrait in 1929, and after Webb's death it was presented to Oriel College, where it hangs in the provost's lodging.[2]

Recapturing some of the insight and vitality of a great mind such as Webb, and recovering some of the intellectual heritage of the moral argument, is one of the crucial benefits to researching the rich history of moral apologetics. Chapters three and four sketch the shape of such research.

[1] H. P. Owen, *The Moral Argument for Christian Theism* (London: Allen & Unwin, 1965), 49n3.
[2] C. S. Lewis, *The Collected Letters of C. S. Lewis*, ed. Walter Hooper (New York: HarperCollins, 2004), 2:537.

# CHAPTER I

# THE COMEBACK OF MORAL APOLOGETICS

*The Christian does not think God will love us because we are good, but that God will make us good because He loves us.*

C. S. LEWIS, *MERE CHRISTIANITY*

IF ELECTRICITY COMES FROM ELECTRONS, does that mean that morality comes from morons?

Okay, that's rude.

Still, sometimes it almost seems so, at least in this day and age, when our collective moral radar appears in need of serious calibration. Today we find ourselves caught in quite the ethical paradox. It is the best of moral times, it is the worst of moral times; it is an age of callous cruelty, it is an age of hypersensitivity; a time of enlightenment, a time of myopia; an age of liberation, an age of bondage; an epoch of free thinking, an epoch of mindless conformity.

What's transpiring at some of our greatest universities provides telling cases in point. No, not the outrageous athletic budgets, but certain agenda-driven protests that so often seem to go awry, setting in motion all manner of bubbling cauldron heads whose collective commentary rivals the blast of a Howler. Some time back, for example, a video went viral of a student at Yale publicly berating a distinguished sociology professor who, in his function as administrator, refused to capitulate to student demands for greater sensitivity over Halloween costumes. We don't want to be callous here because concern and respect for others and resistance to dehumanization are fueled by right motives, but such motives don't always ensure right methods.

Shouts of invective, peppered with feisty expletives and colorful pejoratives that would surely make her grandmother blush, emanated from the livid student. She clearly counted her righteous indignation justified, no matter that it was heavy on indignation and light on righteousness. What, to her thinking, afforded her the moral high ground was what she found to be *offensive* about the professor's administrative decisions. His sin involved endorsing the proposition that students at universities aren't always entitled to protection from every perspective, even derogatory ones. They should cultivate the capacity to engage in rigorous but civil discourse. For this he was demonized with vituperation. Sadly, a plethora of recent examples abound and serve to show how a good moral insight, pushed in isolation, can lead to bad behavior.[1]

Perhaps, though, there is a ready explanation, or at least a partial one, for the moral ambivalence of this age. When a society's moral foundations gradually erode, efforts to compensate for the loss tend to feature a lack of proportionality. Vast swaths of moral terrain can go neglected, such as humility, self-control, and temperance. But a few sacred (or at least coddled) cows remain and irresistibly attract all the pent-up moral indignation. Racism is surely one of those tropes, and understandably so, in light of the hideous track record of race relations in America and elsewhere. Dr. Martin Luther King Jr.'s consensus has been built, and nearly everyone nowadays at least pays lip service to the need for racial justice and equality. A cultural tipping point was crossed, after which racism could be denounced in the strongest of moral terms. Of course, we're not suggesting more progress isn't needed; it surely is.

---

[1]The president of Oklahoma Wesleyan University felt compelled to write this open letter to students because of the frequency of such incidents: Dave Urbanski, "'This Is Not a Day Care': Read College President's Scathing Open Letter to 'Self-Absorbed and Narcissistic' Students," *The Blaze*, November 28, 2015, www.theblaze.com/stories/2015/11/28/this-is-not-a-day-care-read-college-presidents-scathing-open-letter-to-self-absorbed-and-narcissistic-students/.

Racial injustices should of course be denounced, but perhaps what this historical moment reveals is cultural compensation for the loss of much of our collective moral imagination. Rather than recognizing a range of moral victories to savor and, more importantly for present purposes, a wide array of moral failures deserving of our censure and needing healing and grace, our attention has been drawn to but a few notable, sometimes exaggerated, and often inflamed moral fires. This tends to elicit an intensified downpour of indignation that's better distributed more evenly across the moral landscape. Our suggestion is not that all moral sins are equal, for surely they are not, but that the selectivity of contemporary moral outrage is conspicuous and likely unprincipled.

Our sense of moral proportion often needs realignment, not because morality is unimportant but because it's *vitally* important. Like all good things—even a mother's love for her child—morality introduces the possibility of error: a hyperbolic sense of injustice over imagined wrongs, a self-righteous or pharisaical attitude, an artificially manufactured presumed right never to be offended, a failure to empathize as one ought, myriad justifications and rationalizations for wrongdoing, callous disregard for the feelings of others.

Arthur Miller thoughtfully explored this temptation and human tendency in his 1953 play, *The Crucible*. Drawing on the infamous Salem witch trials, Miller's drama is often seen as an allegory of McCarthyism and the House Un-American Activities Committee, intent on rooting out communist sympathizers in America. Although Miller plays fast and loose with the historical record in his fictional recreation, he realistically depicts human failings in the struggle for righteousness. As the Puritan town of Salem, Massachusetts, strives to root out ungodliness in its midst, it sacrifices truth and grace. The courts are overtaken by brute power and authoritarianism, as those are seen as the only means of purification. The result is, well, a witch hunt, with anything but actual justice being served.

And yet this injustice is pursued with the language of the righteous, pitting "good" against "evil" in a facile sorting. Miller's Judge Danforth exemplifies this arbitrary moral line drawing, and he positions himself as arbiter of the good and leverages moral language in support of his immoral rulings: "You must understand, sir, that a person is either with this court or he must be counted against it, there be no road between. This is a sharp time, now, a precise time—we live no longer in the dusky afternoon when evil mixed itself with good and befuddled the world. Now, by God's grace, the shining sun is up, and them that fear not light will surely praise it."[2]

Indeed, the greater something is, as with Danforth's desire for a righteous community or today's social justice warriors' insistence on human dignity, the larger a perversion its distortion becomes. We live at a time when penetrating moral insight is in short supply, when horrific evils are perpetrated with reckless abandon or claimed to have divine approval, when a sense of moral proportion needs to be restored, when clarity about the function and foundation of morality is crucial. Morality can indeed shed light on who we are, on the human condition, and on the meaning of life, but only if, and only after, we grasp its significance and import rightly. This book aims to provide some help to do just that.

## THE TIME IS RIPE

Moral apologetics has experienced a real resurgence in recent years. These things go through phases, and for quite a while moral arguments were frowned upon in many circles for a variety of reasons. But in recent decades the tide has begun to turn.[3] This renewed interest owes a debt to Immanuel Kant, who, after earlier dalliances with arguments for God's existence, became skeptical of nearly all theistic arguments *except* a moral argument. This book doesn't share Kant's negative view toward other arguments for God's existence, but its focus will be on moral arguments in particular. We think these are especially effective at both illuminating the mind and stirring the heart.

Convinced that moral arguments for God's existence possess such great potential and feature a rich history worth recapturing, we started

---

[2]Arthur Miller, *The Crucible* (New York: Dramatists Play Service, 1953), act 3.
[3]Reasons for moral apologetics falling out of favor for a while range from skepticism about speculative metaphysics to the rise of ethical noncognitivism. The new trend, though, has featured Timothy Keller, Paul Copan, William Lane Craig, and numerous others advancing fresh versions of the moral argument.

MoralApologetics.com a few years ago in an effort to bring attention to this important piece of the apologetic endeavor.[4] The site is, first of all, *communal*, tapping into the thoughts and insights of an array of thinkers and academic fields. As an interdisciplinary couple, we see the benefits of crossing disciplinary divides. Such diversity only enriches the overall fruitfulness of the site, better helping readers become more equipped as effective moral apologists. Bible scholars, theologians, philosophers, literary experts, and others all have their distinctive contributions to discussions of moral arguments for God. Moral arguments, *plural*, is not a typo. It's intentional, because there isn't just one moral argument for God's existence—but several. The site aims, in time, to explain and explore them all, and in the process point out their interesting connections and, ultimately, the way together they pack quite the evidential punch.

This makes the site expansive in another sense. Like this book, it discusses moral arguments for God's existence that focus on various *moral facts* ("moral ontology" is the five-dollar word for that), *moral knowledge* ("moral epistemology," to be fancy), *performative matters* (pertaining to the matter of moral transformation—perhaps even moral transfiguration), and *rational issues* (most particularly, the convergence of happiness and virtue). We are especially excited about presenting the power of a cumulative case showcasing all four aspects of the moral case for theism.[5]

To this end, this is the threefold task for the Christian moral apologist: First, such arguments need to be based on some form of "moral realism," objective moral facts. For example, is it actually true that, say, genocide is wrong, or torturing kids for fun is evil? Do such facts obtain irrespective of your opinion or mine but objectively? If so, this is a picture of moral realism, which calls for an explanation.

Second, it needs to be shown that theistic ethics of various types can best explain these realities. For this reason, moral apologists need to

---

[4]This section is lightly adapted from the vision statement of MoralApologetics.com, written by David Baggett, http://moralapologetics.com/about-us/mission-statement/.

[5]The site also hopes to branch out more soon in two directions: (1) the history of the moral argument and (2) the spiritual formation aspects of the foundational truths of moral apologetics, which are useful not only for evidential and evangelistic purposes but as encouragement and edification to believers.

articulate, defend, and advance versions of theistic ethics generally and, in our case, distinctive Christian resources particularly. Again, this is where the distinction between core and secondary convictions comes in handy. At the center of moral apologetics is an appeal to theistic resources to provide the best account of various moral facts. More at the periphery will be particular theistic proposals.[6]

Third, the Christian moral apologist must subject naturalistic and secular ethical theories to various substantive critiques.[7] This needs to be done fairly, acknowledging the strengths of such theories while also pointing out their weaknesses and the way theistic and Christian ethics can avoid those problems and deficiencies. The three main foci of moral apologetics, then, are (1) a defense of moral realism, (2) a defense of theistic and Christian ethics, and (3) a critique of secular ethical theories.[8]

For some insightful discussion of moral arguments for God's existence, let's turn to Alvin Plantinga, longtime professor of philosophy at Notre Dame. Plantinga is a brilliant and winsome philosopher, a combination captured by a story he likes to tell from his days at Wayne State University. He had heard there was a solipsist on faculty there. Solipsism is the theory that the self is all that can be known to exist. Out of curiosity, Plantinga went to speak with the professor. On his way out, he spoke with

---

[6]The core belief in the dependence of morality on God won't include specific theories as to what this dependence looks like. They may incline in the direction of one or more specific theories, but the core commitment is compatible with several theories to choose from, either in isolation or combination. Theistic ethical theories include natural law, divine command theory, divine will theory, divine desire theory, and others. Determining which among such theories is best is a fascinating discussion but not strictly necessary for the moral apologist to settle. It's telling that in broad outline all of the specific theories in question largely agree on the core commitment of the moral apologist that, in some central and ineliminable sense, morality depends on God. This book will gravitate toward a divine nature theory of the good and a divine command theory of the right, but it's less committed to these particulars than the core principle undergirding moral apologetics. We risk belaboring this point because we want our more negotiable particular convictions neither to undermine the more central core concept nor to be perceived as objectionably unecumenical.

[7]Christian moral apologists should also be prepared to identify weaknesses or limitations in other theologies. This isn't a dimension of the project that we'll be focusing on here, though we see it in the contrast between Christianity and Euthyphro's theology.

[8]Jerry Walls and I (Dave) wrote books on the second and third of these tasks, and we intend before too long to write a book defending moral realism. *Good God: The Theistic Foundations of Morality* is a defense of theistic ethics, and *God and Cosmos: Moral Truth and Human Meaning* is our critique of secular ethical theories.

some colleagues who were familiar with the fellow's odd views. They assured Plantinga that they tried to take good care of him, because "when he goes, we all go."

Plantinga has argued throughout his impressive career that rational belief in God does not (in general) *need* argument.[9] He's careful to add that it doesn't follow that there *aren't* any good theistic arguments, among them moral ones. Indeed, he thinks there are a couple dozen or so *good arguments* for God. The arguments are not coercive in the sense that every person is obliged to either accept their premises or be irrational. Instead, it suffices that some or many sensible people in fact do accept their premises. The arguments can serve to bolster and confirm belief in God, perhaps even convince people to believe.

Plantinga recognizes a similar general structure to the moral arguments as the one noted above, as this passage from some famous lecture notes makes clear:

> There are many different versions of moral arguments, among the best being Bob Adams' favored version. . . . (1) One might find oneself utterly convinced (as I do) that morality is objective, not dependent upon what human beings know or think, and that it cannot be explained in terms of any "natural" facts about human beings or other things; that it can't ultimately be explained in terms of physical, chemical, or biological facts. (2) One may also be convinced that there could not be such objective moral facts unless there were such a person as God who, in one way or another, legislates them.[10]

---

[9]Theistic belief doesn't need evidence for deontological justification, or for positive epistemic status, or for "Foley rationality or Alstonian justification." Belief in God, in Plantinga's estimation, is "properly basic" (a concept that will be explained in detail later in this book, which will help those less familiar with it). For now, think of a "properly basic" belief as a belief we tend to accept without argument because it's just that obvious. For example, "the world is over five minutes old." Had the world been created five minutes ago, with all of our memories implanted and with all the signs of age, the evidence we'd have at our disposal would be exactly the sort of evidence we have now for a much older world. Yet none of us are likely to lose sleep over this.

[10]Here consider George Mavrodes' argument that morality would be 'queer' in a Russellian or nontheistic universe (in 'Religion and the Queerness of Morality' in *Rationality, Religious Belief, and Moral Commitment*, ed. Audi and Wainwright). Other important arguments here: A. E. Taylor's (*The Faith of a Moralist*) version, and Clem Dore's (and Sidgwick's) Kantian argument from the confluence of morality with true self-interest, some of the other arguments considered by Bob Adams in the above mentioned paper, and arguments by Hastings Rashdall in *The*

Plantinga then cites various philosophers from the past who have offered forms of the moral argument. This rich history shows both the variety of moral arguments and also their shared core concepts. For now note as well that the same threefold structure of moral apologetics is at work here: objective moral facts, the inability of secular and naturalistic ethical theories to account for them adequately, and the superior explanation provided by theism.

Interestingly, at a 2015 Baylor conference in Plantinga's honor, structured around this legendary lecture on arguments for God's existence, he was asked which of the arguments he thinks to be the best. In terms of the likelihood of the premises and the tightness of the logical connection between the premises and conclusion, he said he would give the nod to the moral argument. William Lane Craig, similarly, has said that, in his experience debating theism on college campuses, the moral argument has been the most persuasive.

What makes this all the more interesting where Plantinga is concerned is his 1967 book titled *God and Other Minds*, inspiration for which occurred to him in a flash while he was in a dingy parking lot at Wayne State University.[11] In that book, a classic itself, Plantinga hardly makes mention of the moral argument. He admitted decades later that much of his skepticism toward most of the arguments for God's existence at that time was because he thought a good argument had to feature premises rationally compelling to all rational people, a requirement he later thought too stringent. His more recent enthusiasm for the moral argument is just one powerful example of a renewed interest in moral apologetics.

Such apologetics is not an argument that just any god or gods exist, however, but rather a God of a particular sort of character. *Who God is* is

---

*Theory of Good and Evil* and by W. R. Sorley, *Moral Values and the Idea of God* which we used to read in college." This is from Plantinga's important paper "Two Dozen (or So) Theistic Arguments," the basis on which a new collection of essays edited by Trent Dougherty and Jerry Walls will soon be published by Oxford University Press. The essay is available online here: www .calvin.edu/academic/philosophy/virtual_library/articles/plantinga_alvin/two_dozen_or_so _theistic_arguments.pdf (accessed August 18, 2016).

[11]I (Dave) am existentially acquainted with those dingy parking lots, having finished my doctorate at Wayne State in 2002. The main flashes of insight they inspired within me involved moving to warmer weather.

a question that is just as important as *whether God exists*. This is a compelling central story line in Lewis's *Till We Have Faces*. Three important characters in the novel are Psyche, Orual, and the Fox. Psyche and Orual believe in "the gods," whereas the Fox, trained in Greek philosophy, is skeptical of their existence. Between Psyche and Orual, however, there is another divide: Psyche considers the gods marvelous and good, whereas Orual considers them dark and consumptive and horrible.

The question of whether God exists is an important one, but just as important, if not more so, is whether God is good. To the question of God's character, therefore, we now turn.

## THE PANTHEON OF GODS

It is unclear what Socrates' particular theological convictions were. Considering Plato's record of his words in, say, the *Apology*, Socrates sounds at points like a monotheist but at other times like the polytheists of his day. Much of Socrates' skepticism is directed at "the gods," though. Usually when speaking of his own convictions he makes reference to the Supreme God.[12] Nevertheless, what is clear is he does not accept the pantheon of Greek gods, or the traditional lore surrounding them, as infallible truth. He does, in contrast, seem to take quite seriously his divine mandate to function as a gadfly, exposing people's pretensions and ignorance.

The difference between belief in a collection of finite and imperfect gods versus a supreme creator and sustainer of all can hardly be exaggerated. To take but one example: Zeus engaged in countless affairs with immortals and mortals alike, sometimes taking to rape to satisfy his lusts. The God of classical theism can be framed in such terms only by the most tortured depictions. But to many atheists, the difference is a minor one. Indeed, the suggestion is often made that the difference is negligible, perhaps even nonexistent. What is held in common is far more important than any disagreement, so goes the suggestion. Some atheists are

---

[12]But this still might make him more of a henotheist than a classical monotheist. Henotheism is the belief in and worship of a single god while accepting the existence or possible existence of other deities. The term was originally coined by Friedrich Schelling (1775–1854) and was used by Friedrich Welcker to depict primordial monotheism among ancient Greeks.

fond of saying that they believe in just one god less than do the mono-
theists, but this is perhaps the wrong way to understand what's going on.
The difference between a polytheistic assortment of this-worldly, morally
flawed gods, on the one hand, and an all-powerful, omnibenevolent God,
on the other, can hardly be starker, so what accounts for the way some
thinkers conflate these two radically different visions of reality?[13]

Perhaps part of what's going on is the distinction between looking *at*
a beam of light and looking *along* it, as C. S. Lewis once put it. Lewis
envisions a toolshed into which is shining a sliver of light through a small
crack. One can look at the beam of light, or one can look through the
crack along the beam of light, and then a whole world bursts into view.
One has to, in a sense, be inside the beam to see what it lights up.

Or for another example: someone with only a cursory knowledge of
music might blur the auditory lines between "Chopsticks" and
Beethoven's Fifth Symphony, but those called to perform the piece understand the differences to a degree no outsider could know. Atheists,
looking from the outside in, fail to see any significant difference between,
say, the gods of the Greek pantheon and the God of Christianity. But for
those for whom God is a living reality, the thought of interchanging the
God of all creation, the God in whom there's no shadow of turning, with
the feckless, fallible gods of Euthyphro is worse than a joke.[14]

The issue at stake is the huge metaphysical difference between Euthyphro's quarreling, contentious gods and the one on whom all that exists
depends for its existence from moment to moment. The imaginary gods
are conceived to be part of the universe, the cosmos, whereas God is the
creator of the universe, vastly greater than the universe itself. Even
putting the point like this risks conveying the wrong impression—as if
the value of the universe and of its Creator can be quantitatively compared. It's no mere difference of degree between God and his creation but

---

[13]David Bentley Hart adroitly pushes the disanalogies between the finite gods of, say, the Greek
pantheon and the God of all creation in his *The Experience of God: Being, Consciousness, Bliss*
(New Haven, CT: Yale University Press, 2013).

[14]Ironically enough, Lewis, in his 1954 inaugural address at Cambridge University (on his fifty-
sixth birthday), discerned greater continuity between paganism and Christianity than between
Christianity and post-Christianity.

a difference of kind. The qualitative incommensurability is the most important difference of all, of which the radical difference between a book and its author is but the slightest intimation. The God of classical theism differs from his creation infinitely more than architect differs from building, as farmer differs from crop, as teacher differs from lesson plan.

The gods, conceived as contingent and finite, are a subset of all the contents of a universe, which itself can't begin to compare with its maker. As Paul said at Mars Hill, "The God who made the world and everything in it, being Lord of heaven and earth, does not live in shrines made by man, nor is he served by human hands, as though he needed anything, since he himself gives to all men life and breath and everything" (Acts 17:24-25).

The issue of the divine identity makes all the difference when it comes to the question of whether moral truth points to God. In the *Euthyphro*, Socrates inquires into the nature of piety or holiness. Euthyphro's first answer is that piety is doing what he himself is doing: prosecuting a wrongdoer. But Socrates wants more than an example.[15] He wants to know the essential nature or essence of piety. Today we might call this the nature of morality, or perhaps the foundation of morality.

Euthyphro then appeals to the loves of the gods, but the problem, as Socrates quickly points out, is that the gods disagree. Hera is none too fond of Zeus's unfaithful ways, for example. If they disagree, they likely disagree about moral matters. Euthyphro finally tries again to salvage his theistic account by saying that the pious is what *all* the gods love, and the impious what *all* the gods hate. And Socrates then challenges him with what's come to be known as the "Euthyphro Dilemma": "Is something loved by (all) the gods because it is pious, or is it pious because it is loved by (all) the gods?"

Put into contemporary terms—replacing reference to the "gods" with "God" and "the loves" with "the commands"—the famous Euthyphro Dilemma is thought by many to be the nail in the coffin of theistic ethics. It goes like this: "Is something moral because God commands it, or does

---

[15]This is sometimes called "definition by ostension."

God command something because it is moral?" As we'll see, neither option presented is entirely satisfying.

Each horn of the dilemma is thought to pose a problem for the classical theist. If she says that something is moral because God commands it, then this generates what seems to be extreme arbitrariness. Morality becomes subject to the whims of what could be a capricious god. For example, what if God were to command us to do something awful, like torture children for fun? Surely nothing, not even divine fiat, could warrant so horrific an action. How could a God like this meaningfully be thought good?

The other horn of the dilemma, though, would suggest that God commands something because it is moral, which seems to suggest that morality has a sort of independent existence and authority apart from God. So the classical theist who wishes to ground morality in God has a problem: to avoid saying morality is arbitrary, she's driven to admit that morality is independent of God. But to deny a dependence relation is to sacrifice the heart of the case for moral apologetics.

This does indeed seem to pose a thorny dilemma for Euthyphro's gods. Quite the sticky wicket. And who wants a sticky wicket?[16] But it's not at all clear that it's as big a problem for the God of classical theism. Suppose we confine our attention for the moment to a divine command theory (DCT) of moral obligations. On this (noncore) specific account of theistic ethics, God's commanding us to perform an action makes it the case that we have a moral obligation to do the action. Now consider this argument:

Premise 1: DCT; that is, God's command to us to perform an action makes it obligatory for us to perform the action.

Premise 2: *It is possible* that God could command us to torture children for fun.

Conclusion: *It is possible* that child torture for fun could become morally obligatory.

---

[16]Maybe *some* do. We have no idea what a sticky wicket is. We'd look it up, but we have a book to write. If anyone knows what a sticky wicket is, feel free to clue us in.

The conclusion follows from the evidence (the premises) and appears to be a devastating case against divine command theory, but are the premises true? Since the conclusion is beyond horrific, one might wish to suggest this shows that DCT is false. Suppose instead we challenge the other premise. This is a possibility introduced because of the theology of classical theism, according to which God is, among other things, perfectly good. Remember that this wasn't an option available to Euthyphro because of the morally corrupt nature of his gods. The God of classical theism, in stark contrast, is all-good (or *omnibenevolent,* to sound sophisticated; or *impeccable,* to sound downright pretentious), practically by definition. Arguably this means that premise 2 is simply false. It's *not* possible that God could command us to torture children for fun.[17]

Some have responded by saying that, even if it's impossible for God to do this, nevertheless, *if* God were to issue such a command, *then* divine command theory would entail that such a reprehensible action would become a moral obligation. They grant that God can't but are still troubled by the implications were this impossibility to materialize. The same could be said for any moral theory at all, however.

If Kant's moral theory (what he calls the "categorical imperative") were to command us to torture children for fun, then it would entail the moral propriety of the action. Likewise with any other moral theory. Adherents of each of these theories would be well within their rights to argue that it's significant that, in fact, their theories entail no such things. Dealing with impossible hypotheticals is not required to set forth a satisfactory ethical system.

The divine command theorist would certainly be within her rights to deny God could do this, and if she's basing her theory on the God of classical theism, she's correct. *Who God is* makes a huge difference. The divine command theorist isn't just endorsing DCT irrespective of who God is or what God is like. And once more, DCT is just one particular example of a theistic moral theory, not at the core of the moral argument. Plenty of moral apologists might choose to flesh out how morality is dependent on God differently.

---

[17]Or at least it's reasonable to assume that such a heinous command isn't possible in light of God's essentially loving nature.

## THE CHARACTER OF GOD

The importance of God's character was a key insight that occurred to Robert Adams during the course of his career. He realized that the nature of God makes all the difference to a defense of divine command theory. It's not the commands of any arbitrary, capricious god that are morally authoritative but the commands of a loving God. The Euthyphro Dilemma poses an insurmountable difficulty for morally deficient deities, but not for the God of classical theism.[18]

In this connection, one more word about Orual and Psyche from *Till We Have Faces*. Rudolf Otto, author of *The Idea of the Holy*, claims that experiences of the Holy are one of the basic sources of religious belief throughout the centuries. He distinguishes and describes several constituent elements of the experience of the numinous, or the Holy, two of which are these, both found in *Till We Have Faces*: (1) *tremendum*, a kind of dread or fear unlike our other fears—as Orual rightly describes it, a fear "quite different from the fear of my father," and (2) *fascinans*, a consuming attraction or rapturous longing. Psyche is poignantly aware of both, Orual mainly only of the former. *Fascinans*, or "joy," to use Lewis's term, is associated with the objects of the imagination, with beauty, with poetry, and above all with the Mountain—all common motifs in Lewis's fiction.[19]

When one such as Richard Dawkins starts a book by writing that the "God of the Old Testament is arguably the most unpleasant character in all of fiction. Jealous and proud of it; a petty, unjust unforgiving control-freak; a vindictive, bloodthirsty ethnic-cleanser; a misogynistic homophobic racist, infanticidal, genocidal, filicidal, pestilential, megalomaniacal," it's clear he's no fan. This led Plantinga with characteristic wit to chide:

---

[18]Also known as the God of Anselm—the possessor of the great-making omni-qualities such as omniscience, omnipotence, and omnibenevolence. Adams's insights furnished various reasons for the resurgence of interest in moral apologetics. If such arguments require God to function at the foundation of ethics, the specter of Euthyphro had to be exorcised. Good theology had to replace bad theology. A theologically and philosophically rich enough understanding of who God is had to be the operative theology among theistic ethicists. Capricious gods are susceptible to arbitrariness objections, whereas the God of classical theism is not.

[19]Adam Barkman usefully points out the way that, in Lewis's larger corpus, a constellation of notions are used to capture this idea of heavenly desire: Platonic *eros*, romanticism, the numinous, *Sehnsucht* ("poets have said more about it than philosophers"), nostalgia, joy, hope, desire. See chapter 3 of Barkman's *C. S. Lewis & Philosophy as a Way of Life* (Allentown, PA: Zossima, 2009).

"Dawkins seems to have chosen God as his sworn enemy. (Let's hope for Dawkins' sake God doesn't return the compliment.)"[20]

Dawkins clearly inhabits the place of Orual throughout most of *Till We Have Faces*, holding God up to critical scrutiny. He seems to grasp an intimation of *tremendum* but precious little of God's *fascinans*. On the other hand, we hazard to guess that plenty of religious believers could be implicated in focusing on God's love to the exclusion of his fear-inducing characteristics. The fear of God is the beginning of wisdom, Scripture teaches (Prov 9:10). Judgment by God is a frightful prospect, but nowadays people seem to feel that judging God is more important. God's "in the dock," as Lewis once put it; it's thought we judge God rather than vice versa. Modern people think they can issue an indictment of God's character. The Old Testament conquest narratives, for example, are cited by many as decisive evidence that God's a monster.[21]

A danger of any particular time period is that those inhabiting it take as sacrosanct its prevailing assumptions. Ours is a cynical and judgmental age, and it's easy to envision ourselves as upholding the moral standards even God must meet. A mere moment's reflection reveals how misguided such confidence is, at best; at worst, how transparent an effort it is to shift the focus away from our own moral failures. We are in no position to judge God, but even if we presume to, Arthur Miller's Danforth provides a telling cautionary tale of just how wrong we can be.

Or imagine the following scene: a man walks into the doctor's office and says, "Doc, I think that I am God."

"How did that start?" asks the doctor.

"Well, first I created the sun, then the earth. . . ."

We aren't God. If there's a reckoning to come, it will involve *us* in the dock, not God. If the hour of ignorance is over, why harbor a hankering to return in spirit to the pantheon of morally immature Greek gods? If the God of all

---

[20]Alvin Plantinga, "The Dawkins Confusion," *Books and Culture*, November/December 2016, www.booksandculture.com/articles/2007/marapr/1.21.html.

[21]Readers interested in that issue are encouraged to take a look at Paul Copan's *Is God a Moral Monster? Making Sense of the Old Testament God* (Grand Rapids: Baker Books, 2011), and Copan and Matthew Flannagan's *Did God Really Command Genocide? Coming to Terms with the Justice of God* (Grand Rapids: Baker Books, 2014).

goodness has shown up and revealed his character once and for all to be perfectly loving and holy, why regress to deficient gods of the imagination?

God is neither a monster nor an innocuous friend. *Tremendum* without *fascinans*, or vice versa, leads to the wrong picture of God. He is indeed to be feared and held in awe. God is life and love itself. Rather than thinking that morality constitutes evidence against God's existence or goodness, we think it rather gives us good reason to believe in a good God. This is the case we intend to lay out.

God's goodness and his holiness do not mean safety. Of the great picture of Christ we find in Lewis's Aslan, we affirm with Mr. Beaver: "'Course he isn't safe. But he's good. He's the King, I tell you." There's nothing soft or indulgent about God's love. He means business. At the culmination of *Till We Have Faces*, after the whole book traces Orual's judgment of the gods, God shows up to judge her. "The earth and stars and sun, all that was or will be, existed for his sake. And he was coming. The most dreadful, the most beautiful, the only dread and beauty there is, was coming."

Morality provides a credible reason to affirm the existence of a God who is good—the most dreadful and the most beautiful.

## TALK BACK

1. In the first section of this chapter, we offer several examples of people who seem to be striving for justice, but in a way that twists it into something unrecognizable and, often, even contrary to true justice. What is it about the human condition that might account for this?

2. In this chapter, we quote Richard Dawkins, who cares very little for the God of the Old Testament (to put it mildly). How prevalent is such a depiction of God (as vindictive, cruel, oppressive)? On what is it based? What answers are there to such charges?

3. Have you ever experienced *tremendum* (one-of-a-kind dread) or *fascinans* (rapturous longing), what Rudolf Otto articulates as the experience of the numinous or the Holy? Explain those experiences and what conclusions you drew about the nature of reality based on them.

# CHAPTER 2

# STUBBORN MORAL FACTS

*The word "good" has many meanings. For example,
if a man were to shoot his grandmother at a
range of five hundred yards, I should call him a
good shot, but not necessarily a good man.*

G. K. CHESTERTON,
"NEGATIVE AND POSITIVE MORALITY"

IN 2005 AMERICAN NOVELIST and essayist David Foster Wallace opened his celebrated commencement speech to Kenyon College with a fish story. As Wallace told it, two young fish happened along an older fish one morning. The older fish greeted them with an affable, "How's the water, boys?" They swam on for a bit, and as they did, the question settled in. Eventually, unable to contain his curiosity any longer, one fish demanded of the other: "What the hell is water?"[1]

Often, the more foundational an aspect of our everyday experience, the more encompassing and omnipresent a reality, the easier it goes unnoticed or even gets taken for granted. Gravity, light, our senses, Pokémon: we leave in-depth understanding of these commonplace phenomena to the experts and go on our merry way. The same often holds true for our culture-specific habits and belief systems. Sometimes a visit to another country affords an opportunity to identify and examine the expectations we have of the world around us.

---

[1]David Foster Wallace, *This Is Water: Some Thoughts, Delivered on a Significant Occasion, About Living a Compassionate Life* (Boston: Little, Brown, 2009).

On a visit to the Louvre a few years back, I (Marybeth) realized how much I took for granted my sense of personal space. While waiting in line to purchase tickets, I left an American-sized gap between myself and the person in front of me. Europeans have different standards for such things, I learned, as a throng of people crowded in to fill the space. My ingrained sense of respectable personal space was clearly culturally conditioned and contingent.

Others of our most elemental commitments, however, are much more obstinate. A mother's duty to her child, proscriptions against rape, forgiveness as crucial for loving relationships. These belong to the realm of moral truths. While these truths are often just assumed as so obvious that they don't need much explanation, consideration of what lies behind them or what might account for them can help us better understand ourselves and our world.

Hastings Rashdall explains the function such inquiry can serve: "So long as he is content to assume the reality and authority of the moral consciousness, the Moral Philosopher can ignore Metaphysics; but if the reality of Morals or the validity of ethical truth be once brought into question, the attack can only be met by a thorough-going enquiry into the nature of Knowledge and of Reality."[2]

For the purpose of just such an inquiry, identifying an assortment of moral realities in need of explanation is the aim of this chapter. As we've mentioned before, the argument we prefer is an inference to the best explanation. Another term for this type of argument is *abduction*, which differs from deductive or inductive argument forms.[3] Generally, the procedure of abduction goes like this: we come across something that

---

[2]Hastings Rashdall, *The Theory of Good and Evil* (Oxford: Clarendon, 1907), 192.

[3]In a deductive argument, the premises aim to provide a logical guarantee for the conclusion, an airtight case between the evidence and conclusion. For example, "All men are mortal. Socrates is a man. So Socrates is mortal." In a good inductive argument, the premises supply strong evidence for the truth of the conclusion, but nothing like certainty. Generalizations, statistical syllogisms, and arguments from analogy are examples. Suppose you have a lot of friends, and I meet most but not all of them. All your friends I meet are nice people. I then infer, on this basis, that *all* your friends are nice. There's no guarantee, but it's not a bad inference. The more of your friends I've met, and the more representative the sample, the more likely the conclusion's true. Abduction shares with induction a less-than-certain inference but has enough of its own distinctive features to qualify as a third kind of reasoning.

needs to be explained, then we identify a range of possible explanations, and then we narrow the list down to the best one. For example, does a Starbucks triple skinny mocha help us write better because it's chock-full of caffeine that stimulates the nervous system, or does it help us write better because the baristas sprinkle it with enchanted fairy dust? While this is an easy question to answer (fairy dust, obviously), the approach can help with more knotty ones such as the moral issues at the heart of this book. This is just one among other ways to structure the moral argument, but it's the one we'll pursue here.

The process of finding the best explanation involves applying standards such as explanatory power and scope to the different theories on offer. Explanatory power is *how well* an explanation explains; explanatory scope is *how much* an explanation explains. The conclusion of this book will be that theism in general, and Christianity in particular, provides the best explanation of morality in terms of both explanatory power and scope. We will thus argue that morality gives us good reason to think that a good God exists.

Once we identify the *best* explanation, we at least tentatively infer it as the *likely true* explanation. As a nonphilosopher, I (Marybeth) sympathize with many of our readers who might find this conclusion less than satisfactory. God is the true explanation of these moral truths—no "likely" about it, I want to say! However, it's important to keep in mind what we are attempting to do here and why. Although we ourselves are committed to the stronger claim, arguing for the less ambitious one is preferable. Our approach relies on and encourages bridge building, which isn't helped by treating difficult questions as easier than they are. Additionally, counterintuitively to be sure, this less ambitious claim actually makes for a stronger argument overall by requiring the evidence to carry less freight. We should also remember the context of this argument: it is but one tool in the apologetic and evangelistic toolbox. The longer we can stay in discussion with others, the more of these tools we can use. Humility, nuance, patience: all of these help the apologetic endeavor in the long run.

Act Two of the book will present the pieces of our actual argument, and Act Three will bring them all together. Since important moral facts function at the foundation of the argument to come (these facts are the data in need of explanation), it's worth spending a bit of time here introducing them.

## VALUE AND OBLIGATIONS

Perhaps the most foundational moral category is that of value. It is human nature to value things—our family, friends, pets, art, to name but a few possibilities. The mere act of valuing something, of course, doesn't mean it's actually valuable. Someone might value Internet trolling, for example, without such an obnoxious practice containing any real value. Presumably, though, some things *deserve* to be valued. They really are valuable.

A good candidate for something of intrinsic value or dignity is human beings. Most people assume that indeed human persons, even Detroit Lions fans (such as our son), have tremendous dignity. But this of course has not always been assumed. Vast swaths of human history have featured denials of human rights, dignity, value, or equality. Carving out the category of intrinsic worth or essential equality for human beings required a protracted process of moral development. Nowadays it's usually assumed as axiomatic, but historically it was hardly considered obvious. In light of the differences between people, this is rather understandable. Over time, though, human rights and the intrinsic worth, inherent dignity, and essential equality of persons have become much more commonly held convictions. They are often thought of as so obvious today, in fact, that they are seen as requiring no defense.[4] (What's water, anyway?)

Moral obligations are closely connected to moral value, but they remain distinct. To have a moral obligation to perform an action is, among other things, to be guilty for failing to perform it, perhaps to

---

[4]The principle was enshrined in the American Declaration of Independence with the claim that all men are created equal and that they are endowed by their Creator with inalienable rights. At times, of course, rather than deny the premise that humans have value, groups in power have excluded segments of the population from that category—the unborn, Jewish people during the Holocaust, African American slaves.

deserve censure of some sort for neglecting it.[5] Binding, authoritative obligations seem to be real phenomena in need of robust explanations. Of course, however, it's always possible to deny their existence—or the existence of moral value, for that matter.

Flannery O'Connor imaginatively depicts such a scenario in her short story "Good Country People." The character Hulga (who has changed her own name from "Joy"), an atheist with a degree in philosophy, claims to be skeptical of a great deal. Having lost a leg and grown disillusioned with life, she's hardened her heart and become jaded. Fancying herself the intellectual, she claims to see *through* things, to explain them *away*. Her education, combined with her sense of personal loss and pain, becomes an excuse for cynicism, even a sort of radical nihilism. This is her situation until she's wooed by Manley Pointer, a traveling Bible salesman in whom she sees, for the first time, real innocence. He pursues her romantically, and she acquiesces to his advances, all the while thinking herself his superior.

In a moment of tenderness, while they recline together in a barn loft, he asks her to show him where her artificial leg attaches, encouraging her to entrust him with her greatest vulnerability. She finally relents and shows him how to remove it, then lets him gently do so himself. To her the experience feels like an epiphany, like her heart has stopped, like she's lost her life and has found it again.

Then, in typical O'Connor fashion, she sucker-punches the reader's soul. The boy's demeanor suddenly changes, he puts the leg out of Hulga's reach, and his reverence and respect disappear. After realization of the horrific reality dawns on her, Hulga tries to lunge for her leg but is easily pushed back down. Her cynical nihilism is revealed for the sham it is as she charges Manley with hypocrisy, for not living up to his moral obligations:

> "You're a Christian!" she hissed. "You're a fine Christian! You're just like them all—say one thing and do another. You're a perfect Christian, you're . . ."

---

[5]An action can be a morally good action to perform without being an obligation.

The boy's mouth was set angrily. "I hope you don't think," he said in a lofty indignant tone, "that I believe in that crap! I may sell Bibles but I know which end is up and I wasn't born yesterday."

He then steals away with her leg, an act whose cruel treachery vividly lays bare the vacuity of moral skepticism. The moral of the story is clear: roll in the hay with nihilism, and you won't be left with a leg to stand on.[6]

Moral skepticism deserves a full-length treatment of its own, of course. For now, we are comfortable assuming that people have great value and that some actions are right and wrong. We have obligations to perform certain actions, and to refrain from doing others, on pain of objective guilt, perhaps censure. Some acts are hideously evil—the Holocaust, Cambodian Killing Fields, or a thousand other atrocities. Typically, outside the philosophy seminar room, such moral truths are obvious. In this book we will assume that our moral sensibilities are often truth revealing, that they have something vital to teach us, so we will reexamine such moral facts and ask what it is about what's real that accounts for them. What is it about reality that's revealed by such obvious and inviolable truths?

## MORAL FREEDOM

One of the most famous attractions in Philadelphia, the great City of Brotherly Love, is the Liberty Bell. Commissioned in 1752, the vaunted and venerable bell in its subsequent history took on the status of an icon, an international symbol of hope and, most importantly, freedom. "Proclaim LIBERTY throughout all the land unto all the inhabitants thereof," it reads triumphantly, taken from Leviticus 25:10.

Almost as famous as the bell itself is its prominent crack, visible to the eye. Closer inspection reveals a smaller hairline fracture extending through much of the bell as well. The bell has needed recasting, and some have even called for its replacement because of shoddy workmanship, damage incurred in transit, and inferior metal composition.

Like the famous bell, the notion of moral and metaphysical free will has also been mishandled and forged with inferior stuff, rendering it by

---

[6]Hat tip to Henry Edmondson.

turns brittle and damaged along the way and, on occasion, making it sound the wrong note. Some practically deify and idolize it, and by extension themselves. They assign to human beings prerogatives not just to choose *to do* the moral thing, but to determine *what is* good and bad, right and wrong, virtue and vice. Some have suggested we ditch the concept of free will altogether, relegating it to the outdated faith of our forebears somewhere in the past tucked between powdered wigs, bell bottoms, and flip phones. Others have called for revisions in our understanding of it to repair its weaknesses and replace its ingredients.

Yet others continue to extol free will, rightly cast, as the symbol of our highest and best selves, a mark of our dignity and our very humanity, perhaps even a way of imaging God. This not only calls for an investigation into what sort of freedom we have; it constitutes a call to arms, a battle over what it means to be human and a meaningful moral agent.

Moral freedom functions at the foundation of the whole moral edifice. Morality is *prescriptive*. In other words, it tells us how we *ought to live*, and this makes sense only if we have sufficient volitional control. But moral agency—meaningful free will with which we can make culpable moral decisions—can't just be presupposed. Whether we have it and what exactly it is are crucial questions, particularly if moral obligations exist. The subjective feeling of genuine agency is common to everyone. What best accounts for such corresponding moral freedom, if it's real, remains the question.[7]

## MORAL KNOWLEDGE

In an iconic scene from Mark Twain's *The Adventures of Huckleberry Finn*, Huck is forced into a difficult decision. His adventure down the Mississippi with the runaway slave Jim has not worked out well. Jim has been captured, and Huck believes the only solution is to inform Jim's owners of his location. However, this will almost certainly result in Jim being sold "down the river," a fate that means separation from

---

[7]We realize that questions regarding free will are vexed and controversial and that plenty of readers might disagree with some of our general claims here. Also, we're not devoting a full chapter to this question, but it's a query that lingers in the background of much of our discussion.

family, hard labor, and cruelly harsh treatment at cotton plantations in the Deep South. To be sold down the river is often as good as a death sentence for a slave.

In the moral high point of the book, Huck rejects the cultural voices that insist this is the right course of action. Huck no longer sees Jim as a slave merely to be bought and sold but as a friend and human being, someone deserving of better treatment than his society allows. This rejection comes at a high price for Huck, costing him his soul—or so he believes because of the cultural message of his day. But he poignantly accepts this fate, crystallizing his decision in this memorable declaration: "All right then, I'll go to hell." Huck is able to make this difficult choice because he sees with crystal clarity that it is the right thing to do, no matter the cost to himself. It's something he knows.

Moral knowledge is different from, say, moral values or moral obligations. A moral value might exist without our being aware of it. Moral metaphysics, concerning which we quoted Rashdall earlier, is about what moral reality *there is*. Moral epistemology, on the other hand, is the matter of *what we know* about morality. Most of us claim to know various moral facts such as how right or good it is to feed the impoverished or house the homeless. In fact, many of our moral beliefs are such that we claim to know them as well as just about anything else. What can best explain the moral knowledge most all of us tend to think we have?

## KANTIAN MORAL FAITH

C. S. Lewis once wrote that there are two facts at the foundation of all clear thinking about ourselves and the universe we live in: First, human beings, all over the earth, have this curious idea that they ought to behave in a certain way and cannot really get rid of it. Second, they do not in fact behave in that way. They know the law of nature; they break it.

While this sounds like a dismal position for us to be in, we also recognize the truth of Lewis's insight. In our struggles to act morally, we might feel like Sisyphus, doomed forever to roll his ball uphill only to watch it tumble back down again. So why do we insist that the moral project is worthy of our commitment? The tenacity of the law is surely one reason. We can't help but feel the force of its authority on us. But what about the second part: Are we doomed always to fall short?

Such questions move us into the realm of moral faith. Moral faith, or "Kantian moral faith" (named after—you guessed it—Immanuel Kant), has two parts: first, the moral life is possible, and, second, a life of true happiness must be a moral life—morality and happiness must converge. Can we be moral, and are moral people ultimately happy? An answer of *yes* bespeaks a kind of moral faith. Let's quickly consider the first of these in a bit of detail, and the second more briefly.

First, is morality possible? When you're sick, you can try suppressing the symptoms, or you can go after the source. Or to alter the analogy, when you see a weed, you can cut off its head or remove its root. A similar distinction holds in the arena of morality. One option is merely to deal with symptoms, settling for marginal moral improvements, avoiding hurtful consequences by our actions, that sort of thing. Merely managing the symptoms, however, will ensure an ongoing battle with them, since the underlying cause remains. True achievement of integrity, virtue, and holiness, though, requires considerably more.

Is such moral transformation possible? And if so, with what resources? Benjamin Franklin once tried to do this on his own, setting himself the formidable task of achieving moral perfection. In "Arriving at Perfection," an excerpt from his *Autobiography*, Franklin writes about his plans to conquer all imperfections, whether they derived from natural inclination, custom, or company. "I soon found I had undertaken a task of more difficulty than I had imagined. While my care was employ'd in guarding against one fault, I was often surprised by another; habit took the advantage of inattention; inclination was sometimes too strong for reason."[8]

In light of what seem to be some deeply entrenched patterns of selfishness and moral weakness characteristic of the human condition, we appear to need profound external resources to meet the moral demand and to effect the needed change in our character. As we will see, this is one of the most important lessons Orual must learn in *Till We Have Faces*.

---

[8]Benjamin Franklin, *Autobiography* (1790), 38, www.ushistory.org/franklin/autobiography/.

Kant saw clearly that the moral demand on us is very high, while also recognizing that we have a natural inclination to resist it. In both Kant and Lewis, the suggestion seems to be not just that we happen to fail to meet the moral demand but that our failure is inevitable. We have a problem, one too deep for us to solve on our own. Is hope rational in the face of such an intractable challenge?

Second, the other aspect of Kantian moral faith pertains to the convergence of happiness and virtue. Even if we were able to be virtuous—completely altruistic and self-controlled—wouldn't that mean a life of asceticism? Where's the fulfillment in that? Can a life of joy and happiness fit with one of duty and sacrifice? If morality is to be a fully rational enterprise, it would seem it must. What features of reality would ensure such a correspondence?

What we have seen in this brief chapter is a bird's-eye view of the range of moral phenomena in need of explanation: evil, moral agency, moral goodness, moral obligations, moral transformation, moral rationality. Moral arguments, at least those advanced by Christian apologists and evangelists, choose some such moral element and argue that classical theism and/or orthodox Christianity constitutes either the best or the only explanation of the phenomenon in question. This book will opt for the former, arguing that theism (and Christianity) provides the *best* explanation. And the phenomena under consideration will run the gamut—from moral facts to moral knowledge, and from moral transformation to moral rationality.

Though we have reasons to prefer our particular approach, other apologists may take a different route. Much of what we say can be adapted to other approaches. We are not claiming that our strategy is sacrosanct, the only acceptable format, or even necessarily the best tack. What's at the core of our case is not the form of our argument but its underlying intuitive force, to which we wish to direct the reader's attention. Part of the import of the next two chapters on the history of moral apologetics is to showcase some of the remarkably rich variety possible in moral arguments.

## TALK BACK

1. Reflect on the moral facts laid out in this chapter—goodness, obligation, knowledge, transformation, and providence. Did any surprise you? Do you have a sense at this point of which you feel is the strongest? Note how often you use such moral language and categories and reflect a bit on what you mean when you do.

2. Drawing on my (Marybeth's) comments about the claims made by our argument (God as the likely true explanation of moral truths), reflect a bit on the role of reason in faith. Why might some be uncomfortable with an apologetic method of evangelism and prefer, say, proclamation or testimony? What advantages does apologetics have? Is there any tension between proclamation, testimony, and apologetics?

3. We used quite a few examples from literature in this chapter, drawing on characters and stories as examples of moral truth in action. What role can literature (or other fictional stories) serve in calling our attention to something true about the nature of reality? Is use of such stories appropriate in our search for truth?

# CHAPTER 3

# MORAL APOLOGETICS
# BEFORE THE
# TWENTIETH CENTURY

*When you read a work of history, always listen out for the*
*buzzing. If you can detect none, either you are tone deaf or*
*your historian is a dull dog. The facts are really not at all*
*like fish on the fishmonger's slab. They are like fish swimming*
*about in a vast and sometimes inaccessible ocean; and what*
*the historian catches will depend partly on chance, but mainly*
*on what part of the ocean he chooses to fish in and what tackle*
*he chooses to use.*

EDWARD HALLETT CARR, *WHAT IS HISTORY?*

IN THIS SECTION, WE TRACE moral arguments for God's existence
that can be found in Western literature.[1] We hope readers will discover
through our coverage the richness of the moral argument and the ways
in which many fine thinkers through the centuries have found this form
of natural theology rife with apologetic potential and power.[2] Another

---

[1]This is challenging to do in short compass because in each case we are wrenching the thinkers
from their historical contexts, which informed so much of their analysis. We're under no illusions
that this brisk survey is anywhere near exhaustive, nor does the discussion traverse all the various complexities and nuances, criticisms and rejoinders.

[2]Recall Plantinga's concise litany of moral apologists: Robert Adams, George Mavrodes, A. E.

important advantage of this history is that it brings into focus the distinction between core concepts of moral apologetics and secondary or peripheral ones.

As we proceed, be sure to listen for the buzzing! We hope you will not find us dull dogs!

## TWO GREEKS

Alfred North Whitehead once said that all of Western philosophy is a footnote to Plato (420s–348/347 BC), so we might as well start there.[3] William Lane Craig writes that the reasoning at the heart of the moral argument goes all the way back to Plato.[4] Why Plato?

Plato recorded the words of Socrates, who, you will recall, saw himself as under a divine mandate. Socrates was also a firm believer in objective moral obligations. C. Stephen Evans points out that Socrates seemed to have thought of obligations much as we do.[5] These obligations, Evans argues, exhibit four features: (1) Judgment about a moral obligation is a kind of verdict on my action. (2) A moral obligation brings reflection to closure. (3) A moral obligation involves accountability or responsibility. (4) A moral obligation holds for persons simply as persons. Plato's aforementioned *Apology* makes clear that Socrates believed in obligations involving all of these features, and Plato doesn't seem to have been different from his teacher in this regard.

---

Taylor, Clement Dore, Henry Sidgwick, Immanuel Kant, Hastings Rashdall, and William Sorley. To this list can be added several other luminaries: Plato, Aquinas, Augustine, Austin Farrer, A. C. Ewing, Angus Ritchie, C. S. Lewis, John Henry Newman, C. Stephen Layman, C. Stephen Evans, William Lane Craig, Mark Linville, John Hare, Paul Copan, and others besides. This chapter offers a whirlwind tour, in chronological order, of many of these figures, quickly fleshing out highlights from their moral arguments for God's existence. Both similarities and differences will become evident as the tour threads its way through history.

[3]Our son insists that all Mexican fast food joints are a footnote to Chipotle.

[4]William Lane Craig, *Reasonable Faith: Christian Truth and Apologetics*, 3rd ed. (Wheaton, IL: Crossway, 2008), 104.

[5]See C. Stephen Evans, *God and Moral Obligations* (Oxford: Oxford University Press, 2013), 16-19. Elizabeth Anscombe argues that the notion of moral obligations as law-like verdicts on our actions is a result of the Judeo-Christian tradition, which certainly has wielded a formidable influence on ethical thought in the Western world. What Evans points out challenges this view, showing that moral obligations have a longer history, however much Christianity may have accentuated their importance.

Apart from that issue, we find in Plato the notion that things have goodness insofar as they stand in some relation to the Good. The Good, Plato believes, subsists in itself. The Good, for Plato, was the "Form" that had primacy over all the others, the ultimate standard for all evaluations of goodness. It is likened to the sun and is said to be the source of all that exists. Craig adds, "With the advent of Christian theism, the Good became identified with God himself."[6] This is hardly to suggest that all moral apologists have to embrace this sort of Platonic picture of the Good. It's just one intriguing possibility among others, but one with a rich pedigree.

George Mavrodes argues that Plato's worldview, though not Christian, has very often been taken as congenial to a religious understanding of the world. He writes that the idea of the Good seems to play a metaphysical role in Plato's thought. In other words, it is somehow fundamental to what *is* as well as to what *ought to be*, much more fundamental than are the atoms. "A Platonic man, therefore, who sets himself to live in accordance with the Good aligns himself with what is deepest and most basic in existence."[7] Evans elaborates by suggesting it is no accident that there is a long tradition of theistic (and even Christian) Platonism, running from Augustine to Robert Adams. He suggests that it seems almost irresistible for a Platonist to ask what it says about the nature of ultimate reality that moral truths are deep truths about the universe.[8]

David Horner draws on Scripture to make this case:

The Psalmist invites us to "taste and see that the LORD is good" (Ps 34:8). Peter draws upon this image, as he invites his readers to grow in Christ:

---

[6]Craig, *Reasonable Faith.*

[7]"Or to put it another way, we might say that whatever values a Platonic world imposes on a man are values to which the Platonic world itself is committed, through and through." George Mavrodes, "Religion and the Queerness of Morality," in *Ethical Theory: Classical and Contemporary Readings*, 2nd ed., ed. Louis P. Pojman (New York: Wadsworth, 1995), 587.

[8]Arguably, in fact, Platonism makes more sense in a theistic world than a nontheistic one. John Rist writes, "Plato's account of the 'Forms' (including the Good) as moral exemplars leaves them in metaphysical limbo. They would exist as essentially intelligible ideas even if there were no mind, human or divine, to recognize them: as objects of thought, not mere constructs or concepts. But, as Augustine learned, and as the Greek Neoplatonists had asserted, the notion of an eternal object of thought (and thus for Plato a cause of thought) without a ceaseless thinking subject is unintelligible. Intelligible Forms, never proposed as mere concepts, cannot be proposed as Plato originally proposed them, as free-floating metaphysical items." John M. Rist, *Real Ethics: Rethinking the Foundations of Morality* (Cambridge: Cambridge University Press, 2002), 40.

"Like newborn babies, crave pure spiritual milk, so that by it you may grow up in your salvation, now that you have tasted that the Lord is good" (1 Pet 2:2-3). What Peter sees as the *result* of his readers' taste of God's goodness is suggested in his immediately subsequent phrase: "As you come to him . . ." (1 Pet 2:4). The picture suggested here is one that is reflected throughout Scripture and the history of Christian thought, viz. that God is good, and we are—and should be—drawn to him for precisely that reason: *as* good. Such an understanding also fits the classical philosophical conception of goodness as essentially desirable.[9]

Plato was Socrates' student, and Plato's famous student was Aristotle (384–322 BC). Although Plato's protégé, Aristotle took a different approach to ethics from that of his mentor. Aristotle was more inclined to speak of a thing's flourishing. A knife's goodness depends on the effectiveness with which it serves its purpose, for example. Likewise with human beings: How effectively do they serve their purpose? And this question raises another, namely, *what is* the purpose, goal, or end of human beings?

Borrowing an image from C. S. Lewis's *Mere Christianity* (book 3, chap. 1), consider a fleet of ships and the analogy they constitute for the moral enterprise. One dimension is that each ship needs to be seaworthy so that it can stay afloat and navigate the waters. The moral analogue is that each of us needs to be morally healthy so that we don't self-destruct from within but rather flourish as we should. A second issue is that the ships need to cooperate, to avoid bumping into one another. This corresponds to the social aspect of morality that pertains to harmony and peaceful interaction.

A third component considers where the ships are headed. What's their destination? This is the notion of teleology, which pertains to the purpose or directive, the goal or destination, of things, including human beings. Regarding ethics, the correlative question is, what are we made for? What fulfills our nature? Aristotle thought that everything in nature had some goal or telos, human beings most certainly.

---

[9]David Horner, "Too Good Not to Be True," *Moral Apologetics*, July 29, 2015, http://moralapologetics .com/too-good-not-to-be-true-a-call-to-moral-apologetics-as-a-mode-of-civil-discourse/.

Much of the Judeo-Christian tradition would affirm a strong sense of human and moral teleology. A life of virtue, for example, is thought to *fit our nature* somehow, Aristotelian and Christian ethicists would agree. Today this idea can still be found, even among many secular thinkers, but it generally plays a less prominent role in the thinking of many ethicists.

For Aristotle the highest activity in which we can be engaged is contemplation of the divine. This is the apex of the life of rational contemplation. Aristotle conceived of God as a magnet drawing people to himself. The Christian conception would add to this picture that God is pursuing us. Still, the ease with which one such as Aquinas could incorporate Aristotle's philosophy into a framework of divine law reveals quite a bit of consistency between aspects of Aristotelian and Christian thought. The strong shared sense of teleology, in particular, stands at odds with naturalism and its dogged challenges in retaining such a category.

## AN EARLY CHURCH THEOLOGIAN
## AND A MEDIEVAL THEOLOGIAN

Plato and Aristotle exerted a huge influence on early and medieval Christian thinkers, including Augustine (354–430) and Thomas Aquinas (1225–1274). Regarding Augustine, David Horner writes, "The goodness of God is a central (perhaps *the* central) feature of Augustine's thought. Augustine endorses the classical moral psychology, according to which we do all that we do in relation to what we take to be our *summum bonum*" (highest good).[10]

Augustine referred to the supreme good as something we seek, the good that somehow serves at the foundation of all we do. He thought we desire it not for the sake of something else but for its own sake. We require nothing further in order to be happy than obtaining *it*. It is truly called the "end," because we want everything else for its sake, but we want *it* only for itself. What is the highest good that everyone is ultimately seeking? God himself, Augustine thought. Horner adds that Augustine's famous words at the beginning of his *Confessions* should be understood

---

[10]Ibid.

in that light: "You have made us for yourself, and our heart is restless until it rests in you."

In book eight of *The Trinity*, Augustine's aim is to show that God is the good and that humans find happiness when they love God. Augustine makes two arguments that human happiness is found in loving God. The first argues from the existence and ranking of finite goods. Augustine begins his argument here with the assumption that humans "certainly only love what is good." Loving what is good Augustine takes to be a natural and obvious thing to do. This is the human telos. Augustine then notes that there are different goods found in different finite things. There is the good of friendship and of the beauty in nature, for example. Humans prefer some of these goods more than others.

In light of this, Augustine thinks two points are in need of explanation: the human ability to distinguish among the goods and a way to make sense of the ranking of different goods. Augustine suggests that God as *the* good explains both of these. God impressed upon the human mind "some notion of good itself."[11] And God is the standard by which all finite goods are ordered so that God is properly thought of as *the* good. Since the human telos is loving the good and God is identical to the good, human happiness or *eudaimonia* is found in loving God.[12]

---

[11] Augustine of Hippo, *On the Trinity*, in *St. Augustine: On the Holy Trinity, Doctrinal Treatises, Moral Treatises*, ed. Philip Schaff, trans. Arthur West Haddan, vol. 3 of A Select Library of the Nicene and Post-Nicene Fathers of the Christian Church, first series (Buffalo, NY: Christian Literature Company, 1887), 244.

[12] Besides this argument, Augustine also makes an argument from the requirements of moral transformation. Augustine begins this argument by noting that a human can be good in two senses: (1) it is good in that it exists, and (2) it is good in that it is an excellent example of its kind. Being good in sense (2) requires a "deliberate choice in order to acquire excellence." Since it is the human telos to love the good, being an excellent human requires a turn to the good. However, in order for moral reform to be possible, the good must be changeless and therefore cannot be the human soul. This changeless good can only be identified with *the* good, which is the only changeless good. Therefore, if humans are going to live according to their telos, if they are going to have happiness in the Aristotelian sense, they must love the good that is God. Augustine then concludes these arguments by saying, "If you cling to him [God] in love, you will straightway enter into bliss." In book 15 Augustine adds, "For this is the will of the best and most wise Creator, that the spirit of a man, when piously subject to God, should have a body happily subject, and that this happiness should last forever." Thanks to Jonathan Pruitt for those thoughts. See ibid., 223.

Born almost a millennium after Augustine, Aquinas is often cast as the original "natural law" theorist, paving the way for natural law's long and distinguished history in Christian thought ever since. More on natural law in a moment. Tom Morris thinks that Aquinas was probably the single greatest Christian thinker of all time.[13] It's true that Aquinas threw his (considerable) weight behind natural law. Theistic natural law theorists believe that God has manifested his moral law by writing it into human nature and into other aspects of his ordered creation.[14] Aquinas's famous "Fourth Way" has been interpreted by some as a type, or potential type, of moral argument. He begins this argument with an observation of something we find in the world: a gradation of values. Some things are better, truer, and nobler than other things. Such comparative terms describe the varying degrees to which things approach a superlative standard: the most good, truest, noblest. There must therefore exist something that is the best and truest and noblest of all. Aquinas believed that whatever possesses a property more fully than anything else is the cause of that property in all other things. Hence there is some being that is the cause of the existence, goodness, and any other perfection of finite entities, and this being we call *God*. This argument has been subjected to various criticisms, but we will defer discussion on this for now.

In Aquinas, Horner notes, at the heart of both his moral psychology and teleology is the classical understanding of the good as desirable.[15] Horner explains that, for Aquinas, the "perfect good" all human desires

---

[13]However, this didn't stop Morris from poking fun at Aquinas's inordinate heft: "A very, *very* fat Dominican, Aquinas was one of the heaviest thinkers at a time when the greatest minds were often housed in the largest, most corpulent bodies, a time not inappropriately known as the 'middle' ages. Corroborating the medieval metaphysical principle that effects resemble their causes, his literary output is often described as 'enormously voluminous.'" T. V. Morris, *The Bluffer's Guide to Philosophy* (South Bend, IN: Diamond Communications, 1989), 37.

[14]In recent literature, theistic ethicists such as John Hare and C. Stephen Evans have argued for a rapprochement of sorts between elements of natural law and divine command theory.

[15]Horner is elaborating on the following excerpt from Aquinas: "Whatever man desires, he desires it under the aspect of good. And if he desire it, not as his perfect good, which is the last end, he must, of necessity, desire it as tending to the perfect good, because the beginning of anything is always ordained to its completion; as is clearly the case in effects both of nature and of art. Wherefore every beginning of perfection is ordained to complete perfection which is achieved through the last end." Citations from Thomas Aquinas, *Summa Theologica*, trans. Fathers of the English Dominican Province (Westminster, MD: Christian Classics, 1981), Ia IIae.1.6c.

ultimately aim at is God himself: "God is the ground or 'Supreme Fount' of goodness and its true fulfillment, as 'the vision of the Divine Essence fills the soul with all good things, since it unites it to the source of all goodness.'"[16]

Horner notes that Aquinas, like Augustine, connected humanity's craving for goodness with its desire to know God: hunger for the good is, essentially, an expression of the longing for knowledge of God. Horner adds, "Aquinas devotes two full questions (Ia.5-6) to the nature of goodness and God's goodness, developing a rich metaphysical account of goodness that underwrites the metaphysical teleology and moral psychology noted above. At the heart of Aquinas's thought is seeing God as good, as the supreme good."[17]

## IMMANUEL KANT AND THOSE HE INSPIRED

Asked when moral arguments for God's existence really began making their appearance, many are inclined to start with Immanuel Kant (1724–1804).[18] Kant was brilliant, but reading his work can pose a challenge. Tom Morris jokes that Kant's writings have done more than anything else to persuade prospective philosophy majors to study business instead.

Generally skeptical of arguments from natural theology, Kant found workable versions of the moral argument, in which God functions as a "postulate of practical reason."[19] In the previous chapter, we noted two aspects of Kantian moral faith: the moral life is possible, and it's conducive to happiness. We must believe in God to give us the needed resources to be holy. We must also believe that God will ensure perfect

---

[16]Horner, "Too Good Not to Be True."

[17]Ibid. One might wonder, if this is so, why Aquinas isn't listed before Kant among the first moral apologists. Perhaps the biggest reason is that much of what Aquinas does when it comes to God and morality is explicate his variant of theistic ethics, which is different from offering an explicit moral apologetic. They're closely related and easily confused but remain conceptually distinct. Still, even if he did less moral apologetics than explication of theistic ethics, much of what he wrote remains relevant to the former.

[18]Anthony Thiselton, for example, writes that the moral argument did not emerge with full seriousness until the time of Kant. Anthony C. Thiselton, *The Thiselton Companion to Christian Theology* (Grand Rapids: Eerdmans, 2015), 601. Incipient moral apologist precursors to Kant arguably include Blaise Pascal, John Locke, and Thomas Reid.

[19]God, freedom, and immortality are *presupposed* by the categorical imperative of moral experience.

correspondence between happiness and the moral life in order for morality to make full rational sense.

Kant held that a rational, moral being must necessarily will "the highest good," which consists of a world in which people are both morally good and happy, and in which moral virtue is the condition for happiness. Kant was less concerned with questions of happiness per se than with questions of what makes us worthy of happiness. Kant held that a person cannot rationally will a virtuous life without believing that moral actions can successfully achieve such an end, which requires that the world be ordered in a certain way. "This is equivalent to belief in God, a moral being who is ultimately responsible for the character of the natural world."[20]

Since Kant, most notable moral apologists have been Protestants—a bit surprising given the influence of Augustine and Aquinas—but one partial exception is the Anglican-turned-Catholic John Henry Newman (1801–1890). In the nineteenth century he developed what could be called an argument from conscience. His most important work containing his moral argument is *An Essay in Aid of a Grammar of Assent*, published in 1870.

He argued that our consciences, particularly our feelings of guilt, lead us to conclude God exists.[21] Feelings of conscience are often directed toward fellow human beings, but sometimes our feelings of guilt or shame, which we take as evidence to suggest that we have offended someone, lack an appropriate human target. If such feelings are appropriate, they must then have a nonhuman target. Our feelings of responsibility, shame, and fear emanating from our conscience imply that there is one to whom we are responsible, before whom we are ashamed, whose claims on us we fear. Newman shared with Socrates and Paul the recognition of moral reckoning. God is more than judge, though. Newman argued that what the human heart most earnestly seeks is communion with God. Guilt sensitizes us to the impediment of sin in the way of that fellowship, a problem calling for a solution.

---

[20]C. Stephen Evans, "Moral Arguments for the Existence of God," in *Stanford Encyclopedia of Philosophy*, Winter 2016 ed., http://plato.stanford.edu/entries/moral-arguments-god/.

[21]This paragraph is lightly adapted from work previously done by David Baggett and Jerry Walls: *Good God: The Theistic Foundations of Morality* (New York: Oxford University Press, 2011).

Henry Sidgwick (1838–1900), an English philosopher, was not a proponent himself of a moral argument, though he nevertheless provides the materials for such an argument. In his *Methods of Ethics*, he identifies the "dualism of practical reason," a dilemma residing in attempting to reconcile morality as requiring both sacrifice and protection of self-interest. The import of this effort is closely aligned with the question of whether virtue and happiness coincide. With the limited resources of this world, a disconnect between them and thus between rationality and morality seems inevitable.

Often morality and self-interest coincide, but what about cases where they don't? What about when a costly and painful sacrifice is made at great variance with self-interest and without any posthumous way in which to experience compensation? Sidgwick himself saw that, if God were to exist, he could resolve the dilemma. A just God could ensure the desired correspondence between joy and virtue, and Sidgwick saw such correspondence as a vital need for morality to be fully rationalized. Although he saw this as a possible solution to the dualism of practical reason, he didn't opt for it, reconciling himself instead to an unresolved dilemma at the heart of ethics. Although Sidgwick didn't take this as moral evidence to suggest the truth of God's existence, the materials are surely there to do so.

American philosopher William James (1842–1910) is one of our favorites. By reputation he was eminently gregarious and had a big heart and lots of dear friends.[22] James once told a class that he knew a person who would poke the fire, set chairs straight, pick dust specks from the floor, arrange his table, snatch up a newspaper, take down any book that caught his eye, trim his nails, waste the morning anyhow, in short, and all without premeditation—simply because the only thing he ought to attend to is the preparation of a noonday lesson in formal logic, which he detests.

Although James wasn't exactly a moral apologist, he made a few relevant contributions to the discussion. For example, he offered a moral

---

[22]William James was the older brother of major American writer Henry James, who by all accounts was, in contrast to William, quite the recluse.

critique of naturalism by pointing to the phenomenon of moral regret. Some tragic elements of this world—dehumanizing, horrific mistreatment of innocents, for example—make for a "crop of regrets." However, in a determined world—at least an approximate likelihood if naturalism is true—"nothing else had a ghost of a chance of being put into their place."[23]

If there is any nagging doubt about James's verdict on naturalism, here's a telling passage from his justly lauded *Varieties of Religious Experience*:

> For naturalism, fed on recent cosmological speculations, mankind is in a position similar to that of a set of people living on a frozen lake, surrounded by cliffs over which there is no escape, yet knowing that little by little the ice is melting, and the inevitable day drawing near when the last film of it will disappear, and to be drowned ignominiously will be the human creature's portion. The merrier the skating, the warmer and more sparkling the sun by day, and the ruddier the bonfires at night, the more poignant the sadness with which one must take in the meaning of the total situation.[24]

The decade after James was born, William Sorley came into the world (1855–1935). He was author of *Moral Values and the Idea of God* (1918) and professor of moral philosophy at Cambridge, replacing Sidgwick. In his work we find arguments centering on this question: What worldview can explain both the natural and moral order? Not pluralism, he argues,

---

[23]These selections are from James's piece "The Dilemma of Determinism," in *The Will to Believe* (New York: Dover, 1956). For readers unfamiliar with the notion of determinism, it's the idea that all events are caused to happen just as they do, including human choices. Sometimes quantum indeterminacy is adduced as an exception, based on a particular interpretation of quantum mechanics, but, even if this interpretation holds, something at least close to determinism at the macro level seems likely on naturalism.

[24]William James, *The Varieties of Religious Experience* (New York: Modern Library, 1994), 159. Germane to questions of moral transformation, James contrasted the emotional and practical difference between acceptance of the universe in the "drab way of stoic resignation to necessity, or with the passionate happiness of Christian saints": "If religion is to mean anything definite for us, it seems to me that we ought to take it as meaning this added dimension of emotion, this enthusiastic temper of espousal, in regions where morality strictly so called can at best but bow its head and acquiesce. It ought to mean nothing short of this new reach of freedom for us, with the struggle over, the keynote of the universe sounding in our ears, and everlasting possession spread before our eyes. . . . This sort of happiness in the absolute and everlasting is what we find nowhere but in religion." Ibid., 41-42.

since moral values are eternally valid and can't reside in temporally finite persons. Nor monism, the notion that everything is essentially of a piece, which conflates *is* and *ought*. So what *could* explain both? Theism, he argues. The moral ideal is nowhere actualized in the finite world but instead in a personal and eternal God.[25] He thought his moral argument completed the cosmological argument: together they show God as the one explanation of both the natural and moral orders. His cast of mind favored a cumulative case for theism, drawing together various arguments so as to combine their strengths.

Anthony Thiselton writes that in the nineteenth and early twentieth centuries the most convincing advocate of the moral argument was perhaps Hastings Rashdall.[26] Rashdall (1858–1924), author of *The Theory of Good and Evil*, writes that from the fact that we are obliged to act in a certain way it must follow that there is an objective moral law. But such an ideal can exist nowhere but in a mind, and, owing to its objectivity, not in human consciousness. An absolute moral ideal can exist only in a mind from which all reality is derived. Our moral ideal can claim objective validity only insofar as it can rationally be regarded as the revelation of a moral ideal eternally existing in the mind of God, Rashdall argues. He thought that being an agnostic about the source of ethics may be reasonable enough but is unreflective. He was convinced that even when God isn't *explicit* in moral propositions, he remains *implicit*. If one starts to harmonize these things, one will be able to see agnosticism as unreasonable. Once we start to reflect and make the relevant connections, we'll see that morality points to a mind, and no mere finite mind will do.

In his Gifford Lectures from 1926–1928, A. E. Taylor (1869–1945) presented material for a powerful moral apologetic. Published in two volumes as *The Faith of a Moralist*, a bona fide classic, his argument stresses that moral values seem to be properties of persons, not mere Platonic abstractions. Taylor writes that, were there only the wills of

---

[25]William Lane Craig gives a nice summary of Sorley's view in his *Reasonable Faith*, 104-6.

[26]Thiselton, *Companion*, 602. For a fuller summary of Rashdall, see Thiselton's entry on the moral argument in that volume.

human beings—who are so often ignorant of the moral law and so often defy it—it is not clear where the moral law's validity would come from. Recognizing the validity of the law seems to carry with it a reference to an intelligence that does not, like we do, need to become aware of it incrementally. Rather, this intelligence has always been in full and clear possession of it. Such a will, Taylor thought, is guided by the law in all its operations, rather than often setting it aside, like we do.

Like some other notables, Taylor placed a premium on the evidential significance of *guilt*, identifying five characteristics that set human moral guilt apart: (1) Human guilt involves true condemnation of our behavior and not just because we got caught. (2) Moral guilt is indelible; even punishment doesn't do away with it. (3) We recognize that our guilt deserves punishment. (4) Justice demands punishment for our wrongdoing, but forgiveness marks love and perfection. (5) We sense that we have sinned against a person, not just against an impersonal principle. With God, though, there's also hope for salvation, forgiveness, and redemption. More explicitly than Kant, Taylor makes it clear that falling short of the moral standard is an offense against God himself. Taylor also distinguishes himself from Kant in explicitly identifying God as the highest good and the ground of value.

In the next chapter, we'll continue the historical fishing expedition begun here. And as you'll see, when it comes to the moral argument, the twentieth century is a fertile fishing hole indeed. Before its end, the moral argument experienced an explosion of renewed interest. It had already begun with the likes of Taylor, but a few decades after him came arguably the most important popularizer of the moral argument to date. We open the next chapter with our sights set firmly on the biggest moral apologetic fish of them all.

## TALK BACK

1. Review the four features of moral obligations as laid out by C. Stephen Evans (in our discussion of Plato). Connect these features to an obligation that you are certain you have and reflect

on how that obligation exhibits each feature. How can this fourfold distinction help us sort out controversial cases from indisputable ones, and why might it be important to do so in making the moral argument?

2. Search Scripture (through a concordance or an online Bible tool) and identify references to the good or goodness. How often do they occur? Where? In what contexts, and how is it discussed?

3. Taylor lays out five features of guilt, the state we find ourselves in when we fail to meet our obligations. Look at these features and connect them to your own experience, a time when you fell short of the moral standard—how did these aspects of guilt make themselves clear to you? Using Taylor's terms, discuss insights that reflecting on guilt offer about ourselves, about our relationship to others, and about the nature of reality itself.

CHAPTER 4

# MORAL ARGUMENTS IN THE TWENTIETH CENTURY AND BEYOND

*People in fact agree on a politics of solidarity, or on human-itarian action, for a wide range of reasons; where one is an atheist humanist, another a Christian, another a Muslim, and so on. This is of the essence of a modern polity which operates on an "overlapping consensus." But within this, we can still ask which is more satisfactory as a basis, not now as an account of how it could come to exist . . . but rather as what I have called a "moral source." I mean by that considerations which (for us) inspire us to embrace this morality, and the evoking of which strengthens our commitment to it.*

CHARLES TAYLOR, *A SECULAR AGE*

IN 1942 ENGLAND WAS EMBROILED in a brutal conflict with Nazi Germany, part of a war so relentless that it left almost no place on the globe untouched. The English had little reason for hope at this moment. The country had endured long stretches of heavy air raids that left London and other major industrial centers devastated. France, England's closest ally in the fight and nearest neighbor, had surrendered to Germany, making England all the more susceptible to invasion. England was struggling to turn the tide, but it was still several years away from the war's conclusion. The year 1942 was a dark time indeed.

Yet this bleak moment also gave birth to one of the most popular contemporary works of Christian apologetics. This was the year C. S. Lewis (1898–1963) began his BBC radio broadcasts, a series of fifteen-minute talks in which he laid out a rational case for Christianity. Eventually these broadcasts were published as *Mere Christianity* (1952), which has become the bestselling (and arguably the most dearly beloved) book of apologetics in the twentieth century. In England's darkest hour, Lewis proclaimed the message of humanity's greatest hope.

## C. S. LEWIS ("JACK")

Born in 1898, Clive Staples Lewis is perhaps the greatest apologist of the twentieth century, and much of the credit for this status stems from the reputation of *Mere Christianity*. The book's influence, at the time of its writing and today, is difficult to calculate, but a *Christianity Today* poll conducted in 2000 found that it received the most nods as the "best religious book" of the twentieth century.[1]

Significantly, Lewis's acclaimed apologetic begins with a version of the moral argument. C. Stephen Evans writes that such arguments are both interesting and important. *Interesting* because evaluating their soundness requires attention to a wide range of philosophical questions. *Important* because of their prominence in popular apologetic arguments for religious belief. He cites as evidence the amazing popularity of Lewis's treatise.[2] In a nutshell, the argument goes something like this:

1. There is a universal moral law.

2. If there is a universal moral law, there is a moral lawgiver.

---

[1]"Books of the Century," *Christianity Today*, April 24, 2000, www.christianitytoday.com/ct/2000/april24/5.92.html. Important to note is the influence of Arthur Balfour on Lewis. A British prime minister trained in philosophy, Balfour was also a Gifford lecturer. One of the books produced by those lectures, *Theism and Humanism*, contains an explicit moral argument for God's existence; Lewis ranks this book in the top ten that most shaped his own life.

[2]C. Stephen Evans, "Moral Arguments for the Existence of God," in the *Stanford Encyclopedia of Philosophy*, Winter 2016 ed., http://plato.stanford.edu/entries/moral-arguments-god/.

3. If there is a moral lawgiver, it must be something beyond the universe.

4. Therefore, there is something beyond the universe.

At this point in his presentation, Lewis says if there's "something more" here, it's analogous to a mind, not a collection of atoms. Recall Newman's earlier argument that our consciences, particularly our feelings of guilt, lead us to conclude that God exists. Feelings of conscience are often directed toward fellow human beings, but sometimes they lack an appropriate human target.

Another important dimension of Lewis's moral apologetic is his argument that there are two fundamental facts that point to the meaning of life and the import of the human condition: there's an objective moral standard, and all of us invariably fall short of it.[3]

## THE EARLY TWENTIETH CENTURY

Although Lewis's argument might have gained the widest hearing, it was most certainly not the only moral argument on offer during the twentieth century. Also educated at Oxford, A. C. Ewing (1899–1973) served as a Cambridge lecturer for more than twenty years. Author of more than a dozen books, including *Value and Reality*, he was a prominent critic of Ludwig Wittgenstein, a twentieth-century pioneer in the philosophy of religion, and one of the foremost analysts of the concept of "good." In his moral argument, he embraces a cumulative case for God's existence, drawing on insights from Sorley, Rashdall, Kant, and others.

Another Oxford scholar, Austin Farrer (1904–1968), was the Anglican whom C. S. Lewis asked to review a portion of *Mere Christianity*. Lewis and Farrer were close friends, and many thought that Farrer would be the natural successor to Lewis's status as public Christian apologist.[4] Unfortunately, Farrer's potential wasn't realized, as he died a mere five years after Lewis's passing. Still, his contribution to Christian thought

---

[3]Two aspects of the fourfold case this book will lay out. Erik Wielenberg and I (Dave) conducted a published exchange on Lewis's moral argument in *C. S. Lewis's Christian Apologetics: Pro and Con*, ed. Gregory Bassham (Leiden: Brill, 2015), part 3.

[4]Michael Ward, "The Next C. S. Lewis? A Note on Austin Farrer," *Transpositions*, February 14, 2014, www.transpositions.co.uk/austinfarrer/.

was notable, with Rowan Williams dubbing him "possibly the greatest Anglican mind of the twentieth century."[5]

As chaplain at Keble College, Farrer went every morning to celebrate the Holy Eucharist. He was devoted, but his friends sometimes wondered why he bothered. "Doesn't it get lonely in there, with just one or two students, and them, half asleep?" Farrer replied, "Quite to the contrary. What with all of the apostles, prophets, saints, martyrs, angels, and archangels—well, it's a wonder there's any room for us at all."

Farrer put forth a moral argument of his own, which can be found in his book *Reflective Faith*. For a taste of Farrer's argument, consider the way we normatively ought to think about other people. It is of great importance, he argues, that we value them rightly, that we think about others in such a way as to regard them properly. The only limitations that such deep regard for others should encounter are those that cannot be avoided—those "set by the conditions of our life," as he puts it. Such regard should be at once so pure and so entire that it leads to a sort of frustration. This frustration derives from the incompleteness of our definition of those we so regard. Thinking of our neighbors in too garden variety a way can't sustain the esteem we intuitively think they deserve. The conclusion to which Farrer feels compelled is that what deserves our regard is not simply our neighbor but God in our neighbor and our neighbor in God.

Across the pond, George Mavrodes (b. 1923) wrote an article, "Religion and the Queerness of Morality," that has proven seminal.[6] A graduate of Calvin College and longtime philosophy professor at the University of Michigan, Mavrodes, echoing J. L. Mackie, argues that moral obligations are an odd fit in a Russellian (naturalistic) world. They seem to possess a sort of authority to which a naturalist account of moral obligations fails to do justice. On a theist picture of reality, in contrast, moral obligations make excellent sense.

---

[5]Rowan Williams, "General Synod: Debate on the Gift of Authority," Dr Rowan Williams, 104th Archbishop of Canterbury, February 13, 2004, http://rowanwilliams.archbishopofcanterbury.org/articles.php/1836/general-synod-debate-on-the-gift-of-authority-archbishop-of-canterburys-remarks.
[6]George Mavrodes, "Religion and the Queerness of Morality," in *Ethical Theory: Classical and Contemporary Readings*, 2nd ed., ed. Louis P. Pojman (New York: Wadsworth, 1995).

Incidentally, in his contribution to Tom Morris's *God and the Philosophers*—a collection of "spiritual-intellectual autobiographies" of contemporary Christian philosophers—Mavrodes recounts an anecdote involving Lewis's *Mere Christianity*. This episode, in fact, initiated what became one of the central concerns of Mavrodes's philosophical work: the intersection of reason and faith. At dinner with a fellow Christian and his atheist friend, Mavrodes was anxious to make a convert through rational argument. He tried out Lewis's moral apologetic because he had found it so convincing himself. As the evening and conversation wound down, he could see that his conversation partner was no closer to belief in God than he was at the start. And the whole affair was, for Mavrodes, "the beginning of a long reflection on the role of argument in religious affairs and in human life generally."[7]

In light of that anecdote, perhaps we should interject a general comment about arguments. Arguments have their role, but all sorts of factors are at play in belief formation. That an argument doesn't persuade someone doesn't mean it's not a good argument—or doesn't have the potential to become one with further elaboration. It may be a perfectly fine argument but still be unable to persuade everyone. How much weight we assign to various priorities, how strongly we are convinced of various pieces of evidence, how tight we perceive the connection to be between premises and conclusions—all of these can vary from person to person.

If we find an argument persuasive, we should often refrain from insisting that everyone else should immediately find it equally compelling on pain of irrationality or insincerity. Arguments inadequately leavened with grace, particularly those that pertain to significant questions about reality, can easily become off-putting and divisive, rather than what they ought to be: collaborative efforts to move toward the truth.

H. P. Owen (1926–1996) offered another version of the moral argument. Owen was a Welsh theologian and academic, educated at Oxford and ordained in the Presbyterian Church of Wales. Had he not pursued an academic career, he may have fared well as a pianist, as he

---

[7]George Mavrodes, "There Was a Wind Blowing," in *God and the Philosophers*, ed. Thomas V. Morris (Oxford: Oxford University Press, 1994), 212.

was extraordinarily gifted in music.[8] In his *Moral Argument for Christian Theism*, Owen argues that it is impossible to derive a moral "ought" from a merely naturalistic "is."[9] Anthony Thiselton summarizes Owen's view by emphasizing that a good conscience is far more than a gratified wish. Against A. J. Ayer and others, Owen argues that moral obligation cannot be reduced to mere corporate or individual approval. Thiselton writes, "We cannot merely rest content with 'disapproving' of the Nazi Holocaust; we must assert that it is wrong or evil. . . . Owen argues that this sense of the moral points beyond itself to God."[10]

Clement Dore is one of those figures specifically mentioned by Plantinga in his earlier litany of moral apologists. Born in 1930, Dore offers a moral argument in the fourth chapter of his book *Theism*.[11] He starts with the Platonic insight that a person's wrongdoing inexorably harms himself. This is an aspect of morality that no Hobbesian view of ethics can adequately explain. According to English philosopher Thomas Hobbes (1588–1679), ethics functions to adjudicate conflicts arising from self-interest. What kind of harm does wrongdoing entail?

Dore argues this harm must be more than merely being a bad person, because some people are perfectly content to be bad people. In fact, some hedonists relish the prospect, while still seeming to avoid harm in this life. But if morality is overriding, such people will be harmed by their significant wrongdoing. Dore contends that a being with "God-like power" and "God-like knowledge" and who is thereby a person provides the best explanation of this.[12] Although Dore's argument doesn't conclusively prove

---

[8]David Edward Pike, "The Story of the Gate," *Welldigger*, February 13, 2013, http://daibach-welldigger .blogspot.com/2013/02/the-story-of-gate.html. This gift ran in the family; Owen's sister was Morfydd Llwyn Owen, a notable Welsh composer, pianist, and mezzo-soprano.

[9]H. P. Owen, *Moral Argument for Christian Theism* (London: Allen and Unwin, 1965). See too the second chapter of his *Moral Skepticism* and the fourth and fifth chapters of his *On the Existence and Relevance of God*.

[10]Anthony C. Thiselton, *The Thiselton Companion to Christian Theology* (Grand Rapids: Eerdmans, 2015), 602. And not just to God in the generic sense but to the specific God of Christianity.

[11]Clement Dore, "A Moral Argument," in *Theism* (Boston: D. Reidel, 1984), chap. 4.

[12]A person at least to that extent. Incidentally, Dore thinks it's possible to show that this being may have a further characteristic that's traditionally been ascribed to God, namely, necessary existence. He argues we are justified in thinking that some moral obligation claims express necessary truths. This applies in every possible world, so significant wrongdoing needs to be able to be punished in every possible world, so in every world there's a Godlike person able to

the existence of the full-fledged God of orthodox theism, he asserts that it does imply that another doctrine, which is normally associated with theism, is true, namely, that human beings survive earthly death.[13]

Dore recently passed away, and his obituary testifies to how fully he embraced the conclusion of his moral apologetic: life does not end with earthly death. The tribute brims with joy and paints a picture of someone who relished life, his family, and philosophy. It tells of his children caring for him during his final days, "cracking arguably inappropriate jokes, remembering his deep loyalty," and "celebrating his inimitable character." Dore's reflections on why many go into philosophy capture a bit of his spirit, as he points specifically to central questions about morality and existence: "I think the reason that many people go into philosophy is because people who are concerned about whether anything is objectively right or wrong are not totally at home in the world, . . . or they wonder whether the world really exists—I mean, that's a good example of not being at home in the world."[14]

## THE LATER TWENTIETH CENTURY

Born in 1937, Robert Adams has done some truly groundbreaking work in theistic ethics and in the process constructed a few variations of the

---

do so. Still, despite the attractions of parsimony, Dore admits he's yet to show that it's the same Godlike punisher who exists in each possible world, or, for that matter, that there is only *one* Godlike punisher in any given possible world. Nor has he shown that this person is perfectly good, or that the person is omnipotent and omniscient. What he has shown, he claims, is that the person is more powerful and knowledgeable than any wrongdoer could possibly be.

[13]We know from observation that the morally innocent are just as apt to suffer in this world as moral reprobates. And since this is a well-substantiated inductive generalization, it would be irrational to claim that all wrongdoers are worse off in this life than they would have been if they had remained relatively morally innocent. So, given the overriding nature of moral obligation, it follows that there is an afterlife in which those wrongdoers who flourish in this world are punished. But all of us are wrongdoers to some degree, and most of us sometimes do what is significantly wrong without suffering (here and now) for it. It follows that there is reason to believe that many of us survive our earthly death. An alternative argument would be that the overriding importance of morality entails not only that the wicked are worse off in the long run than the relatively righteous, but that the latter are better off in the long run than are the wicked, and that those among the relatively righteous who suffer greatly in this world will be compensated in the afterlife. But this would show at least some survive earthly death, which renders it more likely than it would be otherwise.

[14]"Obituary for Clement 'Clem' Joseph Dore Jr.," *Walker's Funeral Home*, www.walkersfuneral service.com/obituaries/Clement-Clem-Dore/#!/Obituary (accessed January 3, 2017).

moral argument for God's existence.[15] His magnum opus, *Finite and Infinite Goods*, is nothing less than a classic. He's also a prominent scholar on Leibniz. In addition to explicating versions of Kant's moral argument, Adams offers one of his own on the basis of his favored theory of moral obligations, namely, divine command theory. According to divine command theory, on his account, when God commands us to perform an action, the action thereby becomes our moral obligation. He thinks it perfectly legitimate to deploy strong moral convictions about right and wrong as premises in a reasoned argument. After defending at length divine command theory as the best explanation of the nature of right and wrong, he observes that since such a theory entails God's existence, he takes this commitment as evidence for God's reality.[16]

Adams's wife, Marilyn McCord Adams, was also a preeminent philosopher of religion who wrote extensively on the problem of evil, tackling even the most difficult cases of what she calls "horrendous evils" that require defeat by nothing less than the goodness of God. She writes, "My strategy for showing how this can be done is to identify ways that created participation in horrors can be integrated into the participants' relation to God, where God is understood to be the incommensurate Good, and the relation to God is one that is overall incommensurately good *for the participant*."[17]

Linda Zagzebski, born in 1946, writes on epistemology, philosophy of religion, and virtue ethics. She is a fine philosopher who has done terrific work, including in the arena of theistic ethics, most particularly with her major book *Divine Motivation Theory*. Rather than asking the question

---

[15]For space constraints, and no small amount of indolence, we refrained from elaborating on John Warwick Montgomery, born in 1931, who offered a variety of evidential arguments for God's existence. *The Law Above the Law* and *Human Rights and Human Dignity* put forth a moral argument to the effect that classical theism provides the necessary explanation of human dignity and human rights.

[16]The two main advantages Adams cites in favor of divine command ethics are (1) that it presents facts of moral rightness and wrongness as objective, nonnatural facts, and (2) that it is relatively clear, certainly more so than, say, intuitionism or Platonism. He spends a fair bit of time defending divine command theory against objections, most especially arbitrariness concerns. Most relevantly in that regard, he predicates his divine command theory on a loving God.

[17]Marilyn McCord Adams, *Horrendous Evils and the Goodness of God* (Ithaca, NY: Cornell University Press, 1999), 156.

"Why be moral?" she asks another question in the same vicinity that is not so easily answered: "Should I try to be moral?" Why is this question different? Because, in short, it doesn't make sense to attempt something one can't do. If we are relegated to depend on our moral powers and capacities alone, our moral effectiveness seems to be in serious jeopardy, thus rendering the whole enterprise of morality, in an important sense, futile (not unlike Marybeth's attempts at singing). Since morality presumably isn't futile, we have reason to think we are not relegated to depend on our own moral capacities and powers alone.

Zagzebski identifies three ways in which we need moral *confidence*, particularly in light of the sometimes costly nature of doing the moral thing: (1) We need confidence that we can have moral knowledge—good reasons that our individual moral judgments, about both obligations and values, are correct. (2) We need confidence in our moral efficacy, both in the sense that we can overcome moral weakness and in the sense that we have the causal power to bring about good in the world. And (3) insofar as many moral goals require cooperation, we need confidence in the moral knowledge and moral efficacy of other people.

As it happens, she also thinks that deep skepticism is warranted in each of these three areas if all we have to go on morally is our own moral intuitions and reasoning and the intuitions and reasoning of others. We all know how flawed we ourselves and others can be! Again, such resulting moral despair, she assumes, cannot be rational, so she concludes that we must be able to rely on more than our own human powers and those of others in attempting to live a moral life.

C. Stephen Evans, born in 1948, a prolific philosophy professor at Baylor, educated at Yale, is author of *God and Moral Obligations*, among other books, including a half-dozen important works on Søren Kierkegaard. His *Natural Signs and Knowledge of God* won the C. S. Lewis Book Prize in 2012 from the University of St. Thomas, which is awarded to the best recent book in religious philosophy written for a general audience. Evans privileges language of "natural signs," which serve as pointers toward God—though these are nothing like absolute demonstrations. Natural signs, on his view, provide a measure of good evidence for belief in God.[18] (Notice that this is yet another of the negotiable noncore ways in which to couch the moral argument.) He refers to two moral natural signs: human dignity/worth and moral duties.

J. P. Moreland, Distinguished Professor of Philosophy at Talbot School of Theology at Biola University, was born the same year as Evans. On a personal level, Moreland is a prince of a man: bighearted, hilarious, encouraging, engaging, and warm. We also consider him one of the top two or three Christian apologists in the world today. Moreland's evidential considerations for God's existence from the arena of morality focus on central philosophical insights and the strictures imposed by what constitutes a workable worldview. His book *The Recalcitrant Imago Dei: Human Persons and the Failure of Naturalism* is one place among others where he lays out this type of case.

One of the roles of a worldview, Moreland emphasizes, is to provide an explanation of facts, of reality, the way it actually is. Indeed, it is incumbent on a worldview to explain what does and does not exist in ways that follow naturally from the central explanatory commitments of that worldview.[19] In this light, Moreland characterizes a "recalcitrant fact" as one that is obstinately uncooperative in light of attempts to handle it by some theory. Such a fact resists explanation by a theory. The particular recalcitrant moral facts on naturalism are threefold: (1) objective, intrinsic value and an objective moral law; (2) the reality of human moral action; and (3) intrinsic human value and rights.

John Hare, born in 1949, is the son of the eminent Oxford don and ethical theorist R. M. Hare. He currently teaches philosophical theology at Yale University and Divinity School. In his book *The Moral Gap*, Hare gives a particular version of the moral argument. It's a "performative" variant of the argument, according to which God is needed to make up for the gap between our moral status and what morality calls us to achieve. He argues that secular theorists tend to puff up

---

[18]Evidence that satisfies the Pascalian constraints of wide accessibility and easy resistibility.

[19]J. P. Moreland, *The Recalcitrant Imago Dei: Human Persons and the Failure of Naturalism* (London: SCM Press, 2009), 3.

human capacities to close this gap, lower the moral demand, or generate secular substitutes for God's assistance.

The performative variant of moral apologetics focuses on one aspect of Kantian moral faith—that the moral life is possible. Hare's book actually touches on the other variant as well by arguing that without God we lose reason to believe that the virtuous are ultimately happy and fulfilled. In late 2015 Hare published a new and groundbreaking book to add to his previous ones, *God's Command*, aspects of which will be discussed in a later chapter. *God's Command* deserves to be ranked alongside *Finite and Infinite Good* (by Adams) as the best books on divine command theory in the last quarter century. Hare's encyclopedic work in the history of philosophy has powerfully demonstrated the important role theism played in the work of several philosophical luminaries.[20]

Reading Hare is inspiring but also intimidating. He makes it easy for his readers to heed the biblical dictum to "count others better than yourselves" (Phil 2:3). This brings to mind the time he was in the audience when I (Dave) delivered my first conference paper (at Oxford, crazily enough). Not only was Hare in attendance; he asked me a technical question about John Duns Scotus, about which, at the time, I didn't have a clue. Awkward.[21]

Also born in 1949, William Lane Craig, with his two doctorates in hand, is arguably the greatest living Christian apologist. He has used a version of the moral argument to powerful effect on a plethora of college campuses across America and around the world. He has also been involved in numerous debates on a variety of subjects, but many times on the question of morality and God. The form of moral argument he advances is deductive and easy to understand. It's valid and straightforward. A deductive and valid argument is an argument whose premises (evidence) decisively demonstrate its conclusion, such that, if the premises are true, the conclusion must be true as well. His argument goes like this:

---

[20]The way he shows how "natural" contrasts with "artificial" rather than "supernatural," in Aristotle's work, is just one small but potent example of his perspicacity. See John E. Hare's *God and Morality: A Philosophical History* (Oxford: Blackwell, 2007) and *God's Command* (Oxford: Oxford University Press, 2015).

[21]Still gives me nightmares. Let's never mention this again.

Premise 1: If God does not exist, objective moral values and duties do not exist.

Premise 2: Objective moral values and duties do exist.

Conclusion: God exists.

The conclusion follows from the evidence, so detractors need to try calling into question one of the premises.[22] Craig has said that, though the moral argument is not his personal favorite, it's the argument that has had the biggest effect on his listeners.[23]

C. Stephen Layman (no relation to C. Stephen Evans), emeritus professor of philosophy at Seattle Pacific University, was born in 1955, and he's proposed a different formulation of the moral argument. He thinks it works best as part of a cumulative case. Layman begins his argument with the *Overriding Reason Thesis* (ORT), which says "the overriding (or strongest) reasons always favor doing what is morally required."[24] He then introduces the *Conditional Thesis* (CT), which says that "if there is no God and no life after death, then the ORT is not true."[25] The intuition behind ORT is this: "If considerations of prudence and morality conflict, and if the prudential considerations are momentous while the results of behaving immorally are relatively minor, then prudence overrides morality."[26]

Now, it might appear that CT casts doubt on ORT, and it undoubtedly does from the atheist's point of view. But Layman adds that it is hardly

---

[22]The fancy name for an argument of this form (A implies B, not-B, so not-A) is *modus tollens*. Since the argument form is valid (meaning the truth of the premises entails the truth of the conclusion), every specific instance of the general argument form is a deductively valid argument. To refute such an argument, then, one must try to call into question the truth of at least one of the premises. The logical form itself is flawless.

[23]Note that it focuses on the ontological matters of deontic and axiological morality. Incidentally, one might think that all that is needed to render the conclusion more likely true than false is that each premise be more likely true than false, but in fact what's needed is that the premise set, taken collectively, is more likely true than false. We owe the following example to Tim McGrew: Consider rolling a six-sided die. It's more likely true than not that the roll will yield a 1, 2, 3, or 4, and more likely true than not that it will yield 3, 4, 5, or 6. Deductively it follows that it will yield 3 or 4, but such a roll is less likely true than not (a one-in-three chance).

[24]C. Stephen Layman, "A Moral Argument for the Existence of God," in Robert K. Garcia and Nathan L. King, *Is Goodness Without God Good Enough?* (Lanham, MD: Rowman & Littlefield, 2009), 52. He's referring to more than merely prima facie duties.

[25]Ibid., 54.

[26]Ibid.

fair simply to assume that atheism is true when an argument for theism is being offered. Surely we ought to be reluctant to jettison ORT.[27] Instead, he would encourage readers to remain open to the possibility of both ORT and CT being true. If they are both true, what follows is this: either God exists, or there is life after death in which virtue is rewarded. Note that this leaves open the possibility of something like karma instead of a theistic universe, so an atheist could consistently accept both ORT and CT. In light of the incalculable complexity of a system of karma, Layman's response to this approach is to argue that "the moral order postulated by nontheistic reincarnation paradoxically provides evidence for the existence of a personal God."[28]

Born the same year as Layman was Jerry L. Walls, whom I (Dave) still remember well walking into the first class I took with him at Asbury Theological Seminary in July 1989. Wearing a Mickey Mouse T-shirt that day, he was first my teacher, then my friend, then my tennis doubles partner, then a collaborator. Walls has done simply superlative work in Christian eschatology, writing a trilogy on heaven, hell, and purgatory. He's also one of the world's leading Arminian critics of Calvinist soteriology. He has argued, notably in his final chapter of *Heaven: The Logic of Eternal Joy*, and also in other places, that Christian theology accounts for morality more naturally and fully than does naturalistic evolutionary theory.

In *Heaven* he advances three connected arguments for this claim. Not only can Christian theology, unlike evolutionary theory, account for altruism in a way that reinforces our instinctive admiration of it, but it also has a ready explanation for why moral obligation has an objective ground. In a Christian account, he adds, morality is not tarnished with the sort of deception and illusion that naturalistic accounts rely on at certain points.

Moreover, the doctrine of heaven provides moral philosophy the resources to resolve one of the most difficult problems it has been plagued with for the past several generations, namely, the conflict between egoism [by

---

[27]Ibid., 56.
[28]Ibid., 58-59.

which he primarily means self-interest] and altruism. Each of these arguments has force in its own right, but taken together they provide strong reason to prefer a Christian account of morality to naturalistic ones.[29]

R. Scott Smith, born in 1957, a philosophy professor at Biola, studied under Moreland and attributes much of his analytic approach to Moreland's influence. Smith's moral argument against naturalism and in favor of theism is heavily epistemic and ontological. In his *In Search of Moral Knowledge*, Smith offers an epistemic variant of the moral argument.[30] He carefully articulates, in very insightful ways, a number of specific ethical theories. In addition to that very large task, he attempts to construct a master argument able to critique all naturalistic ethical theories in one fell swoop. We should completely reject naturalism if indeed his argument goes through. He asks us to consider a paradigm naturalist, Daniel Dennett, one who takes both cognitive science and the implications of naturalism seriously. Although Dennett is not entirely consistent, to the degree he is consistent about what he takes to be the implications of naturalism, he's hoisted by his own proverbial petard. He encounters deep difficulties that undermine many of

---

[29]Jerry L. Walls, *Heaven: The Logic of Eternal Joy* (New York: Oxford University Press, 2002), 193. His trilogy also contains a book on hell and one on purgatory. Jonathan Pruitt and I (Dave) have written a paper on purgatory in which we try to reconcile Walls's insistence on the need for a posthumous process of sanctification with the common evangelical insistence that it takes place in a very short interval. Walls and I have teamed up to write a few books on theistic ethics and moral apologetics. The first was *Good God: The Theistic Foundations of Morality*, in which we defend theistic ethics against an assortment of Euthyphro-inspired objections. Later, in *God and Cosmos: Moral Truth and Human Meaning*, we extend our abductive moral argument by critiquing the adequacy of various secular theories of morality and building our fourfold moral apologetic. We are currently writing a third book in our series, a much more richly developed history of moral apologetics, and after that intend to round out the series by writing a book defending moral realism. With Gary Habermas, Walls and I (Dave) have also edited a book called *C. S. Lewis as Philosopher*, an expanded version of which will be published in 2017. New chapters come from Will Honeycutt, Stew Goetz, Bruce Reichenbach, and Sloan Lee, and new topics broach issues such as myth, epistemology, and the argument from desire.

[30]His is an ambitious and sweeping account, canvassing the whole Western and ancient Near Eastern ethical traditions, starting with the Old Testament, moving to the New, traversing ancient Greece. Then it provides a very rich examination of aspects of medieval thought and modernity, including the Renaissance and Enlightenment, their points of emphasis and innovations and a whole plethora of subsequent trends. This elaborate tracing of the history of ethical analysis proves tremendously useful in accounting for many of today's trends in ethical thought. Smith helps us get a better handle on them, understand their genesis, and subject them to scrutiny rather than simply assuming them as axiomatic or sacrosanct.

his claims, including what he considers to be any principled commitment to naturalism itself.

Mark Linville, born in 1957, has done outstanding work on the moral argument, not to mention that he's one of the funniest people on Facebook. In Linville's entry on the moral argument in *The Blackwell Companion to Natural Theology* (titled, unsurprisingly, "The Moral Argument"), he offers two independent moral arguments for God's existence. The first is an argument from evolutionary naturalism, which itself has two parts: First, that on evolutionary naturalism our moral beliefs are without warrant. This argument canvasses a variety of (meta-ethical) theories to test their adequacy in accounting for moral knowledge. Those predicated on naturalism are found wanting in light of challenges posed by evolutionary moral psychology. The second part of Linville's first argument is that theism is able to avoid such moral skepticism.

Linville's second argument in this landmark article is an argument from personal dignity, in which he tests an array of normative ethical theories to account for the essential moral standing of human persons, aiming to determine their explanatory adequacy. Egoism, utilitarianism, and virtue ethics are all shown to be ill-equipped to accommodate the Kantian principle of humanity to treat people as ends in themselves and not merely as means. Naturalism per se is further implicated for failing to account for the existence of persons themselves, whereas theism, he argues, is well situated and equipped to explain human persons, moral agency, and personal dignity.

Paul Copan, born in 1962, a former student of William Lane Craig's, has proven himself both a formidable moral apologist and a master of puns. In truth, his pun problem has, sadly, gotten a bit out of hand. An intervention was recently held to help him break the freakish addiction.[31] Do pray for Paul before it's too late.[32] At any rate, in between the ubiquity

---

[31]See for yourself. It's sad. "MNL: Intervention on PBA&E," April 12, 2011, www.youtube.com/watch?v=X6hQxjxRjmw. Evidence suggests he's still caught in the throes of it all, saying, for example, "My students just don't see things the way I do. Even though they're my *pupils*. They just see things *askew*. So I *ask you*, what do you think?" Yeah, that's what we're dealing with here. The torrential tornado of puns is spiraling out of control.

[32]It's too late.

of puns, he's managed to write one of the most anthologized versions of the moral argument. Copan has also advanced moral apologetics by showing the reconcilability of certain Old Testament conquest narratives with nonnegotiable moral intuitions.

Angus Menuge was born in 1963, and he's offered a compelling epistemic version of the moral argument.[33] After identifying apparent reasons to be skeptical of naturalism explaining objective moral truth, he distinguishes between two sorts of evolutionary ethics (EE): strong EE and weak EE. Strong EE dictates that moral facts themselves would be different had evolution played out differently. If, for example, we had been raised to kill our brothers and sisters or children, then such behaviors would have been morally right. Weak EE, in contrast, says it's only moral psychology (our moral beliefs) that would be different if we had been raised like hive bees.

Strong EE holds no realistic hope of sustaining objective moral facts. On the other hand, weak EE, Menuge suggests, gives us no grounds to think our moral beliefs are true, for they would be formed for reasons potentially quite unrelated to their truth. To make his point, he uses an example of looking at what turns out to be a broken clock, unknown to you. It reads 7 p.m., and suppose that it is indeed, by sheer coincidence, 7 p.m. No knowledge results, though, since your reason for thinking it is seven o'clock has nothing to do with its actually being seven o'clock.[34]

Unfortunately for weak EE, if it is true, then we are in a precisely similar situation regarding our moral beliefs. On that view, natural history is causally relevant to our moral beliefs but does not account for moral reality. Menuge writes,

> So if we had been raised like hive bees we would think fratricide and infanticide were right even if they were not. And, it could be that we think fratricide and infanticide are wrong (because we were not raised like hive

---

[33]This section on Angus Menuge and Angus Richie is lightly adapted from an article by David Baggett, published at MoralApologetics.com, "Battle of the Angi," *Moral Apologetics*, November 19, 2014, http://moralapologetics.com/battle-of-the-angi/.

[34]Philosophers call this a Gettier case. The "Gettier problem" in epistemology arises when cases are adduced in which a justified true belief obtains but presumably not knowledge, which seems to indicate that the right account of knowledge isn't "justified true belief." Menuge seems to be implicating weak EE in a "moral Gettier case."

bees) even though they are right. But now suppose that our belief that fratricide and infanticide are wrong happens to be true. Still, it is not knowledge, because what made us believe this has nothing to do with why our belief is true.[35]

Angus Ritchie, born in 1974, has offered his own epistemic variant of the moral argument, and an impressive one indeed. Whereas Menuge focuses on the way naturalism functions to preclude moral knowledge, Ritchie's focus is more on the way naturalism has an intractably difficult time explaining moral knowledge. His *From Morality to Metaphysics* does an admirable job identifying weaknesses in a broad array of secular meta-ethical theories. He also convincingly advances the claim that the teleological nature of theistic ethics is needed to overcome the central epistemic problem he identifies. Ritchie doesn't deny that secular ethics can justify moral beliefs but rather that its weakness is accounting for how our cognitive faculties can be reliable.

Whew! That lightning-quick, bird's-eye synopsis was like speed dating—except without the uncomfortable silences. Needless to say, this history of the moral argument is far from comprehensive. It is intentionally cursory but serves present purposes by giving readers a brief sketch of the breadth and scope of moral apologetics up to the present. And the story continues. That a new generation of younger scholars is beginning to focus its attention on theistic ethics and moral apologetics bodes well indeed for future developments in this area.

What we have seen in Act One is what is in need of explanation—an array of moral facts—and the operative theology that we will use to provide that explanation. We've also captured a hint of the rich history of moral arguments for God's existence. After a brief intermission, in which by returning to Athens we'll identify ways to defend theistic ethics against standard objections, the book will turn to our own case for moral apologetics. It is a fourfold argument that will avail itself of, and feature points of resonance with, many of the theorists just discussed.

---

[35]Angus Menuge, "The Failure of Naturalism as a Foundation for Human Rights," available at http://moralapologetics.com/the-failure-of-naturalism-as-a-foundation-for-human-rights/ (accessed August 21, 2016).

Finally, a quick word about the following intermission: It is a bit more technical than most of the book, but it's dealing with something specific. Namely, the challenge posed to theistic ethics and divine command theory by the so-called Euthyphro Dilemma, discussed briefly in a previous chapter. For those up to the challenge, feel free to read it. We think it's important and valuable, but it's not for everyone. It's useful for anyone who might like additional resources to know how to answer criticisms of theistic ethics such as arbitrariness objections.[36] If readers prefer to skip to Act Two of the book, though, that is entirely workable.

## TALK BACK

1. In our introduction, we talk about the importance of noting the core elements of the moral argument (morality is dependent on God) and the more peripheral elements (*exactly how* morality is dependent on God). Reviewing the many variations of the moral argument on offer in this history, trace some of the core concerns across these theorists. How do they cash these out differently?

2. What surprised you about these arguments? Which one did you find most intriguing, and why?

3. William Lane Craig has said that he finds the moral argument most effective in his talks on college campuses. Based on what you've been exposed to in this book so far, do you have any sense about why it might move people?

---

[36]William of Ockham is often associated, fairly or not, with a version of divine command theory susceptible to intractable arbitrariness objections. For a serious scholarly treatment of him, read the magisterial two-volume work of Marilyn McCord Adams on Ockham, and the work of Lucan Freppert, which Adams largely endorses. For a laugh about Ockham, consider this: he has the enduring distinction of being the only great philosopher whose place of burial is marked by a plaque in a parking garage (in Munich, Germany).

# INTERMISSION

# ANSWERING EUTHYPHRO

*Philosophy begins in wonder.*

SOCRATES, IN PLATO'S *THEAETETUS*

AS PREVIOUSLY MENTIONED, this intermission will tend toward the more technical, so it's not for everyone—even among those in the land of the living.

But for those who are willing to wade through what follows, you will discover the ultimate cure for the Euthyphro Dilemma. Read this intermission, and arbitrariness objections will disappear! But wait, there's more! Vacuity issues will be knocked down! Read the intermission in the next twenty-four hours, and your moral argument will be unassailable!

[*Warning*: Such claims are somewhat hyperbolic, perhaps bald-faced lies. Also, this intermission will cause some readers to experience migraines and dizziness. Other possible side effects include hostility and depression, inflated ego, gout, a penchant for pretension, a goiter or two, constipation, spontaneous combustion, and so on. Talk to your doctor if you experience any of these symptoms and stop reading immediately. Stay away from the intermission!]

What are you waiting for? Start reading the intermission today to be the best apologist you can be![1]

---

[1]Individual results will vary.

Let's return to the olive trees and craggy hills of ancient Greece and the conversation between Socrates and Euthyphro that reverberated through the centuries. In the context of that discussion, Socrates pushes Euthyphro to identify the essential nature of piety or holiness. Euthyphro's ultimate answer is that the pious is what all the gods love, and the impious or unholy is what all the gods hate. Socrates in reply raises what has become known as the "Euthyphro Dilemma": Is something loved by the gods because it's pious, or is it pious because it's loved by the gods? Expressed in contemporary terms of a single God and God's commands rather than the gods' loves, the Euthyphro Dilemma sounds like this: Does God command something because it is moral, or is it moral because God commands it?

This challenge has spawned a whole range of criticisms of theistic ethics, critiques thought by many to show that ethics needs to look elsewhere for an account of moral foundations. If such critics are right, moral apologetics would be in serious trouble. Fortunately, theistic ethics, and even divine command theory (for those inclined to embrace such a view), can withstand such criticisms.[2] Divine command theory, again, is the view that in virtue of God's commanding us to do something—call it $x$—we are morally obligated to do $x$. In light of the fact that the Euthyphro Dilemma has inspired a wide variety of objections to theistic ethics (and divine command theory), in this intermission let's identify seven key distinctions that collectively can help defuse such objections and, in the process, contribute to understanding the explanatory power and scope of theistic ethical foundations.

To begin, let's quickly review the main objections that various critics pose against a generally supernatural understanding of morality and a specifically Christian one. The Euthyphro Dilemma gives us two options: God commands something because it's moral, or something is moral because God commands it. Assuming the first stance makes it sound as if God is beholden to an independent morality that gives him

---

[2]Again, this book is treating theistic ethics as the more central aspect of moral apologetics, and divine command theory as secondary at most. Nonetheless, a discussion of Euthyphro broaches questions at the heart of God as moral authority, so it's important either way.

instructions to follow. On such an answer, morality seems to exist apart from God. This understandably is thought to detract from God's sovereignty and independence.

Saying instead that morality is whatever God commands (which sounds a lot like divine command theory) raises another set of concerns. First and foremost, there's the problem of *arbitrariness*. If the content of morality depends on divine whim, then wouldn't it mean that God could issue commands to do simply awful things such as torture children? Second, *vacuity* is a concern, because if morality is whatever God says it is, what do we mean when we ascribe moral goodness to God? The claim "God is good" seems empty of content and only trivially true. Other concerns raised include epistemic and autonomy concerns, but we'll confine our attention mainly to arbitrariness and vacuity issues.

How might the theistic ethicist, particularly a Christian theistic ethicist, answer such questions? The following list offers seven useful distinctions for navigating this challenge. At least some of these distinctions can be helpful for the theistic ethicist who doesn't happen to embrace divine command theory (opting for a different specific formulation instead).

The seven distinctions to come encompass the following categories: scope, semantic, modal, moral, epistemic, meta-ethical, and ontological. And respectively, the distinctions are (1) definition versus analysis, (2) univocation versus equivocation, (3) conceivability versus possibility, (4) good versus right, (5) difficulty versus impossibility, (6) knowing versus being, and (7) dependence versus control. In one way or another each of these distinctions can be found in the literature on theistic ethics. Their cumulative force, all of them taken and applied together, enables a defense of theistic ethics against various objections. Combined with a positive moral apologetic, this defense of theistic ethics enables an advancement of the case for moral arguments for God and thus against the problem of evil.

First, the *analysis versus definition* distinction. If we take insights from the so-called direct reference theorists about "natural kinds" and generalize the points, we can usefully employ this distinction in the area of ethics as well. Let's quickly begin with a natural kind to get our bearings. Take water, with its presumably essential property of being $H_2O$ (if that example doesn't strike your fancy, choose some other, like gold's atomic number of 79). Linguistic competence in the use of the term *water* for a long time involved merely the knowledge that it referred to the liquid found in lakes and streams that folks drank and bathed in. People were qualified to use the term and understand the concept of water well before scientific discovery made its structural composition commonplace knowledge.

Such competence didn't require knowledge of water's essential makeup, which was later empirically discovered. Arguably even today it doesn't require such knowledge. Plenty of kids can, with little difficulty, define water in the sense of demonstrating ample linguistic competence in using the term adequately to pick out its referent in the vast range of cases. If, as seems plausible, we tie the workable definition of *water* to such linguistic competence, we can apprehend the distinction between *definition,* on the one hand, and proper *metaphysical analysis* of water itself on the other, involving experientially discoverable chemical microstructures.

It was just this distinction, when applied to ethical theory, that enabled Robert Adams to leave behind the way he had earlier relativized the import of moral terms to linguistic communities. Since atheists don't tend to mean by moral terms anything associated with God, it was thought that moral terms can't rightly be defined in theistic terms. Actually, though, this does nothing to detract from the possibility of theistic ethics because, as with water, linguistic competence in using a term doesn't have to penetrate to the most essential foundation of the thing to which the term applies. So atheists can use moral terms without intending to refer to anything pertaining to God, yet still display linguistic competence in their moral language usage. This provides no evidence against theistic ethics.

Second, what about *univocation versus equivocation*? John Stuart Mill was famous for insisting that God's goodness must be *just like* that of human beings or he wouldn't countenance calling God good. In other words, God must be good in precisely the same way a human being is good. Swing the pendulum to the other side, and you find folks who embrace the radically voluntarist horn of the Euthyphro Dilemma. According to this, whatever God says goes, pretty much no matter what. Describing God as good, in that case, potentially bears no similarity at all to describing a human being as good. These thinkers might insist that even if God predestined someone for hell with no chance at redemption, such a God would still be good, because goodness after all is whatever God happens to make it.

Mill insisted on univocation, perfect consistency in language usage, whereas those radical voluntarists would be guilty of committing a pretty flagrant case of equivocation, using a term in radically different ways. One wonders why we should bother calling God "good" if the term bears no resemblance to its traditional meaning. It seems likely designed to capture what the word connotes, but that can't really be done if the denotation is so radically subversive.

The majority tradition in the history of Christianity, though, features neither univocation nor equivocation but rather *analogical predication*. On this view, God's moral goodness and unspeakable holiness are infinitely greater than anything merely human. Yet we are still able to recognize his love and his goodness as love and goodness. In fact, God can be seen as the ultimate exemplar or archetype of love and goodness. God's love doesn't suddenly become hate. As C. S. Lewis once put it, human goodness is like a child's first attempt to draw a wheel. God's goodness, in contrast, is like the perfect circle. There is both sameness and difference, but the difference doesn't involve God's inversion of the picture so radically that his goodness becomes utterly unrecognizable.

This means that if God is impeccable, perfectly sinless, and omnibenevolent, as classical theism and Christian theology teach, then instances of God's actions will never ultimately be utterly unrecognizable as consistent with his love and goodness. This avoids arbitrariness and vacuity objections to divine command theory specifically or theistic ethics more generally. We can't turn justice into injustice in the name of love, nor can we turn love into hate in the name of justice. God loves everyone. A God who does not wouldn't be an adequate foundation for ethics, wouldn't qualify for the office of deity.[3]

Third, *conceivability versus possibility*. Suppose someone were to argue against an impeccable God in this way: "We can conceive of God's sinning, and conceivability entails possibility, so God's sinning is possible. Therefore, God's not impeccable, that is, essentially sinless." Can we truly conceive of God sinning, though? Can we have whatever sort of clarity and distinctness that conceivability requires when we try to imagine the God of classical theism, the possessor of the omni-qualities, sinning? We rather doubt it. We suspect we're just instilling into the office of deity something less than the classical conception. It's useful to refer to this classical conception as the "Anselmian God," after the medieval thinker Anselm, who affirmed both God's omni-qualities and the deliverances of Christian Scripture about God's nature.

Nevertheless, let's suppose we *could* conceive of such a thing. What reason would there be to think that conceivability would entail real possibility in such a case? To get your mind around this, consider a different example for a moment. Suppose Goldbach's conjecture to be true. Goldbach's conjecture is the mathematical idea that every even number greater than two is the sum of two prime numbers. If we suppose it's true yet we can still conceive of its falsehood, we've thereby shown that conceivability doesn't entail possibility. This is because, as a mathematical truth, its truth means it's necessarily true, not possibly false. So conceiving of its falsehood wouldn't genuinely mean it's possibly false, because it can't be false.

Similarly, suppose someone insists that he can conceive of God's moral imperfection. But suppose that God indeed is morally perfect, such that it's impossible for God to be imperfect, just as it's impossible

---

[3]Jerry Walls recently wrote in personal correspondence, "The Christian faith is indelibly marked by a distinctively beautiful account of a God whose essential nature is holy love. The nature of God as love is intriguingly revealed in the Trinity, as an eternal dance of joyous, mutual loving and giving among the Three Persons. And that love was communicated to us in definitive fashion in the incarnation and death of Jesus, the Second Person of the Trinity. 'As the Father loved me, so have I loved you.' The time is long overdue to face up to what it says about a religion that rejects this vision of love, not only denying one of the best attested facts of ancient history (the death of Christ on the cross), but also failing to discern in that death the heart that moves omnipotence."

for Goldbach's conjecture to be false if it's true. Even if someone can in some vague way conceive of God's moral imperfection, it wouldn't show that this is a real possibility. So either conceivability doesn't entail possibility, or, if it does, what some call a conceiving or imagining is too fuzzy to infer from it anything of much metaphysical significance.

In this way, we have a ready answer when pressed on the question of what to say about the prospect of God issuing a horrific command such as child torture for fun. Put simply: God can't do such a thing, because it would go contrary to his nature. If he could, he'd be less than who he is, less than what deity requires. It's not that God isn't free to do such a thing. It's that he's completely free from sin; it has no power over him. If he could sin, it would have power over him, for he would be vulnerable to it. Remember that the question of *who God is* is just as important as *whether God is*.

Fourth, *good versus right*. Confining attention to moral goodness, we are here distinguishing moral goodness from moral rightness. Following Adams, moral rightness is best understood as a deontic category pertaining to moral obligation, forbiddenness, and permissibility. We see this best by taking the notion of wrongness, negating it, and playing with its scope. "Not wrong" means permissible; "wrong not" means obligatory. So if something is right, morally speaking, it's permissible to do and potentially obligatory to do.

Moral goodness, on the other hand, pertains to broader moral considerations than those associated with deontic ethics. And there's of course no perfect correspondence (or isomorphism) between good and dutiful actions. Plenty of good actions, though permissible, aren't obligatory. Otherwise there's no room for the category of *supererogation, actions praiseworthy to do but not blameworthy for not doing.* Serving in a soup kitchen five days a week, or giving away 70 percent of your income, for example. These would potentially be quite morally good actions, but not obligatory. Typically they would be actions said to go above and beyond your moral duties.

This distinction between the good and the right is useful in a number of ways when discussing theistic ethics and divine command theory.

One way is that we can follow the late William Alston's advice and tie divine commands to moral obligations and God's nature to moral goodness. But there are other applications too. For example, suppose God were to command something in some sense bad. This would not necessarily implicate God for a reprehensible command or the divine command theorist in an intractable arbitrariness conundrum. Perhaps God's command is to do the lesser of two evils when we're faced with a situation in which one of the two has to be done. It's wrong, then, to insist that all of God's commands be commands to do something good, though most typically this is probably the case.

It is certainly true, we think, that God's commands are consistent with his impeccable nature of perfect love, but this leaves room for the possibility that some of God's commands may be to perform an action that is in some sense bad. This insight gives very useful help in dealing with, say, the biblical examples of the binding of Isaac or the conquest narratives. Divine command theorist or not, those who take biblical revelation seriously had better have something insightful to say about those passages. The recent work by Copan and Flannagan is especially helpful on that score.

The fifth distinction is the *difficult versus impossible* distinction. On occasion I (Dave) ask my students why God may have commanded the killing of the Amalekites and such. Usually after just a brief pause various possibilities are mentioned. It's not easy to understand such a thing, admittedly. It's very difficult. But maybe, just maybe, God knew that unless he commanded them to slaughter their enemies the Jewish remnant wouldn't survive, the remnant through whom the light of the world was to come. Or perhaps there's some other possibility. This exercise often leaves us thinking it difficult, perhaps excruciatingly difficult, to make sense of, to reconcile with our most nonnegotiable moral intuitions. But perhaps not impossible.

In principle some things *would* be impossible. Suppose unconditional perdition, for example: God created someone with the express purpose of torturing them forever, with no chance at deliverance. That would be an excellent candidate for a proposition we have to say is (to understate it) well-nigh impossible to square with our best moral intuitions. Some such principled line exists between cases merely hard, even if very hard, to make sense of, and cases rationally impossible to make sense of and reconcile with our best most nonnegotiable moral intuitions. This is a very useful distinction. *Good God* tries drawing a principled line here using an algorithm of sorts bearing a salient structural resemblance to Alvin Plantinga's free-will defense.

Sixth, *knowing versus being.* The medievals phrased this distinction as follows: the order of being is different from the order of knowing. *Ordo essendi* versus *ordo cognoscendi.* Moral knowledge likely functions bottom up. As children we begin with an egoistic perspective. Then our scope of concerns expands to those around us, then our neighbors, then wider still. Eventually we feel a kinship with people everywhere. Ultimately we may well discover that the foundations of morality find their locus in God himself.

Reality may well turn out to be top down in that sense, but that doesn't mean we started with that knowledge. We arrived there bottom up. So when an atheist advocate such as Sam Harris or Richard Dawkins identifies naturalistic mechanisms by which we come to acquire moral knowledge, they have not done anything to provide evidence against theistic ethics. Thinking otherwise is to confuse epistemology and ontology. You may have learned that six times eight is forty-eight from your elementary school teacher, but this hardly suggests that she is in any way responsible for the result of the calculation.

Seventh and last, *dependence versus control.* Suppose that God is the locus of the necessary truths, perhaps by thinking just the thoughts he does in this and all possible worlds along the lines suggested by Tom Morris in *Anselmian Explorations* or Plantinga in "How to Be an Anti-Realist."[4] The necessary truths would thus depend on God, at least for their modal status, yet not even God could alter their truth or falsity. Such truths would be, on this picture, insights into aspects of God's very

---

[4]Thomas V. Morris, *Anselmian Explorations: Essays in Philosophical Theology* (Notre Dame, IN: University of Notre Dame Press, 1987), and Alvin Plantinga, "How to Be an Anti-Realist," *Proceedings and Addresses of the American Philosophical Association* 56, no. 1 (1982).

nature. Just as God can't deny himself or commit suicide, he can't alter such truths. They are part of him, reflections of his character and essence. But if such necessary truths depend on God even though God can't change them, this helps answer the Euthyphro Dilemma. Recall that the dilemma is based on the assumption that dependence entails control, and invariance (constancy) entails aseity (absolute ontological independence). If it doesn't, then we have all the resources we need to answer the dilemma.

This foray to Athens was meant to provide resources to play defense against Euthyphro-inspired objections to theistic ethics. Collectively, this set of distinctions helps answer such objections, thereby bolstering the case for moral apologetics. Armed with this full set of distinctions, theistic ethicists have powerful resources to answer standard criticisms of their view. Again, this portion of the book was written with a bit more rigor and technical jargon than the rest of the book, so if you struggled with it, take heart. That was the toughest going.

The rest of this book is going to look at positive reasons in favor of theistic foundations for morality and our version of the moral argument. So let's now turn to Act Two of the book, which makes the case for theistic ethics by simultaneously arguing for its explanatory potential and the difficulties and deficiencies besetting various secular alternatives.

## TALK BACK

1. Distinguishing between linguistic competence and metaphysical analysis is extremely helpful in avoiding the challenges posed by the Euthyphro Dilemma—we can know what water is, for example, without understanding its chemical composition. In morality, too, we can know on some level what goodness is without tracing it back to its source. Why, then, might it be helpful or important to know more than that?

2. How helpful is the C. S. Lewis example of a child drawing a circle in our thinking through what love and goodness are? Look at 1 Corinthians 13, the descriptions of love found there and especially

1 Corinthians 13:12, and think through how Lewis's example can help us better understand the similarities and differences between that perfect love and our imperfect love.

3. How do you understand the distinction between something difficult to make sense of and the impossible (distinction number five here)? What might be some guidelines to use in interpreting difficult biblical passages? Appealing to mystery is on occasion entirely appropriate, but are there times when we push the mystery button prematurely?

# THE MAIN
# CHARACTERS

A couple drove down a country road for several miles, not saying a word. An earlier discussion had led to an argument, and neither of them wanted to concede their position. As they passed a barnyard of mules, goats, and pigs, the husband asked sarcastically, "Relatives of yours?"

"Yep," the wife replied, "in-laws."

The word *argument* often conjures up unpleasant situations like this. Over the course of the next several chapters, we will lay out our moral argument. But rest assured that we will vigorously avoid engaging in what's often meant by *argument* in common parlance. Instead, we use *argument* as shorthand for an attempt to point out some evidence that makes a conclusion likely.

Act Two systematically builds a cumulative, abductive moral argument for God's existence. Here we will simply attempt to cite some evidence that we think points in a particular direction. But persuasion is a hard thing. Human psychology is complicated, background assumptions can differ, and sometimes what appears rational to various people can seem disparate indeed. So we're not insisting that readers see all of this the way we do, but we think it worthwhile to share some of the considerations that we have found to be persuasive.

The argument will cover four main dimensions of morality: (1) moral facts (ontology), which includes moral goodness (values) and moral duties (obligations); (2) moral knowledge (epistemology); and the two aspects of moral faith that Immanuel Kant recognized, namely, the issues of (3) grace, or how we can be morally transformed and even perfected; and (4) providence, or whether happiness and virtue are ultimately consistent. By putting all four parts of the argument together, we hope to show the overall cumulative effect.

Again, the argument provided will be an abductive argument. Such an argument involves an *inference to the best explanation*. The basic structure of such an argument, once more, is this: it identifies various moral phenomena in need of explanation. In this case, what needs explanation is the four sets of moral phenomena involving moral metaphysics and epistemology and the two aspects of moral faith. Then various explanation candidates are scrutinized, particularly for their adequacy in terms of explanatory power and scope. Eventually the best explanation is identified. We are then positioned to tentatively infer to that best explanation as the likely true one. This is how the argument of the book will culminate in the conclusion that morality gives us reasons to believe that God indeed exists.

For now, though, consider a simplified abductive argument just to be sure you get it. Suppose you go to the store and park next to a white car. When you come out, the white car is gone, and you have a dent in your car with white paint on it. This state of affairs needs explanation. You'd naturally assume the white car next to you hit yours and left behind the dent and paint. But actually what you're doing is making an abductive inference. There could be other explanations, of course. Perhaps it was a second white car that replaced the first and then, when leaving, left the dent and paint. Or perhaps no car hit yours at all. Rather, some philosophically precocious kids from the university were intent on making you draw a false inference. So they intentionally dented your car with a hammer and splashed some white paint on it. Kids nowadays.

All sorts of potential explanations could account for what you've found, but the best explanation, in this case the one to which you'd naturally gravitate, is the likely true one. It might be false, as far as you can know, but it's at least likely true. So there's nothing scary or intimidating about an abductive inference. We use such arguments all the time. Here we're just going to slow the process down and walk you through the abductive steps a bit more carefully than usual.

After all, we all need a little help from time to time. I (Dave) have a sister who told me, some years back, that there were no community colleges where she lived. I found this hard to believe, so I asked her the name of the closest college to her. She immediately replied, "*Fort Pierce Community* College." Then, after a slight pause, "OHHH!!"

Sometimes it takes a moment for the light to dawn. Discerning the signs of truth and signals of transcendence around us can sometimes be genuinely tricky. We're inclined to think the existence of real moral truth is just such a sign and signal, one easily overlooked. What we intend to do here is help you see in a fresh way some quite telling evidence that surrounds us all.

# CHAPTER 5

# MORAL GOODNESS

*We are not to reflect on the wickedness of men*
*but to look to the image of God in them, an image*
*which, covering and obliterating their faults, an*
*image which, by its beauty and dignity, should*
*allure us to love and embrace them.*

JOHN CALVIN,
*INSTITUTES OF THE CHRISTIAN RELIGION*

THE GRUESOME IMAGES have haunted our computer and television screens for a while now. Innocent men, women, and children tortured, drowned in acid, strung up, burned alive, or beheaded by radical Islamic State terrorists. The world looks on in horror at the atrocities, marveling at how anyone could have become so twisted and corrupt as to perpetrate these evils with such zeal and reckless abandon.

In truth, however, as sad as this is to say, history is replete with unspeakable evils foisted by humans on other human beings. The institution of chattel slavery in the United States and elsewhere, the degradation and exploitation of poor labor, incessant sex trafficking in so many places, indignities and cruelties imposed on women and children, callous disregard for the unborn (even the selling of baby parts for profit): these are but a smattering of the sorts of despicable treatment of human beings that history reveals.

When we speak of objective value, we could take the discussion in a great many directions. We could talk about various theories of the good, or the sense in which God is good, or the difference between different kinds of goods, or between moral and nonmoral goods. Instead we will focus our attention on just one aspect of the discussion, but an eminently important one. Namely, we intend to discuss human value and what it suggests about reality. When we see or hear accounts about horrific and heart-wrenching actions like the recent mass shooting at a nightclub in Orlando or the ensuing celebration of the perverse Westboro Baptist Church in reply, few of us doubt that there is real evil in the world.

Evil has for its salient contrast goodness, the topic of this chapter. Immanuel Kant noted that the term *good* is ambiguous. Sometimes it's contrasted with *bad*, by which is usually meant something like "painful," and issues of pleasure and pain are certainly relevant to ethics. Arguably, however, the more distinctively moral use of the term *good* contrasts with *evil*. Clearly, the examples cited above are instances of evil, if anything qualifies. Surprisingly enough, however, some do doubt that anything at all actually is evil.

## IS EVIL REAL?

Joel Marks has claimed that whereas he *used* to be sure genocide (or animal cruelty) was wrong, now he's fairly sure it is *not*. It's not that he intends to engage in either behavior; he personally despises both practices. He just happens to think that nothing is evil at all. To him, the category of morality is bogus.

He writes that he is

> not merely skeptical or agnostic about it; I had come to believe, and do still, that these things are not wrong. . . . Now I will call a spade a spade and declare simply that I very much *dislike* it and want it to stop. . . . I must accept that other people sometimes have opposed preferences, even when we are agreed on all the relevant facts and are reasoning correctly. My outlook has therefore become more practical: I desire to influence the world in such a way that my desires have a greater likelihood of being realized.[1]

---

[1]Joel Marks, "Confessions of an Ex-Moralist," *New York Times*, August 21, 2011, http://opinionator .blogs.nytimes.com/2011/08/21/confessions-of-an-ex-moralist/?_r=0.

His position is an intriguing one that's well worth exploring. Of course it isn't altogether novel. It echoes aspects of both Hume and Nietzsche. However counterintuitive the position is, that is not decisive evidence that it's false, any more than the longstanding skepticism about human flight precluded air travel. In fact, there's a good reason that Marks has lost confidence in moral truth: the naturalism he espouses has a difficult time making sense of such truth.

For present purposes, we do not need to argue that it's impossible for naturalism to account for moral values. In fact, depending on how values are defined, naturalism can in fact account for them. For example, suppose we were to domesticate the concept into something readily explainable: moral values are values on which most rational people agree, or values on which most sensitive, compassionate, and empathetic people agree. In this way, a group of like-minded secular thinkers could agree to call mistreating children a morally bad thing, or even an objective moral value in some sense. And there you have it: objective value furnished by the resources of naturalism alone.

Someone like Marks sees through the futility of such an exercise, however. He realizes that it takes more than a consensus or unanimity of opinion to generate or locate a real objective moral value. A roomful of people can agree to call a cat a dog, but it's still a cat. Real objective moral value requires more than some group of people happening to "value" something. Another example makes this clear: a group of men with a penchant for pedophilia doesn't give such an inhumane practice value. Something that is valuable should be valued, but valuing something is hardly enough warrant to show that it should be valued or is in fact valuable.

The aim of this chapter is to explore the question of how best to explain objective moral value, more specifically human dignity or value. Since Marks doesn't believe in such a thing, as it's an objective moral value he denies exists, a view like his goes beyond the scope of this discussion. On another occasion we intend to scrutinize his position at greater length. Before setting his view to the side, however, allow us to share just one major misgiving about it.

Consider a question: On what basis might one try to defend a view like his? Let's suppose that Marks is right that naturalism can't sustain objective moral facts. Does it follow that such facts should be rejected? Only if one should be a naturalist, for one could just as easily renounce naturalism and retain commitment to those moral facts instead. Since naturalism shouldn't be presumed as a default position, or merely assumed to be true by definition, rational belief in it requires evidence. But what is the evidence for naturalism?

We hazard to assert on balance that there's precious little if any evidence for naturalism that outweighs, even remotely, the compelling reasons to believe in the wrongness of child torture. Naturalism is a hugely ambitious metaphysical thesis dictating that nothing except matter and energy make up the inventory of reality. Everything arises from the natural world, leaving no room for the supernatural or spiritual. Naturalism features a bold conclusion predicated on next to no evidence, flies in the face of common sense, and is a distinctly minority position in the history of the world.

The attempt to infer naturalism simply from science shows a common confusion and constitutes a naive non sequitur. Indeed, naturalism can't even define itself within the boundaries of its own terms, as David Bentley Hart writes, because "the total sufficiency of 'natural' explanations is not an identifiable natural phenomenon but only an arbitrary judgment." For this reason Hart argues it can never be anything more than a guiding prejudice, "an established principle only in the sense that it must be indefensibly presumed for the sake of some larger view of reality."[2]

If Marks would exercise his obvious skeptical powers when it comes to the thesis of naturalism, perhaps he would come to see there's no particularly good reason to be a moral skeptic. Is it really more obvious that naturalism is true than that setting fire to cats is just fine? What we find in Marks is someone who thinks that we can first embrace a particular theory of reality (naturalism) and then turn to ethics. We think this is a mistake.

---

[2]David Bentley Hart, *God: Being, Consciousness, Bliss* (New Haven, CT: Yale University Press, 2013), 17.

We're rather inclined to think that ethics itself can help us figure out the right overall view of reality (metaphysics). To be clear, what we are suggesting is not that by our ethical practices we glean insight into reality, although it's true that what we are able to grasp about reality is often conditioned by who we are and who we're becoming. But that's not our present point. Rather, apprehending ethical reality is the concern; by allowing what we're able to understand clearly about right and wrong, good and evil, vice and virtue, to shape our understanding of ultimate reality, ethics thus construed can shape our metaphysics, can shed light on reality.

So take the well-rehearsed moral dictum that it's wrong to torture children for the fun of it. We freely admit we could be wrong about this. Perhaps we're making a mistake taking as reliable our sense that this is a clear and veridical moral deliverance. But frankly, if we're wrong about that, we're likely wrong about most everything else. We're happily willing to take the risk. Philosophizing has to start somewhere. We're confident our starting point is about as good as it gets.

Marks used to be a committed Kantian ethicist. His departure from Kantianism seems regrettable to us, for Kant, laudably, thought it altogether legitimate and fitting that we use the deliverances of morality and our moral consciousness—among them the intrinsic value of persons—as insight into ultimate reality. In fact, this is the very methodology on which a moral argument for God's existence is based.

To be effective, an argument needs to rest on evidence that at least most people find reliable. And most people assume as axiomatic the inherent dignity and value of persons—despite notable exceptions like a decent person such as Marks and indecent people such as jihadist terrorists. So we intend not to check our moral common sense at the door but rather to assume without further argument inherent human dignity, that good and evil are real. We will save further engagement with moral skeptics for another occasion.

## THE DIGNITY OF PERSONS

To focus this discussion, we will zero in on the dignity and value of human persons. We wouldn't deny that objective value attaches to other things—chimpanzees and azaleas, for example—but for now our focus is on human beings. That an account of the value of nonhuman entities is readily on offer is actually an apologetic point in favor of a theistic ethic. Understanding such living things as part of the created order imbued with meaning and significance by God stands in contrast with many secular ethical theories that assign exclusive primacy to human beings as morally valuable. Such theories leave something like animal rights without much of an explanation. Other secular theorists fail to recognize the uniqueness of human beings—Princeton's Peter Singer and his views on infanticide come to mind. For our purposes, we will be discussing the inherent dignity and worth of human persons, leaving other considerations for another time.

Because of the moral status of human beings, their indiscriminate torture or slaughter constitutes evil (and thus morally blameworthy) behavior. On occasion taking human life is likely permissible, but only when there's morally sufficient justification for doing so. Pacifists—who think violence, or at least killing, is never morally justified—would likely be all the more eager to affirm the dignity of persons. When Kant discussed human dignity, he contrasted it with *price*. Whereas it makes perfect sense to speak of the worth or cost of a watch or house, it isn't appropriate or proper to speak of a person's price, as if he or she could be replaced with some corresponding quantity of compensation. Human beings, Kant thought, are incommensurable in this way, radically distinct from artifacts or things. They are in fact infinitely valuable. Kant considered this fact to be a veridical deliverance of the moral law—not a conclusion to draw but an inviolable truth to apprehend or premise to start with.

In Kant's case, he associated human dignity with autonomy. He deemed it necessary, in order to show adequate respect for others, to treat them as ends in themselves, particularly in terms of their moral agency. Although we are inclined to see the concept of human dignity as broader than that, it's worth quickly noting that Kant was certainly on to something here. As we write this, we just survived a particularly contentious election season, featuring two major-party candidates with polling negatives in the stratosphere. This has led no small number of partisans on each side of the aisle to pontificate about not only where they came down in the race, but where anyone who is rational, sane, or morally sensitive should have come down too.

In a case like this, we suspect Kant would caution against allowing other people to function as our conscience or arbiter of rationality. He would counsel thinking for oneself and remaining averse to imposition. One should think long and hard enough about the issues at hand and come to one's own settled and autonomous conclusions. Without deliberately appropriating for oneself the various principles at play, one is not behaving autonomously. Moreover, anyone who would coerce or impose a belief and try to circumvent a moral agent's autonomy or attentiveness to the evidence is likewise failing to respect that person's dignity.

We will be extending the notion of human dignity beyond those Kantian parameters, but we don't deny the power of Kant's insight, which retains its potency and relevance today. If more people in the public square and blogosphere respected the "mental freedom" of others (to use a phrase from William James), it would likely lead to an appreciable improvement in the caliber and tone of public civil discourse. Indeed, the insight even seems to be a scriptural one, because the apostle Paul encourages that "every one . . . be fully convinced" (Rom 14:5) with love, when it comes to several peripheral matters of practice on which, for various reasons, early believers didn't always agree. The enjoinder to engage in agreeable disagreement is a sermon that can't be preached enough, an art form we should all intentionally cultivate.

For present purposes, the salient feature of human dignity we'll discuss will be that human beings are the legitimate bearers of basic human rights. In other words, because of the dignity of human persons, their inhumane treatment is morally treacherous. What the Nazis did, what Pol Pot did, what certain terrorists are doing today, is morally odious. We live at a time when the pejorative "evil" tends to be eschewed by many, suggestive for some of colonialism, jingoism, or xenophobia. In truth, however, whatever aversion one may feel about the term, altering the example is usually enough to effect a change in tune and a reaffirmation of the category.

History reveals that evil behavior knows no ethnic, cultural, or national limitations. This is important to show that the level of this conversation is different from the standard political and partisan divides that epitomize current discussions. A political conservative might not hesitate in calling radical jihadism evil, whereas a political liberal might wish to avoid doing so for appearing to paint all Muslims with a broad brush into the category. That same left-leaning individual, however, is unlikely to think the category of evil is empty—corporate greed, slavery, rape, and racial profiling, for example, would all neatly fit the bill.

The point is that this is not a left-versus-right divide but rather a good-versus-evil and right-versus-wrong distinction. We know this sounds almost cliché, but we think it deeply important to stress. While the examples and instances adduced might differ, none but the most ardent moral skeptics would deny the categories altogether.

The question that arises is, what best explains this intrinsic human value that confers our moral standing and makes us the legitimate bearers of basic human rights? The descriptor *basic* is strategic here, because the point under discussion doesn't pertain to vexed and controversial debates about various political or identity rights demands. Such political rights discourse may be altogether legitimate, but here the focus is more specifically on claims that most people would agree are non-negotiable: children should not be tossed into meat grinders for the amusement of onlookers anxious for entertainment, women should not be forced into sex trafficking, those with opposing or no religious convictions should not be buried alive in acid, and so on. This is, obviously enough, unadulterated moral common sense, about as basic as it gets. Such examples show, to the satisfaction of most, the obvious silliness of denying that there are any moral absolutes.

For example, what's the exception that makes some outlying case of child torture for fun morally okay? We are convinced that there isn't one. Those uncomfortable with such simple assumptions will, we warn you, not find much of what we say persuasive. There's simply not enough common ground for us to build much of anything on. Fortunately, Nietzsche's prediction was accurate that the "death of God" would only slowly result in a loss of moral conviction. Most people—rightly we think—would quickly agree that such obvious moral truths need little defense and are a key to understanding the world and the human condition.

## CONSEQUENTIALIST THEORIES

Let's begin our examination of various ethical theories in accounting for inviolable human dignity and certain basic human rights by considering a few consequentialist moral theories. First we wish to stress that our aim is not merely to point out deficiencies in various ethical theories. Some theists, for example, may wish to subscribe to a utilitarian analysis, properly nuanced. What we think inadequate is not utilitarianism per se, though we do have reservations about it. Rather, what's most deeply driving our analysis is the inadequacy of moral theories across the board when the theistic element is left out of the picture.[3]

Consequentialist moral theories explain the moral rightness and wrongness of actions by appeal to their consequences. The first example is *egoism*. *Ethical* egoism contrasts with *psychological* egoism, which is the view that all of us, by nature, inevitably behave in ways we consider to be in our self-interest. Of course we can be mistaken about what's actually in our self-interest, but our choices are inevitably shaped by our estimations, correct or not, of what's best for us. Psychological egoism claims to be a *descriptive* theory about how we in fact behave as humans, whereas ethical egoism is *prescriptive*. It says that we *should* act in a way that maximizes our self-interest.

Ethical egoism declares that privileging one's own interests resides at the heart of moral obligation. Ayn Rand, Russian-American novelist and author of notable works such as *The Fountainhead* and *Atlas Shrugged*, advocated for a form of egoism. Having suffered under the oppressive communist regime in Soviet Russia, her overcorrection is perhaps understandable. But the spirit of egoism, and its inherent flaw, is apparent

---

[3]Thus our criticism of particular ethical theories and their efforts to stipulate conditions of rightness and wrongness is of secondary importance compared with the case we are trying to build for God as the most robust explanation for the existence of various moral phenomena such as moral values.

in her 1938 dystopian novel *Anthem*. Here she tells the story of Equality 7-2521 throwing off the yoke of collectivism and proclaiming the preeminence of the individual as the pinnacle of value. This triumph culminates in her protagonist's hymn to himself: "I am done with the monster of 'We,' the word of serfdom, of plunder, of misery, falsehood and shame. And now I see the face of god, and I raise this god over the earth, this god whom men have sought since men came into being, this god who will grant them joy and peace and pride. This god, this one word: 'I.'"[4]

Rand's literary depiction notwithstanding, the theory is not as altogether mercenary as it initially seems. If someone is transparently and callously selfish and self-serving in his dealings with others, his behavior is likely to ostracize and create tensions. Such behavior might prove workable in the short term, perhaps even beneficial or lucrative. Over the long term, however, it is likely to catch up with the moral agent and would prove not to be in his interests after all.

So an "enlightened" egoist would engage in behaviors that are in his long-term interests—forging relationships of mutual respect, reciprocity, and goodwill. And, in fact, such enlightened egoism alone would lead people to behave in quite civil, agreeable, and cordial ways. Gratuitous meanness, patent disrespect, offensive put-downs, and other antisocial behavior would not likely be seen as appropriate. They would all be ruled out by enlightened egoism alone. Counterintuitive as it might seem, then, egoism is not a moral theory with nothing going for it.

In a memorable series of sermons in the eighteenth century, Bishop Joseph Butler made the case that the problem isn't that humans are too egoistic. Rather, it's that they are not concerned *enough* about issues of self-interest. In what were bona fide philosophical treatises of the first order (a challenge to preachers today), Butler pointed out myriad ways in which greater attention paid to what's legitimately in our long-term interests would enable us to see that showing more respect for others, listening with greater attentiveness, and caring with more empathy would lead to a much better quality of life.

---

[4]Ayn Rand, *Anthem* (New York: Penguin, 1995), 97.

In a later chapter we'll argue that a generally theistic and specifically Christian ethic makes impeccable sense of how self-interest can be reconciled with a life of altruism. We will be careful not to claim that egoism per se can be reconciled with altruism and the morally good life. Rather, altruism is reconcilable with a judicious and altogether proper self-regard. Such self-regard, however, isn't the *sole* moral criterion that matters, which is what egoism at its heart entails. Legitimate self-regard can be salvaged, but egoism as a whole rules too much of value out, such as any genuine truly altruistic motivation.

To take another specific example, how does egoism fare in accounting for the intrinsic moral value and dignity of human beings? What seems clear is that someone professing ethical egoism can at least claim to believe in something like human dignity and value, perhaps even for egoistic reasons. Believing or claiming to believe in such a moral phenomenon might well prove to be in his own long-term, enlightened self-interest.

What is quite a bit harder for the egoist to make sense of is the *very category* of intrinsic human value. Why is my egoistic rationale for claiming to believe in intrinsic human value evidence that such value is real? None that we can see. After all, my rationale, in light of the logic of egoism, serves the ultimate purpose of securing my own long-term self-interest alone. Nor does egoism provide much of a bulwark against denying such dignity when the denial conduces to one's own self-interest. Indeed, egoism would offer, in such a case, reasons to affirm the opposite, to deny human dignity and fail to respect certain persons.

Consider an example that some might consider to be controversial: a case in which a woman, for the sake of convenience, opts for an abortion. Suppose she wants to take a vacation in Europe, and carrying the child to term would make this trip difficult or even impossible. Suppose she could, with a measure of difficulty, wait, defer the vacation, have the baby, and, if she doesn't want the baby, give the baby up for adoption to a couple that would like to raise the child. Instead, she chooses to abort.

If pressed to explain her rationale, she might, if she's taken an ethics class, point to the vexed nature of the question as to when personhood begins. She might say that if the "fetus" were a "person," then she might have an obligation to carry it to term. But in light of the difficulty of knowing this to be the case, she's morally, not to mention legally, entitled to abort. The denial of full human status to the fetus is, of course, one ostensible effort to salvage an appreciation of human value. The idea is that, of course, human beings are entitled to live, not be killed, but the fetus just isn't a human being, or at least hasn't been shown to be one.[5]

Often detractors and defenders of abortion both attest to the value of human persons. The former affirm that unborn children are human persons or human beings and thus deserve protection, while defenders of abortion contend that the full value of women includes their ability to determine what to do with their bodies. We are decidedly pro-life ourselves and hold deep convictions about how the most helpless and vulnerable of our species need to be cherished and protected. But our point is not about that for now. It's rather a quite nonpartisan point that both sides generally agree on an underlying issue: human beings have rights and deserve our protection. This is an affirmation of human dignity across the political aisle; again, this book is not about left versus right. Egoism is eminently hard-pressed to provide the basis for such human dignity.

One doesn't have to be a religious believer to recognize intrinsic human value. Believers, nonbelievers, and agnostics alike can typically apprehend such a truth. Not every worldview, and not every ethical theory, however, is equally effective at undergirding such a conviction. Consider a different example.

Take the distorted moral logic that the Nazis demonstrated toward Jews (and other people groups), and that slave owners did too when they denied the full humanity of their slaves to project a justification for patently hideous behavior. Each abysmal institution featured its own exalted rationale—the purity of the race, the success of the economy—and

---

[5]One could also point out that, in light of the great value of human beings, and the possibility (some would say exceeding plausibility) that the fetus is in fact a human being, one should err on the side of life, at least in such cases as just described.

each strikes us as a variant of a thinly veiled egoism.[6] If someone is looking for a substantive moral theory with adequate resources to protect and account for intrinsic human dignity and value, he's well advised to do better than egoism. Egoism alone would have never inspired a dream like Dr. Martin Luther King Jr.'s that his four little children would one day live in a nation where they would not be judged by the color of their skin but by the content of their character.[7]

One might wonder how another estimable consequentialist theory fares on the question of respect for persons—the theory of utilitarianism. How does it explain and protect inherent human dignity? Utilitarianism comes in different varieties, but what matters for present purposes is what utilitarians hold in common. Utilitarianism in general terms says what matters for morality is the maximizing of utility—flourishing, happiness, pleasure, well-being, or something in their close proximity—for all affected by an action. Usually utilitarianism (like egoism) is taken to be what is called a "normative" ethical theory, designed to explain the nature of our moral obligations. The question under consideration here is how well such a theory, particularly such a theory cast without any theistic elements, safeguards human dignity and the human rights that such dignity entails.

Let's begin by making a preliminary point about utilitarianism that parallels a point we made about egoism. Recall that a judicious consideration of self-interest is an altogether legitimate moral motivation and in itself not enough to render one an egoist. To be an egoist, such considerations have to be what *always trump*. Likewise, a realistic anticipation of the full array of consequences of our behaviors is morally relevant. But no mere consideration of such consequences as morally relevant is enough to render one a utilitarian. Consequences are among what's relevant to our moral decisions. Utilitarians, though, insist that consequences are the *only* relevant moral factor. This is why, just as egoism per se can't be reconciled with altruistic motivation,

---

[6]In at least many instances, though not likely all.
[7]Martin Luther King Jr., "I Have a Dream," speech, August 28, 1963, Washington, DC, www.archives.gov/files/press/exhibits/dream-speech.pdf.

pure utilitarianism is hard if not impossible to reconcile with an approach to ethics that insists there are some actions, irrespective of consequences, that should or should not be performed.[8]

On the one hand, utilitarianism certainly seems to care about issues of well-being: happiness, pleasure, flourishing, and the like. On the other, Jeremy Bentham, one of its most important advocates, finds the entire notion of natural rights to be nonsensical. When it comes to "natural and imprescriptible rights," existing prior to a government invested with the authority to confer such rights, Bentham thinks they don't exist. Natural rights, he writes, is simple nonsense: natural and imprescriptible rights, rhetorical nonsense—nonsense on stilts.[9]

It isn't that he rejects the idea of rights altogether. However, he thinks that any rights that do exist aren't inherent but rather are based on the circumstances of society, on what is advantageous in utilitarian terms. Whether rights should be recognized and protected, on his view, depends on what benefits society. Ursula LeGuin's powerful short story "The Ones Who Walk Away from Omelas" puts this feature of a utilitarian ethic on colorful display. The story describes a utopian society whose inhabitants live blissful, fulfilling, peaceful lives. They experience no hardship or pain; all members cooperate and are enabled to reach their full potential. As the story progresses, readers learn that the happiness of the community depends entirely on the horrific mistreatment of a small child, kept locked in darkness, immersed in filth, and left to its misery.

The problem with utilitarians affirming inherent rights is that, in principle, social circumstances might conspire in such a way (as described vividly by LeGuin) to warrant their invalidation, which is to say that there's no such thing as such rights in the first place. It is hard to see how human dignity or human value could exist in an intrinsic sense within Bentham's moral paradigm.

---

[8]This kind of moral theory is called deontological.

[9]Jeremy Bentham, *Rights, Representation, and Reform: Nonsense upon Stilts and Other Writings on the French Revolution*, The Collected Works of Jeremy Bentham, ed. P. Schofield, C. Pease-Watkin, and C. Blamires (Oxford: Oxford University Press, 2002), 317-401.

Before moving on to Bentham's most famous apprentice, here's a story we can't resist. On his death in 1832, Bentham left instructions for his body to be first dissected and then permanently preserved as an "auto-icon" (or self-image), which would be his memorial. The auto-icon is now on public display at University College London, save for the head, which, let's just say, proved problematic. A wax head eventually replaced the original.[10]

Bentham's protégé was the great John Stuart Mill. Mill tries to carve out more space for rights than Bentham does, especially in the fifth chapter of his *Utilitarianism*. Mill identifies duties of justice with the "perfect duties" discussed by philosophers, which involve the rights of individuals.[11] For example, if I have a perfect duty to help you, you have a right to my help. So notions of justice and individual rights are inextricably tied together. Now, why ought society protect such rights? Mill says he can give no reason other than general utility. In this way Mill and Bentham agree wholeheartedly, whatever other differences might obtain between them. And so the notion of inherent or natural rights is just as fanciful by Mill's reckoning as by Bentham's.

The problem seems to be that utilitarianism allows people to fall through the cracks, as it were. Mark Linville points out that there appears to be no necessary connection between an action maximizing utility and its being fair or just. The consistent utilitarian would be in a position of justifying, say, slavery, rape, or torture of innocents, if doing so would maximize utility in particular instances. Linville is willing to grant that, perhaps, the principle of utility, rightly understood, has none of these iniquitous consequences. He maintains, however, that any and all versions of utilitarianism worthy of the name must fail to account for that portion of commonsense morality that affirms that *individuals have moral standing.*

---

[10]Blame David for this story. He insisted. I'm just sorry I couldn't protect you from it. I hereby promise to do better in the future.—Marybeth

[11]The following four paragraphs are lightly adapted from an article by David Baggett, published at MoralApologetics.com, "Mark Linville's argument from Personal Dignity, Part 1," *Moral Apologetics*, December 16, 2014, http://moralapologetics.com/mark-linvilles-argument-from-personal-dignity-part-i/.

In maximizing overall utility, particular persons in principle could be treated unjustly. The possibility of violating a person's "rights," on a view like Mill's, is not sufficient to show that Mill's view accords requisite standing to individuals within the moral community. The utilitarian explanation of the wrongness in question appeals to the generally injurious *consequences for the community* rather than the fact that the person *simply shouldn't be treated that way.* Any rights people have are derivative on such a view, a function of the circumstances of social utility. They are not intrinsic. This means that in principle they can be overridden.

When confronted with the fact that a majority may be made happy by the genocide of a minority, utilitarians typically retort that in the real world and over time, most people are made unhappy by such atrocities. Even if true, this would imply that had a tyrant been more effective in brainwashing or slaughtering those who disagreed, genocide would have been right. As Angus Menuge puts it, "It is surely absurd to suggest that genocide is only wrong in the actual world because of administrative incompetence!"[12] As Linville reminds us, we must not lose sight of the logic of the utilitarian analysis. The principal concern is to maintain the greatest possible net pleasure or satisfaction, which is not for the sake of any individual persons. Rather, any regard for the individual is ultimately a concern for increasing net utility, not for the individual per se.

Sometimes it is suggested that a utilitarian ethic dovetails with a Christian perspective. It is certainly true that particular Christians can and have embraced utilitarianism, and it's surely plausible to consider consequences relevant to morality. In fact, John Hare argues that utilitarianism has religious roots. It was founded not just by Bentham and Mill but also by Francis Hutcheson and, especially, William Paley, "whose work preceded Bentham and indeed the success of whose book at Cambridge provoked Bentham to write his own version of the

---

[12]Angus Menuge, "The Failure of Naturalism as a Foundation for Human Rights," *Moral Apologetics*, December 13, 2014, http://moralapologetics.com/the-failure-of-naturalism-as-a-foundation-for-human-rights/.

theory. The point is that utilitarianism starts with Christians, and works out the view that, as Butler puts it, benevolence, especially God's benevolence, 'seems in the strictest sense to include in it all that is good and worthy.'"[13]

Bentham, Hare thinks, but not Mill, cut himself off from the roots of his own theory. Mill once argued, in response to the charge that utilitarianism is a "godless doctrine," that a utilitarian who believes in the perfect goodness and wisdom of God necessarily believes that whatever God has thought fit to reveal on the subject of morals must fulfill the requirements of utility in a supreme degree.[14]

We would contend, however, that utilitarianism, at least taken in isolation, potentially denies persons their natural rights and treats some as eliminable casualties on the way to a maximization of overall utility. We thus think that utilitarianism remains rather at odds with a theistic and Christian understanding of moral reality and affirmation of human dignity.[15] Some aspects of utilitarianism seem eminently correct—like the assumption that all persons are morally equal. What utilitarianism fails to do is anything other than assert this is so—despite that this is a distinctly minority view in the history of the world, and a hard-fought moral victory largely owing to the influence of Judeo-Christian thought. Any principled justification for such a foundational truth comes from resources other than anything utilitarianism itself provides.

---

[13]See John E. Hare, *God's Command* (Oxford: Oxford University Press, 2015), 288-89. We would qualify this by the reminder that Paley thought that being commanded by God and being felicific (productive of a greater balance of pleasure over pain than any alternative) are necessarily coextensive, but it's only being commanded by God that makes a given action obligatory. This is what many might call a distinct departure from utilitarianism in important respects.

[14]John Stuart Mill, *Utilitarianism, Liberty, and Representative Government*, intro. A. D. Lindsay (New York: Dutton, 1951), 26.

[15]Hare argues that Mill defended a version of the argument from providence—that there's ultimate correspondence between virtue and happiness. Hare thus thinks that a utilitarian like that can hold a utilitarian metamorality to be consistent with the pursuit of individual happiness. To this we would respond with two points: it's not clear how consistent utilitarianism and an argument from providence can be, particularly in light of the utilitarian's appeal to overall utility for the aggregate; and, even if that problem can be solved, the resources for an argument from providence don't come from utilitarianism itself. We agree with Hare, though, that without something like an argument from providence augmenting utilitarianism, the latter features severe moral deficiencies.

## VIRTUE THEORY

A different sort of ethical theory, and another with features certainly reconcilable with a theistic ethic, is virtue theory.[16] This is a view according to which what we're morally obliged to do is what conduces to virtue. The focus of this sort of approach is less on what our moral obligations are and more on *what sort of people we're becoming* by the actions we perform.

William James once wrote that the hell to be endured hereafter, of which theology tells, is no worse than the hell we make for ourselves in this world by habitually fashioning our characters in the wrong way.

> Could the young but realize how soon they will become mere walking bundles of habits, they would give more heed to their conduct while in the plastic state. We are spinning our own fates, good or evil, and never to be undone. Every smallest stroke of virtue or of vice leaves its never so little scar. . . . Nothing we ever do is, in strict scientific literalness, wiped out.[17]

C. S. Lewis echoed the sentiment when he once wrote about the "mark which the action leaves on that tiny central self which no one sees in this life but which each of us will have to endure—or enjoy—forever."[18] A morally bad choice to indulge one's anger, expressed by one man in dramatic fashion or by another in a private setting, is something that, unless he repents, will make it harder for him to keep out of the rage next time he is tempted. It will also make the rage worse when he does fall into it. "Each of them, if he seriously turns to God, can have that twist in the central man straightened out again; each is, in the long run, doomed if he will not. The bigness or smallness of the thing, seen from the outside, is not what really matters."[19]

Lewis had the insight, shared with James and various virtue theorists, that our choices put us on trajectories, shaping the people we're

---

[16]We've been calling these "normative" ethical theories, but when virtue theory gets included in the list the category might be broader. Robert Adams calls the broader category "substantive ethical theory." Now, the theory may cover what are right or wrong actions by a moral agent, or what is virtuous or nonvirtuous character in a moral agent.

[17]William James, *The Principles of Psychology* (New York: Holt, 1890), 127.

[18]C. S. Lewis, *Mere Christianity*, Signature Classics ed. (New York: HarperOne, 2002), 81.

[19]Ibid.

becoming. This invests our moral choices with tremendous signifi-cance, and this is an insight about which virtue theorists seem exceed-ingly right. Virtue theory surely has its merits, but suppose now that we wish to extend a virtue ethic to a wider ethical field and attempt to explain essential human dignity with the resources it provides. Might that work? It is difficult to see how.

On a virtue account of morality, the wrongness of an action is ulti-mately explicable in terms of the damage done to the soul, integrity, or character of the *person performing the action*. Henry David Thoreau's "Civil Disobedience" has surely done much good, especially in its in-fluence on Mohandas Gandhi and Martin Luther King Jr. In that treatise Thoreau puts forth a political philosophy advocating passive resistance to government injustice. In his specific case, Thoreau justified his refusal to pay taxes that inevitably supported the Mexican-American War and, by extension, the spread of American slavery. Yet, curiously enough, much of the argument Thoreau articulates centers on the way such ac-tions shaped his own character. As such, he is able to claim the following: "It is not a man's duty, as a matter of course, to devote himself to the eradication of any, even the most enormous, wrong; he may still properly have other concerns to engage him; but it is his duty, at least, to wash his hands of it, and, if he gives it no thought longer, not to give it practically his support."[20] Thoreau's essay doesn't articulate or defend a full-fledged ethical system, and we are not casting him as a virtue theorist here. However, something of his essay captures the shortcoming of virtue theory when it comes to accounting for dignity.

Although gross violations of moral law arguably do effect great damage in those who perform them, surely such an account leaves something of tremendous significance out, namely, the *nature of the action itself*. In cases where the dignity of other persons is violated, such violations aren't wrong solely because of the damage done to the moral agent. They are much more plausibly thought to be wrong in and of themselves. They

---

[20]Henry David Thoreau, "Civil Disobedience," 1849, repr. in *A Yankee in Canada, with Anti-Slavery and Reform Papers*, ed. Sophia Thoreau, William Ellery Channing, and Ralph Waldo Emerson (Boston: Tickor and Fields, 1866).

simply fail to accord the dignity and worth to another person that morality demands. It's for *this* reason that they are the sort of actions a virtuous person would not perform.[21]

## A THEISTIC PICTURE

A better account of human worth and essential human dignity is needed
than what utilitarianism, egoism, or virtue theory can provide, either
individually or together. Each has its insights, and elements of each are
perfectly reconcilable with a theistic picture. The theistic elements,
though, in our estimation, are not secondary or eliminable but crucial
and central.

Remember that the issue isn't whether secular ethicists can apprehend human value and significance. We're inclined to think they can,
just as we all can. This is not to say that such recognition is innate and
unrelated to advances made in society. Depending on one's accultur-
ation, one may grow up mistakenly thinking that racist and bigoted
attitudes toward persons of color are normative and entirely permissible. All of us are liable to have been shaped to believe things that are
patently false. Once coming to see the light, as it were, we're ashamed
to have thought about it differently. What is true for individuals can be
true of whole cultures.

Throughout much of human history, sadly, the notion of essential
human equality has been a relative rarity. To see something of value in
disabled children, or the mentally ill, or the desperate refugee is a quin-
tessential humanistic value. But it is not one that comes at all naturally.
The ideological shift that had to take place to see such value was huge.

Historically it was intimately tied to the influence of a Judeo-Christian
ethic and its influence on the reigning ethos of civilizations. As David
Bentley Hart writes,

---

[21]Mark Linville writes that standard accounts of virtue ethics have no conceptual room for the
moral standing of individuals and that this counts against such theories. "We should be able to
say simply that rape and genocide are wrong because people ought neither to be raped nor ex-
terminated." Linville, "The Moral Argument," in *The Blackwell Companion to Natural Theology*,
ed. William Lane Craig and J. P. Moreland (Hoboken, NJ: Blackwell, 2009), 391-448.

To look on the child whom our ancient ancestors would have seen as somehow unwholesome or as a worthless burden, and would have abandoned to fate, and to see in him or her instead a person worthy of all affection—resplendent with divine glory, ominous with an absolute demand upon our consciences, evoking our love and our reverence—is to be set free from mere elemental existence, and from those natural inclinations that pre-Christian persons took to be the very definition of reality.

And only someone profoundly ignorant of history and of native human inclinations could doubt that it is only as a consequence of the revolutionary force of Christianity within our history, within the very heart of our shared nature, that any of us can experience this freedom. We deceive ourselves also, however, if we doubt how very fragile this vision of things truly is: how elusive this truth that only charity can know, how easily forgotten this mystery that only charity can penetrate.[22]

Theism offers an account of human persons that permits the *irreducibility of human consciousness and purposes*, as a ground for human rights. According to the theist, God is personal and is the source of all value. The value of personhood is found in the fact that the metaphysically, axiologically, and explanatorily ultimate Being is personal.[23] To love one's neighbor as oneself, as the Bible enjoins, is not to conjure artificial warm sentiments toward them. It's rather to recognize their intrinsic worth and dignity and honor that obtain irrespective of whether there is reciprocation.

This makes insightful indeed the recognition that we have been endowed by our Creator with certain inviolable human rights. To have been made in God's image, created for a reason and purpose, imbued with inalienable rights, to be loved infinitely by him: this is the deepest source, and best explanation, of human dignity and value.[24]

---

[22]David Bentley Hart, *Atheist Delusions: The Christian Revolution and Its Fashionable Enemies* (New Haven, CT: Yale University Press, 2009), 213-14.

[23]Linville, "Moral Argument."

[24]As Linville puts it, "On a Judeo-Christian worldview, human personal dignity, though intrinsic, is derivative. The value of human persons is found in the fact that, as bearers of the *imago dei*, they bear a significant resemblance to God in their very personhood. God and human persons share an overlap of kind membership in personhood itself, and human dignity is found precisely in membership in that kind." Ibid.

In his 1940 novel *The Power and the Glory*, a hauntingly beautiful story of a disgraced priest, Graham Greene charges his readers to recognize and respond rightly to this intrinsic value: "When you visualized a man or woman carefully, you could always begin to feel pity—that was a quality God's image carried with it. When you saw the lines at the corners of the eyes, the shape of the mouth, how the hair grew, it was impossible to hate. Hate was just a failure of imagination."[25]

Marilynne Robinson's *Gilead*, too, offers a compelling meditation on human value, couched in the memoirs of her fictional preacher, John Ames. This preacher's imminent death has brought him a fresh awareness and a deepened appreciation of the inherent worth of every person. For Ames, this truth awakens in us the moment we truly attend to the image of God in another person: "Any human face is a claim on you, because you can't help but understand the singularity of it, the courage and loneliness of it. But this is truest of the face of an infant. I consider that to be one kind of vision, as mystical as any."[26]

God's concern for humanity, moreover, isn't merely for the aggregate of human persons, permitting some to fall through moral and metaphysical cracks as utilitarianism allows. God's love is intensely personal. Robert Adams argues that God himself can be said to be the ultimate good itself, and lesser, finite goods are good in virtue of relevant resemblance to God. Adams thus thinks the value of persons, for example, derives solely from what they have in common: a shared, relevant resemblance to God.

John Hare demurs at this point, however, and in doing so adds an important element about how human dignity can be both intrinsic and derivative. His point is that an account of goodness rooted in God must emphasize not just what good things humans share in common but the distinctive ways they are different, for in those very differences are reflections of disparate aspects of God. Human beings aren't called to reflect God only in virtue of their collection but also as individuals.

---

[25]Graham Greene, *The Power and the Glory* (New York: Penguin, 1940), 131.
[26]Marilynne Robinson, *Gilead* (New York: Farrar, Straus and Giroux, 2004), 66.

Hare writes:

There is a call by God to each one of us, a call to love God in a particular and unique way. Revelation 2:17, in the instructions to the church in Pergamos, refers to a name about which God says, "and [I] will give him a white stone, and in the stone a new name written, which no one knows except the one that receives it." If we think of this name, like "Peter" meaning "rock" (the name Jesus gives to Simon), as giving us the nature into which we are being called, and if we think of this nature, as Scotus does, as a way of loving God, then we can think of the value of each of us as residing in us, in our particular relation to God.[27]

A theistic and Christian picture of the human condition provides a compelling account of human dignity, of incommensurable worth, not just for humanity as a whole but for each and every individual, far better than can standard normative ethical accounts divorced from a theistic context. This is an account strong enough to sustain our deepest intuitions about the inestimable value of every human person.

## TALK BACK

1. Can drawing a distinction between badness and evil help us understand some difficult passages in Scripture? What qualifies as truly evil?

2. What concerns do egoism, utilitarianism, and virtue theory share with Christian theology? Where do they depart, and what correction might Christianity bring?

3. How is it that, as David Bentley Hart claims, only charity can know that a person, especially one on the margins of society, is worthy of affection, due respect, and honor?

---

[27]"What we have here is an intrinsic good in a slightly odd sense; not that we have value, each of us, all by ourselves . . . since we have our value in relation. But the value is not reducible to the valuing by someone outside us, on this account, but resides in what each of us can uniquely be in relation to God." Hare, *God's Command*, 29.

# CHAPTER 6

# MORAL OBLIGATIONS

*What honest boy would pride himself on not picking pockets? A thief who was trying to reform would. To be conceited of doing one's duty is then a sign of how little one does it, and how little one sees what a contemptible thing it is not to do it. Could any but a low creature be conceited of not being contemptible? Until our duty becomes to us common as breathing, we are poor creatures.*

GEORGE MacDONALD, "THE WISE WOMAN"

A RENOWNED PHILOSOPHER was held in high regard by his driver. The chauffeur listened in awe at every speech while his boss would easily answer questions about ethics. Then one day he approached the philosopher and asked whether they could switch roles for the evening's lecture. The philosopher agreed, and for a while the driver handled himself remarkably well. When it came time for questions from the guests, a woman in the back asked, "Is your epistemological view of the universe still valid in an existentialist world?"

"That is an extremely simple question," he responded. "So simple, in fact, that even my driver could answer it, which is exactly what he will do."

I (Dave) once asked a famous thinker a question as well. It was the fall of 2006, if memory serves, when the esteemed visitor took the stage. The hall was packed, and a frenzied excitement filled the air. The well-known speaker, outspoken atheist Richard Dawkins, was about to hold the audience in rapt attention as he chatted, read from his recent book, and answered questions. The location for the event was a college across town from where we live, so I took the opportunity to hear him.

It was a fun evening, and that night anyone there could sense in the crowd a physical embodiment of reigning cultural conflicts. On the one hand, many were persuaded by Dawkins about how misguided belief in God is and how miserable a character the God of the Old Testament is. On the other, a sizable group was profoundly skeptical of Dawkins's skepticism. Although I found Dawkins to be an engaging and likeable enough fellow, I confess to belonging in the latter category.

When the question-and-answer period began, I went up to ask a question. I thought it preferable to start with a bit of a disarming ice breaker: "I always knew you were smart, but then when I heard that accent, I thought you're a genius." The crowd politely laughed, and then I resumed, "But . . ." He immediately interjected, "I knew there'd be a 'but.'" To which I answered, "Well, this is Lynchburg."

Then I asked my question about the foundations of ethics. On his worldview, I pressed, what makes it the case that anything is morally right or wrong? The question was about moral obligations—the duties we have to perform or not perform certain actions—and their explanations or foundations. In his answer he pointed out that a variety of secular ethical theories are on offer, most specifically a utilitarian analysis.

*God and Cosmos* considered a range of such theories, arguing that, in each case, a theistic ethic provides the better and stronger explanation of moral obligations. Rather than delving into a large representative variety of possible secular accounts of moral obligations here, our approach will instead be to identify some key features of moral obligations, based on their language and logic. We will try to provide some general reasons to think that a theistic explanation will be stronger than anything our secular and naturalist friends can provide with the resources they have at their disposal, including a utilitarian account shorn of its theistic elements.

## THE IMPORTANCE AND NATURE OF OBLIGATIONS

Among the approximately couple of dozen arguments for God's existence from Alvin Plantinga's famous and seminal article on natural theology is one that, in his estimation, may be the best of the lot. The argument in question infers God's existence on the basis of moral obligations. In terms of the strength of the premises and the evidential connection between the premises and conclusion, this argument is the one that he thinks is perhaps second to none among arguments from natural theology.

Moral obligations are part of the deontic family of ethical concepts. Deontic ethics includes issues of moral permissibility, moral obligation, and moral forbiddenness, and they often employ language of "right" and "wrong." An action that is *wrong not to do* is a *moral obligation*. An action that is *not wrong to do* is *morally permissible*. An action that is *wrong to do* is *forbidden*. Although moral duties do not cover the whole moral terrain, they are one important part of it and cry out for adequate explanation.

Here is one reason obligations are important. Suppose someone were to say simply that ethics is about cultivating the right virtues or character. Their list of virtues might be entirely right, and it may well be true that the cultivation of such traits makes for a moral person. Still, though, an important question looms: *Ought* we to become people of virtue? Perhaps the answer is obvious that we should. But that doesn't mean the oughtness eliminates the need for moral obligations. Rather, it *presupposes* it.

Another answer is that we ought to become people of virtue because our lives will go better with those virtues than without them. This is also likely true in numerous respects and lots of cases, but presumably there's also something valuable in itself about becoming virtuous persons. The reason we should become people of virtue is stronger than merely the advantages and benefits we get from it. The moral demand is less contingent and more binding and categorical than that. Virtue ethics doesn't rid us of the need for moral obligations but rather makes best sense *only if* there are real moral obligations.

It would be an easy task to explain moral obligations if by *obligations* we simply meant *feelings of obligation*, but the latter are neither necessary nor sufficient for the former.[1] Perhaps someone neglects a particular duty for so long that she has ceased to feel it to be one. Conversely, one can have the feeling one ought to do something yet have no obligation to do it at all—like Huckleberry Finn's conviction that he should turn in his friend Jim, the runaway slave. Usually, though, feelings of obligation at least roughly correspond to actual obligations.

Moral obligations are not just rules or, worse, suggestions, like the rules of the road in Rome. Moral obligations are not mere options for us, even options supported by good reasons. They are thought to be *inescapable*. Another word for "duty" or "obligation" is *imperative*. Immanuel Kant was well known for distinguishing between hypothetical and categorical imperatives. *Hypothetical imperatives* depend for their legitimacy on some goal desired by the subject of the prescription. For example, to lose weight you *ought* to eat less and/or exercise more. The hypothetical prescription to eat less isn't universally applicable, obviously enough. A *categorical imperative*, though, on a Kantian construal, *is* universally applicable, not dependent at all for its legitimacy on any goal desired by the subject of the prescription. To treat others as ends in themselves and not merely as means, to use Kant's famous example, is a categorical imperative, something everyone has a moral duty to do.

Moral obligations construed as categorical imperatives require more than inescapability. They need an additional vital ingredient, which Richard Joyce characterizes as *authority*. This, he notes, gives us a normative system enjoying both features (inescapability and authority), one that possesses "practical clout."[2] Such practical clout dictates that the obligatory is what we have to do, what we must do—not in the sense of the *causal must* but of the *moral must*. When C. S. Lewis speaks of the moral demand at the beginning of *Mere Christianity*, he refers to it as a "law" but distinguishes it from the laws governing the operation of the physical world in just this sense. We can't opt out from

---

[1]Just as we saw last chapter: a feeling that people have intrinsic value is not the same as accounting for such value.

[2]Richard Joyce, *The Evolution of Morality* (Cambridge, MA: MIT Press, 2007), 57.

being governed by gravity. We can, however, choose to ignore the moral law. And too often we do.

Paul Copan and Matthew Flannagan write,

> *Moral obligation is not identical with what one has good reasons to do.* Obligations involve a certain type of reason to act: one that involves a demand with which we must comply, one by which others can rationally blame us and reproach us for failing to do so, one for which we can rightly be held accountable and feel guilty for violating, and one that is rational to inculcate into others.[3]

This illustrates the way that language about moral obligations points to the *authority* of moral requirement, which leads to another characteristic feature of moral duties. We can see this additional feature most clearly when we consider that we often act in violation of the moral law. One result of these violations is the experience of *guilt* discussed before. To reiterate here, guilt should be understood as a moral condition in need of rectification and not merely a subjective feeling. Two more features of moral obligations are responsible for much of the human significance of guilt. One is *harm* caused by one's (wrong) action, and the other and yet more pervasive feature of guilt is *alienation* from other people, to some degree or other.

Of the various aspects of moral duty, perhaps authority is the most important distinguishing feature. The notion of authority is not much in vogue today, smacking as it does of oppression, hypocrisy, and illegitimacy. But anyone who would reject the notion of moral obligations would quickly change their tune if they became the victim of someone else's wrongdoing. As we noted in chapter two, Flannery O'Connor's Hulga is a textbook example of such a reversal. Literature can be helpful in another way here, offering illustration after illustration of obligations met and obligations forsaken.

---

[3]Paul Copan and Matthew Flannagan, *Did God Really Command Genocide? Coming to Terms with the Justice of God* (Grand Rapids: Baker Books, 2014), 165. Perhaps an example can help. Say your neighbor's cat had a litter of kittens, and these kittens need homes. You already have three cats, but your neighbor is having trouble finding homes for two remaining kittens. You are certainly equipped to welcome the two kittens, you have reason to adopt them to help your neighbor, who is on a fixed income and cannot keep up with the added expenses. These kittens need a good home, which you could provide. But these reasons most likely don't rise to the level of obligations.

Phoenix Jackson of Eudora Welty's short story "A Worn Path" treks untold miles through the woods against overwhelming odds to retrieve medication for her grandson. The child is her charge, her responsibility, and he will surely die if not for her fierce commitment to her obligation. So too in Cormac McCarthy's *The Road* an unnamed father sacrifices all for the possibility of his son's survival. He is rightly recognized as the hero of the story, unlike his wife, who abandons the family and fails to live up to her responsibilities. The power of examples such as these—both positive and negative—demonstrates how elemental our recognition of moral authority is.

An important task for the ethicist is to explain such authority.[4] The challenge of doing so, at least in part, led J. L. Mackie to reject such obligations as too metaphysically odd.[5] What is so special, and potentially strange, about moral obligations? To have a moral obligation is to have a special reason to act. An obligation conveys the notion of an absolute verdict. This distinguishes moral obligations from a picture of morality like we find in Aristotle. Aristotle's use of terms such as *should* or *ought* relates to what is good and bad for something. They bespeak what is needed for something to flourish or achieve its potential. And so justice, for example, is a virtue needed for human flourishing.

By contrast, in modern moral philosophy, terms such as *should* and *ought* often bear a special moral sense, in which they imply some absolute verdict.[6] Cambridge philosopher G. E. M. Anscombe attributes the difference to the intervening influence of Christianity, with its law conception of ethics. If such a conception of a law-giving God is dominant for many centuries and then given up, it is hardly surprising that the concept of *obligation*, of being bound or required as by a law, should remain for some time even though it has been cut off from its root.

---

[4]The following three paragraphs are lightly adapted from an article by David Baggett, "Summary of C. Stephen Evans, *God and Moral Obligation*, Chapter 1," *Moral Apologetics*, January 7, 2015, http://moralapologetics.com/stephen-evans-god-and-moral-obligation-chapter-1/.

[5]Leading to his "error theory."

[6]G. E. M. Anscombe, "Modern Moral Philosophy," repr. in *The Collected Philosophical Papers of G. E. M. Anscombe*, vol. 3, *Ethics, Religion, and Politics* (Oxford: Basil Blackwell, 1981), 26-42.

This is just what Anscombe thought had happened, resulting in vestiges of moral language retaining the "atmosphere" of its more traditional
use but with its soul lost and clout removed. This is why Anscombe,
writing in the 1950s, thought it might be best to leave the modern conceptions behind and go back to Aristotle's understanding, because she
thought the theoretical underpinnings of modern morality were irre-
trievably lost. Anscombe, a devout Catholic, may have been pleasantly
surprised to live to see the more recent resurgence of interest in theistic
ethics, including interest in variants of a divine command account of
moral obligations.

What is important for present purposes is to note what Evans dubs the
"Anscombe intuition": the idea that moral obligations as experienced
have a unique character, and attempts to explain moral obligations must
illuminate that special character. Four features stand out to Evans as
comprising moral obligations: (1) A judgment about a moral obligation
is a kind of verdict on my action. (2) A moral obligation brings reflection
to closure. (3) A moral obligation involves accountability or responsibility. (4) A moral obligation holds for persons simply as persons.[7]

More could be said to spell out various features of moral obligations,
but enough has been said to proceed to the next phase of our argument.
To summarize, then, perhaps the most important distinguishing feature

---

[7]C. Stephen Evans, "Moral Arguments for the Existence of God," in *Stanford Encyclopedia of Philosophy*, Winter 2016 ed., http://plato.stanford.edu/entries/moral-arguments-god/. Interestingly
enough, Evans wishes to suggest, contra Anscombe, that Socrates seemed to operate with the
concept of moral obligation. In his *Apology*, for instance, all four features are present. Evans
thinks this is significant because the notion of moral obligations as verdict-like and rife with
authority may not simply be a function of special revelation but something more generally accessible. This is potentially important for a reason most relevant to this chapter's concern. If the
features of moral obligation are defined in a question-begging sort of way, then the failure of a
moral theory to satisfy the strictures that emerge as conceptual features of moral obligations may
not be seen as a significant failure after all. If, for example, moral obligations construed in such
a way as to satisfy the Anscombe intuition came about only or primarily as a result of Jewish and
Christian teachings, then a secularist could reply, "That's fine; so much the worse for moral
obligations understood along those lines." For that reason, recognizing that Socrates himself
entertained an understanding of moral obligations in such close proximity to the modern conception is an important point, and one that should discourage us from dismissing modern conceptions too quickly. Joyce, too, thinks that it is part of the conception of moral judgments
generally and moral obligations particularly that they possess moral clout, "oomph," the sort of
binding authority to which Anscombe's intuition points.

of moral obligations, classically construed in the Socratic and theistic traditions, is that they are *authoritative*, offering us compelling reasons to comply with them. Failure to discharge our moral duties typically results in objective guilt, alienation from others, and, where damage is rendered, even greater guilt.

## LOSING HOLD OF OBLIGATIONS

In the previous chapter we identified one reservation about utilitarianism, namely, that it potentially overlooks individual persons' rights because of its emphasis on overall utility. Now we wish to raise another concern, particularly in light of Dawkins's assumption that utilitarianism provides a fruitful direction to look for an account of moral obligations. Let's begin with an example and then take a look at another well-known contemporary atheist who seems to embrace something in the vicinity of utilitarianism.

Suppose you come across a child who was just hit by a car. He's in terrible pain, and nobody else is around to help. If you don't provide help to the child, his life will clearly be in real danger. You have a cell phone, and it would be quite easy for you to call for an ambulance. Do you have a moral obligation to make the call?

Now, first let's acknowledge that moral skeptics would say there are no such things as moral obligations. They're just figments of our overactive imagination or vestiges of old-fashioned ways of looking at things. Second, let's recall the distinction between a feeling of obligation and the obligation itself. Sometimes, at least, we might feel we have an obligation that we don't in fact have. In this instance, most people would feel a sense of obligation, but that's not enough to assure us that there's a real obligation, as the aforementioned moral skeptics would readily remind us.

Third, if we were to help the boy, as most people would, it would and should likely be for reasons other than that we believe we're obligated to help. We may well help because we want to help, not just out of a sense of duty. That is no argument against our having a duty, however. It's just to say that we need not be always motivated by duty and many times should be motivated by something else.

With those potential confusions out of the way, let's ask again: Would we have a moral obligation to call for help? We hazard to guess that most people would say yes, and they seem clearly right. The question is, where does the authoritative obligation come from? What is it about the world, about reality, about the human condition, that generates such a binding moral obligation? Obviously this is a question only for those who are convinced that such an obligation obtains, but most people are already convinced that it does.

A utilitarian answer is that by calling for help you're likely to produce better overall consequences than by not calling. Your call will ensure (or at least make much more likely) that the boy will get the treatment he desperately needs. This is not in dispute. The question the utilitarian needs to answer, in addition, is *why* we have a binding moral obligation to maximize utility in this way. The answer to this question *cannot* be this: because it maximizes utility. The question at issue is prior: Why are we obligated to maximize utility? How does the utilitarian, especially a secular utilitarian, account for the authority of moral obligations?

Punting to the maximization of utility at this point is to beg the question. It amounts to a large assertion but no argument. Once we distinguish the various components of the discussion and rule out of court rhetorical evasion, the deficiency of this analysis taken in isolation begins to become clear. To explore the adequacy of a utilitarian account further, let's take a look at Sam Harris and what he says about obligations in his book *The Moral Landscape*.

The outspoken atheist Harris makes several interesting points here about moral obligations. His account deserves critical scrutiny, particularly because, in our estimation, these points are indicative of some deep but common mistakes in this discussion. We might begin by pointing to an interesting analogy he uses, a comparison of morality and medicine. Harris believes this can clear up "philosophical confusion." "The simplest way to see this," he writes, "is by analogy to medicine and the mysterious quantity we call 'health.' Let's swap 'morality' for 'medicine' and 'well-being' for 'health' and see how things look."[8]

---

[8]Sam Harris, *The Moral Landscape: How Science Can Determine Human Values* (New York: Simon & Schuster, 2011), 199.

In this way he tries to answer various objections to his ethical proposals, be they value, persuasion, or measurement problems. In each case, he argues, the practice of medicine confronts similar challenges without undermining medicine. By parity in reasoning, he argues that morality can be founded on the scientific foundations Harris identifies and can escape unscathed from various objections.

We bring the analogy up because it is indeed instructive, but in a way rather different from how Harris envisions it to be—for the practice of medicine, rightly construed, very often does not affect healing in the body but simply helps the body heal itself. We see this most especially regarding chronic diseases, where the best medicine can do is treat the symptoms. Doctors don't heal. The body heals itself, or it doesn't heal at all. Medical technologies are wonderful, but medicine isn't the source of health. Proper exercise and nutrition, in contrast, get us quite a bit closer to what genuine health requires. They can help give the body the resources it needs to function optimally, resist diseases, and heal itself. To mistake medical treatment for the essence of health is to confuse genuine health with a mere treatment of symptoms.

In a similar sort of way, we consider much of what Harris says about ethics to involve skating the surface. It answers the easy questions and bypasses the hard ones. It settles for a superficial analysis that fails to explain what needs explanation. In Harris's insistence on the goodness of creaturely flourishing and well-being, for example, it's not that we're inclined to disagree with him that such a thing is indeed good. But that hardly settles the matter.

What makes these things good? Recognizing the goodness of something is not the same as explaining why it's good.[9] And even if something is good, it doesn't follow that we have an obligation to bring it about. Our becoming cancer specialists and battling it the rest of our lives might well be a good thing to do. But it's not thereby a duty. So how do moral obligations arise? Harris does little to answer such a query. Instead he deals with the surface issues and leaves the core questions behind.

---

[9]Thinking otherwise is to confuse epistemology and metaphysics.

For example, note how Harris responds to a very fundamental question. He mentions moral skeptics who ask, "How could it be objectively true . . . that we *ought* to be kind to children?" This is indeed a most important question, and any moral theory worth its salt should be able to answer it effectively.

Harris, however, seems not to recognize the question's import:

> But this notion of "ought" is an artificial and needlessly confusing way to think about moral choice. In fact, it seems to be another dismal product of Abrahamic religion—which, strangely enough, now constrains the thinking of even atheists. If this notion of "ought" means anything we can possibly care about, it must translate into a concern about the actual or potential experience of conscious beings (either in this life or in some other). For instance, to say that we ought to treat children with kindness seems identical to saying that everyone will tend to be better off if we do.[10]

Rather than taking up the challenge, Harris pivots. He suggests the question itself is suspect, insisting that it is predicated on a vestige of faith-based religion. Then he cashes out appeal to obligations in terms of issues of well-being. Let's consider each of these moves in turn, in reverse order.

First, to affirm moral obligations based only on considerations of well-being misses the importance and centrality of the question of what gives obligations their authority. With his characteristic prescience, C. S. Lewis anticipated just this sort of inadequate reply:

> If we ask: "Why ought I to be unselfish?" and you reply "Because it is good for society," we may then ask, "Why should I care what's good for society except when it happens to pay *me* personally?" and then you will have to say, "Because you ought to be unselfish"—which simply brings us back to where we started. You are saying what is true, but you are not getting any further. If a man asked what was the point of playing football, it would not be much good saying "in order to score goals," for trying to score goals is the game itself, not the reason for the game, and you would really only be saying that football was football—which is true, but not worth saying. In the same way, if a man asks what is the point of behaving decently, it is

---

[10]Ibid., 38.

no good replying, "in order to benefit society," for trying to benefit society, in other words being unselfish (for "society" after all only means "other people"), is one of the things decent behavior consists in; all you are really saying is that decent behavior is decent behavior. You would have said just as much if you had stopped at the statement, "Men ought to be unselfish."[11]

Second, what seems to make Harris nervous is the requirement to spell out a theory of moral obligations. He seems to harbor the concern that such explicit talk of moral duties smacks of religion. He finds the whole discussion unseemly from the start. But is there anything seriously dubious about asking whether or not we have a moral obligation to refrain from hurting children, or more positively to be kind to them? Of course not. This is the quite garden-variety language and logic of morality that most everyone uses and that calls for an explanation. Its very obviousness makes it *more* pressing, *not less*.

To affirm that we have a moral obligation, though, introduces the challenge of accounting for the authority of moral duties. What is Harris's account, as a naturalist and consequentialist, of the force of moral law? That we are obliged to maximize utility? Why? What is it about his worldview that would make such a claim true?

There's more. Ought (generally) implies can. It doesn't make sense to say I ought to jump to the moon when it's impossible for me to do so. Harris, however, denies free will. This creates for him a predicament. Free will seems essential for the moral project and, well, for lots of other human projects.

A young couple came into the church office to fill out a premarriage questionnaire form. The young man, who had never talked to a pastor before, was quite nervous, and the pastor tried to put him at ease.

When they came to the question, "Are you entering this marriage of your own free will?" there was a long pause.

Finally, the woman looked over at the apprehensive young man and said, "Put down yes."

At any rate, Harris's denial of freedom means that, on his view, the actual failure of anyone to maximize utility in any particular circumstance

---

[11]C. S. Lewis, *Mere Christianity*, Signature Classics ed. (New York: HarperOne, 2002), 26-27.

could not have been avoided. It was bound to happen. So what sense does it make to say such a person *should* have done it? Harris's account fails to explain how obligations derive from what's good, why obligations have authority, where we get the moral freedom we need to make sense of having obligations, and whether anyone is genuinely blameworthy for failing to discharge a moral duty. This does not bode well for his case.

Harris eschews moral obligations of a certain sort. He rejects as wrong-headed any sense of moral obligation as something intrinsically good or right. However, isn't it intuitive that some behaviors are simply beyond the pale, not possibly justified, however good the overall consequences may be by their performance? Consequentialists such as Harris have a difficult time ruling anything out. In principle, just about anything at all would be morally permissible as long as it ultimately maximizes utility.

In a famous 1958 article by Anscombe, she points this out, lamenting the way utilitarianism, especially since Sidgwick, had pervaded the ranks of English academic ethicists, who feature an overall similarity despite their differences.[12] On their ethical system, killing the innocent is not a forbidden action. She writes:

> Now this is a significant thing: for it means that all these philosophies are quite incompatible with the Hebrew-Christian ethic. For it has been characteristic of that ethic to teach that there are certain things forbidden whatever consequences threaten, such as choosing to kill the innocent for any purpose, however good; vicarious punishment; treachery . . . ; idolatry . . . adultery. . . . The prohibition of certain things simply in virtue of their description as such-and-such identifiable kinds of actions, regardless of any further consequences, is certainly not the whole of the Hebrew-Christian ethic; but it is a noteworthy feature of it; and if every academic philosopher since Sidgwick has written in such a way as to exclude this ethic, it would argue a certain provinciality of mind not to see this incompatibility as the most important fact about these philosophers, and the difference between them as somewhat trifling by comparison.[13]

---

[12]Namely, they all endorse a philosophy according to which it is impossible to hold that it can't be right to kill the innocent as a means to any end whatsoever and that those who disagree are mistaken.

[13]Anscombe, "Modern Moral Philosophy," 26-42.

Whereas Anscombe, herself a committed and devout believer, wasn't one to disparage religious faith and conviction, Harris's view of "faith-based religion" is notoriously and consistently derogatory and condescending. We might briefly note that this is perfectly understandable in light of Harris's understanding of faith. The condition of faith itself, he writes, is conviction without sufficient reason. To Harris, faith is hope mistaken for knowledge, bad ideas protected from good ones, good ideas obscured by bad ones, wishful thinking elevated to a principle of salvation.

Needless to say, we do not recognize Christian faith in such a formulation. Biblical faith, when understood rightly, is trust in the faithfulness of God to do what he has promised he will do. This trust, in our estimation, rests on solid foundations—God's pattern of faithfulness and a long-established record of his trustworthiness. God does not coddle us, giving us all we desire; rather, he demonstrates his love by fulfilling his promises to us and, most of all, by lavishing on us his salvation.

## GOD AND MORAL OBLIGATIONS

What can better account for the authoritative nature of moral obligations? Dawkins, when pressed, mentioned utilitarianism, but this raises difficult questions. For example, utilitarianism assumes the essential equality of persons, which is right. On what basis does a utilitarian claim to believe this, though? We once asked a utilitarian what he thought to be the basis of the equality of persons. His answer gave us a smile (followed quickly by a frown): *we're all equally unimportant.* Not the most inspiring answer!

Perhaps, though, some theistic ethicists might try to salvage utilitarianism by combining it with theistic components that offer hope for answering some of the harder questions of ethics. That's one approach, though not our particular stance. It's not central to our case that we spell out just the right theistic theory of moral obligations, only that theism provides a binding authority not clearly available in naturalistic systems. Still, for what it's worth, we're happy to share our own favored account of moral obligations.

Our preferred theistic answer (one among other possibilities) is a divine command theory. This theory has experienced quite a resurgence in recent years. Ever since Robert Adams's groundbreaking *Finite and Infinite Goods*, a number of others have followed suit and defended their own versions of divine command theory—from C. Stephen Evans to John Hare, to name but a few. Many are drawn to such a theory because it seems to make sense of the "oomph" of morality. God seems to be the one with the requisite authority to invest morality with the sort of clout most intuitively think it has. This becomes clear especially after obligations are seen as part of the social frameworks we find ourselves in. The inclusion of a personal God within that framework can integrate and fulfill the legislative, executive, and judicial functions for the moral law in a way that no merely finite person could.

Usually the most important objection raised to a divine command theory (DCT) is an arbitrariness concern: What if God were to tell us to perform some hideous action? Wouldn't DCT entail that such an action would become our moral duty? In short, such an objection mistakenly assumes DCT is the culprit. In fact the problem is instead the deficient conception of God in operation.

As we discussed earlier, if God is the God of classical theism and orthodox Christianity, then his very nature is love. In God there's no shadow of turning, no vulnerability to moral corruption. He is by nature essentially loving and altogether perfect in every way. Just as he could not commit suicide, he could not tell us to torture kids for fun. His inability in this regard doesn't owe to his imperfection but to his perfection.

The objection we intend to discuss here is a different one. In a dialogue with John Shook, I (Dave) made mention of this objection, and with jocularity he offered to name it after me. It was tempting, because I'm desperate for something to be named after me—an asteroid, hurricane, viral strain, social phobia, heresy, anything! But alas, I couldn't lay dibs on this objection as it had already been advanced by Ralph Cudworth (1617–1688) and others.

The objection bears a striking resemblance to the challenge we issued earlier against utilitarianism. Recall how we asked the utilitarian why

maximizing utility is itself a moral duty. Now the divine command
theorist is asked, "Why is obeying God a moral duty?" The question
isn't a matter of mere prudence: we ought to obey God because he's so
much stronger than us and will punish us if we don't. That misses the
point completely.

Nor is the question whether we have good reasons to obey God. Presumably we do, especially if God loves us, knows what's best for us, and
issues commands that are anything but arbitrary or quasi-arbitrary rules
to test our obedience. The real question is this: Where does God's authority derive, which is the foundation of the authority of the moral law
for which he is in some real sense responsible?

The divine command theorist faces a dilemma at this juncture: the
answer "Because God commands us to obey him" would be circular reasoning. It would be just as circular as the utilitarian saying that we have
an obligation to maximize utility because it maximizes utility. Even if
God does command us to obey him, why do we have an obligation to
obey that command? Evans, in his book defending divine command
theory, tries his hand at providing a variety of responses to this objection,
which he dubs the "prior obligations objection."[14]

Here's another angle, one Jerry Walls and I (Dave) cover in *Good God*
that's worth quoting at length. To answer questions about divine authority,

> consider the reasons we normally ascribe authority to someone. Some-
> times it is a simple matter of power. A person who has the legal power to
> enforce his will, for instance, has a certain kind of authority. Another
> source of authority is knowledge and information. We recognize as au-
> thorities those persons who have sufficient mastery of a field or discipline
> that they can command respect for what they know and understand. A

---

[14]Possible replies Evans adduces include that the prior obligation to obey God may be merely
hypothetical, rooted in God's authority, but actual obligations come into operation only once
God issues commands. Another is that all that DCT needs is the conditional "If God commands
X, then X is morally required." A third possible reply is that the prior "ought" comprises moral
reasons to do the action in question or a "nonmoral ought," not necessarily a moral obligation.
Fourth, he notes, as we did with utilitarianism, that it's an objection that extends to other moral
theories too. Fifth, God in fact does command us to obey him. And sixth, even if the objection
goes through, a divine command could still function as a sufficient condition for a moral obligation, even if it's not a necessary one.

third source of authority is moral integrity and character, the sort of authority that appeals to our conscience and demands respect in a deeper sense than the authority that comes from mere power or even knowledge. Indeed, a person who has mere power or legal authority but who lacks moral integrity lacks the authority to command our respect, even if he has the power to enforce his will on us.

Now then, God has supreme power, knowledge, and goodness, and all of these underwrite his moral authority. He created us and this world and stamped us with his image, and he has the power to hold us fully accountable for our actions. Since he has perfect knowledge of us, he understands perfectly what is good for us and our flourishing. Moreover, since he is perfectly good he desires our well-being and does everything short of overriding our freedom to promote it.

In view of his nature as a perfect being, there are no good grounds for doubting his authority. There can be no being blindsided, no bias, no imperfect understanding, no possibility of misuse of power, or having obtained it wrongly. If all rational withholdings are blocked, we ought to accept God as an authority. And part of what is involved in that is accepting his commands, unless we have good reason to do otherwise. Again, with a perfect being, there can't possibly be good reasons to do otherwise. In short, we think the issue of authority is a matter of power, knowledge, and character, all of which add up to *moral* authority.[15]

John Hare cites a related solution to Cudworth's objection that can be found in John Duns Scotus and Samuel von Pufendorf. Both philosophers say that the justification of obedience to God terminates in something that does not itself need justification. For Scotus, the principle that God is to be loved is known from its terms. So it does not require any justification from any prior principle. We know that God is to be loved, and thus obeyed, simply because we know that God is the supreme good. Pufendorf, similarly, regards God's authority as axiomatic, in the same way mathematics has axioms or first principles that merit belief upon their own evidence.[16]

---

[15]David Baggett and Jerry L. Walls, *Good God: The Theistic Foundations of Morality* (New York: Oxford University Press, 2011), 122-23.

[16]John E. Hare, *God's Command* (Oxford: Oxford University Press, 2015), 58.

We have outlined several related solutions here because the issue of God's moral authority is so central to this discussion. The salient feature of moral obligations in particular, the feature at the heart of the Anscombe intuition, is their binding, prescriptive authority. Exploring this notion of moral authority, especially consideration of what lies behind it, can help us better understand the nature of the reality in which we live. As Lewis makes clear in *Mere Christianity*, right and wrong together clue us in to the meaning of the universe.

We seem to be going through a crisis of authority today, if the most recent election and its aftermath are any indication. *Establishment* has become a pejorative, with institutions such as the press and political parties crumbling from within and attacked from without. Historians will judge and explain the reasons for this, and human authorities are surely flawed and need to be held accountable. But the moral law that binds us has for its authority a being beyond reproach.

Obviously we can reject that authority, as our earlier discussion of free will notes. But if this moral authority is part of the fabric of the reality in which we find ourselves, rejecting our obligations is not a neutral undertaking. There is a price to pay. John Updike sought to make this plain in his literary response to Jack Kerouac's 1957 novel *On the Road*. Kerouac's semiautobiographical account is a celebration of a free-spirited life, where the main characters reject 1950s domesticity and take to the open road, with adventures filled with promiscuous sex, drugs, and music. The novel epitomizes the countercultural lifestyle of the Beat poets and the hippies, their cultural offspring.

Before he had even read it, Updike recognized a mistake at the heart of Kerouac's story: "I resented its apparent instruction to cut loose; *Rabbit, Run* was meant to be a realistic demonstration of what happens when a young American family man goes on the road—the people left behind get hurt."[17] Theism offers a convincing explanation both of the authority behind a father's obligation to his family and an account of how that authority is connected to the social frameworks in which we live.

---

[17]John Updike, *Rabbit Angstrom: A Tetralogy* (New York: Knopf, 1995), x.

Naturalism offers little to compare. This is what is at the heart of Plantinga's recognition of the almost unique ability of obligations to provide moral evidence in favor of theism, because secular and naturalistic theories consistently show themselves wanting when it comes to furnishing such authority.

Time and again what we find in a variety of secular efforts to explain moral obligations falls short of what's needed. Plantinga gives a recent example of this in the writing of Philip Kitcher, who offers a naturalized virtue ethic. Kitcher is the author of the recent *Life After Faith: The Case for Secular Humanism*. He thinks the primary function of morality is to extend and amplify our primitive altruistic dispositions, through which we became social animals in the first place.

This, then, has the secondary effect of promoting social cohesion. On Kitcher's view, elaborated in his 2011 *The Ethical Project*, evolution has put into place certain capacities to empathize with others, feel their pain, identify with their desires, and the like. Since these imaginative faculties remain limited, morality on this view has for its function to extend such empathy. As moral creatures our function is to extend our empathetic responses, widen our altruistic tendencies, and by so doing choose an objectively better way of living.

For present purposes, it bears emphasis that Kitcher's view is particularly ineffectual at explaining moral obligations. Rather than trying to explain such obligations, he denies their existence. He acknowledges that we do not have access to ethical truth or reality but argues that the ethical community can function as an approximate equivalent to ethical truth by forging what are believed to be progressive ethical principles and choices. This becomes quite clear in his latest book, the ethics chapter of which Plantinga describes like this:

> [Kitcher's] aim in this chapter, then, is to give a naturalistic vindication of values; an account of ethics that fits with secularism but doesn't reduce the ethical life to the expression of subjective attitudes. As he notes (p. 28) it is common to think of moral or ethical standards as independent of human desires and aspirations, having a sort of objectivity that fits well with their being divinely commanded. On Kitcher's account, of course,

these standards don't originate in anything like a divine command, and Kitcher's account of ethics and morality doesn't give it that sort of objectivity. What status *do* ethical standards have, according to him? It's not easy to tell. As far as I could make out, Kitcher believes that ethical rules have simply evolved over the centuries as a means to the reduction of "functional conflict" (p. 53) and the promotion of harmony in a society. It's a good idea for us (as members of a society) to follow these rules, and to coerce the unwilling also to follow them, in order to introduce and maintain functional harmony in our society. On this prudential account, of course, there isn't any such thing as objective moral obligation, and there would be nothing wrong, morally speaking, in my flouting current ethical precepts (provided I could escape detection).[18]

Again, a thorough approach to this question requires patience in carefully analyzing the full range of secular ethical theories on offer. Such a task is too big for this volume. Even in *God and Cosmos*, the treatment, though much more comprehensive, remains a work in progress and merely a promissory note. However, what tends to recur on a critical assessment of such theories is a real challenge to account for the authority of moral obligations. Often this amounts either to a *denial* there are such obligations or a subtle *domestication* of moral obligations that is more easily explicable.

The advantage of theism and Christianity is that it can provide an account of moral obligations that does not water them down. The discussion of God's authority, helpful in defending divine command theory, is equally helpful in various other sorts of theistic ethics. What all of them have in common is that, in one way or another, the final source of moral authority is God himself. Secular theories, either individually or in various combinations, have their insights to offer. As far as we can see, however, secular and naturalistic approaches on offer are hard-pressed to provide as good an explanation of moral obligations as theism.[19]

---

[18]Alvin Plantinga, review of Philip Kitcher, *Life After Faith*, *Notre Dame Philosophical Reviews*, January 1, 2015, https://ndpr.nd.edu/news/54977-life-after-faith-the-case-for-secular-humanism/.
[19]Jerry Walls and I (Dave), tongue in cheek, concluded our analysis of this dimension of moral apologetics in our recent book in this way: "If we were wont to engage in a bit of hyperbolic rhetorical flourish, we might bring the chapter to a dramatic end by saying that naturalists who,

Perhaps there's no better way to end this chapter than by letting C. S. Lewis point beyond its content:

> I think all Christians would agree with me if I said that though Christianity seems at first to be all about morality, all about duties and rules and guilt and virtue, yet it leads you on, out of all that, into something beyond. One has a glimpse of a country where they do not talk of those things, except perhaps as a joke. Everyone there is filled full with what we should call goodness as a mirror is filled with light. But they do not call it goodness. They do not call it anything. They are not thinking of it. They are too busy looking at the source from which it comes. But this is near the stage where the road passes over the rim of our world. No one's eyes can see very far beyond that: lots of people's eyes can see further than mine.[20]

The road goes past Sinai but doesn't stop until Jordan. One more quote from Lewis is necessary:

> *Mere morality* is not the end of life. You were made for something quite different from that. J. S. Mill and Confucius (Socrates was much nearer the reality) simply didn't know what life is about. The people who keep on asking if they can't lead a decent life without Christ, don't know what life is about; if they did they would know that "a decent life" is mere machinery compared with the thing we men are really made for. Morality is indispensable: but the Divine Life, which gives itself to us and which calls us to be gods, intends for us something in which morality will be swallowed up. We are to be re-made. All the rabbit in us is to disappear—the worried, conscientious, ethical rabbit as well as the cowardly and sensual

---

despite the writing on the wall, assiduously strive to salvage their dysfunctional relationship with objective morality are in an abusive relationship. They replace obligations with rules, objective guilt with subjective guilt, intrinsic goods with instrumental ones; moral goals bereft of sufficient teleology are foisted on hapless and unsuspecting listeners. In the process their ostensible beloved (morality) gets toppled from her throne, stripped of her riches, and in reductive fashion domesticated to perform lowly chores—like helping us merely 'get along.' Cruelly clipped are the wings of her higher and most ennobling of reaches. The result is a watered-down, emaciated, deflationary account of morality, a shell of her former glorious self, emptied and divested of her most enchanting and winsome distinctives and charms. We would respectfully suggest perhaps it's time morality refuse to settle, declare it's time to see other people, and say to naturalism, her ignoble suitor, 'It's not me. It's you.' But we're not thus wont, so we won't." David Baggett and Jerry Walls, *God and Cosmos: Moral Truth and Human Meaning* (New York: Oxford University Press, 2016), 178.

[20]Lewis, *Mere Christianity*, book 3, chap. 12.

rabbit. We shall bleed and squeal as the handfuls of fur come out; and then, surprisingly, we shall find underneath it all a thing we have never yet imagined: a real Man, an ageless god, a son of God, strong, radiant, wise, beautiful, and drenched in joy.

"When that which is perfect is come, then that which is in part shall be done away" (1 Cor. 13:10). The idea of reaching "a good life" without Christ is based on a double error. Firstly, we cannot do it; and secondly, in setting up "a good life" as our final goal, we have missed the very point of our existence. Morality is a mountain which we cannot climb by our own efforts; and if we could we should only perish in the ice and unbreathable air of the summit, lacking those wings with which the rest of the journey has to be accomplished. For it is from there that the real ascent begins. The ropes and axes are "done away" and the rest is a matter of flying.[21]

## TALK BACK

1. Why might people ignore their moral obligations despite the fact that doing so leads to guilt—which involves harm (to themselves or someone else) and alienation from others?

2. Compare Sam Harris's understanding of faith with the contrasting vision of faith we lay out. How would you respond to Harris? What scriptural examples of faith can you think of?

3. Often we think of *inability* as a deficiency, but we've argued that God's inability to sin, or to be anything other than perfectly loving, is actually a mark of his perfection. What do you think of that claim?

---

[21]C. S. Lewis, "Man or Rabbit?," in *God in the Dock* (Grand Rapids: Eerdmans, 1970), 112-13, emphasis added.

# CHAPTER 7

# MORAL KNOWLEDGE

*Thou dost show me the path of life;*
*in thy presence there is fullness of joy,*
*in thy right hand are pleasures for evermore.*

PSALM 16:11

A LOGICIAN'S WIFE IS HAVING A BABY. The doctor immediately hands the newborn to the dad. The wife says, "Is it a boy or a girl?" The logician says, "Yes." Of that he could be *sure!*

A woman awoke excitedly on Valentine's Day and announced enthusiastically to her husband, "I just dreamed that you gave me a pearl necklace for Valentine's Day! What do you think it means?" With *certainty* in his voice, the man said, "You'll know tonight." That evening the man came home with a small package and handed it to his wife. With anxious anticipation she quickly opened the package to find a book titled *The Meaning of Dreams.*

Cordell Hull, Franklin Delano Roosevelt's secretary of state, was famed for being extremely cautious in his judgments, as one would expect a senior diplomat and professional bureaucrat to be. He was ever careful to draw conclusions in strict proportion to the evidence and nothing more. On one occasion, he was waiting at a level crossing with a friend, watching a trainload of sheep pass by.

"Looks like those sheep have just been sheared," said his friend.

"Yes," said Hull, "at least on the side facing us."

Certainty is notoriously difficult to achieve. This is much of the lesson learned from Descartes's elaborate thought experiment to uncover what can be known indubitably. Owing to all manner of possible errors or delusions, countless mistaken knowledge claims are possible. Something like absolute certainty seems well-nigh beyond our grasp, except perhaps for a few claims inside our individual heads—such as "I seem to see a computer in front of me right now." Perhaps there's no actual computer, just an elaborate illusion, or even a dream, but it at least *seems* to be a computer.

A quick aside here: We understand that discussions like this are fodder for the bad rap philosophy often gets. And we sympathize. How relevant can a field be, so the popular opinion goes, if it promotes ideas like this, suggesting we have to second-guess whatever conclusions we might draw? Bill Nye's unintentionally farcical characterization of philosophical questions captures this sentiment: "Can we know that we know? Are we aware that we are aware? Are we not aware that we are aware? Is reality real, or is reality not real and we are all living on a ping pong ball part of an interplanetary ping pong game and we cannot sense it? . . . I think therefore I am. Well, what if you don't think about it? Do you not exist anymore?"[1]

Nye's mischaracterization aside, we would suggest that there really is something valuable in philosophy's insights on this certainty score. And we are quick to say that this is the beginning, rather than the end, of the discussion. Bear with us, and you'll see in due course that we are not encouraging skepticism at all—far from it. We merely want to take care with this discussion—acknowledging human limitations, establishing definitions, and teasing out our premises—to help us think through together this question of moral knowledge, what it is and what best explains it.

Back to the question of whether we can know anything for sure: The wrongness of child torture for fun seems to be a decent candidate for complete certainty. But there are some who would deny even that. It's at

---

[1]"Hey Bill Nye, 'Does Science Have All the Answers or Should We Do Philosophy Too?," February 23, 2016, www.youtube.com/watch?v=ROe28Ma_tYM.

least possible we could be wrong, they might say. Even such moral certainty seems to exceed our cognitive reach.

Once we decide, however, that the quest for absolute certainty[2] is not an appropriate aim, we can see that knowledge claims don't depend on it. Plenty of things can be known without categorical certainty. On the other hand, we may retain a subjective sense of certainty about the beliefs in question, but that sort of "certainty" provides no guarantee we are right. Plenty of ideological zealots, for example, harbor strong feelings of certainty that they are absolutely right, when in fact they're flat wrong—Dallas Cowboys and Ohio State Buckeyes fans, for example. Subjective certainty sets the bar for knowledge too low, while objective certainty sets the bar for knowledge too high. Knowledge and certainty in fact usually have little to do with one another. The few exceptions are more anomalous outliers than regulative norms.

Knowledge is the topic of this chapter, moral knowledge in particular. This extends the discussion beyond the moral facts about value and obligations canvassed in the previous two chapters. Even if such facts obtain, knowledge of them is another matter entirely. We are shifting the discussion, then, from moral ontology or metaphysics to moral epistemology, which has for its main concern the issue of moral knowledge. If knowledge isn't certainty, however, what is it?

## WHAT IS KNOWLEDGE?

Knowledge comes in a variety of forms. Sometimes we talk about "know-how" knowledge, or *competence* knowledge. "I know how to ride a bike," for example. Other times we speak of knowledge of a person or city, which is knowledge by *acquaintance*. "I know Chicago," for example. Interestingly, an important biblical use of knowledge can be found in a passage such as "Adam knew Eve." A particularly intimate knowledge by acquaintance, suffice it to say.

The sort of knowledge that will occupy most of our attention here is "propositional knowledge," which is just what it sounds like. Propositional

---

[2]Or "Cartesian certainty," named after Descartes.

knowledge is knowledge of propositions, and propositions depict some slice of life in a way that's either true or false. "I know that people are intrinsically valuable," for example.

Now, one long-standing account of such knowledge is that it can be analyzed as "justified true belief," which is to say that knowledge requires three conditions to be satisfied: justification, truth, and belief.

So take a proposition such as this: twice two is four. If you *believe* the proposition, and the proposition is *true*, and you have enough *evidence* for its truth, then you'll have knowledge. At least on the JTB (justified true belief) model of knowledge. Let's consider each of these three conditions (belief, truth, and justification) in turn.

First, *belief*. What does it mean to believe a proposition? Truthfully assenting to it is usually a good indication of belief, but not always, for on occasion we might believe something, down deep, without being altogether conscious of the belief.

Incidentally, this raises an interesting question to ponder: Can you identify a belief of yours that, on reflection, you'd say is likely false? The question isn't whether you can identify someone else's belief you think false, which is easy. Rather, find a belief of your own that, on reflection, you think is likely false. This might be thought to be impossible. Identifying a belief of your own that you recognize on reflection to be likely false means you don't really believe it, right?

Well, sometimes appearances are deceiving. There's a distinction that can prove helpful here between two kinds of beliefs. Sometimes we think we believe something when we really don't, or think we don't when in fact we do. This is what makes it occasionally possible for someone genuinely to assent to a proposition as true when, in fact, down deep, she doesn't believe it. The relevant distinction here is between what we may think we believe, on the one hand, and what our dispositions to behave reveal about our actual, deeper beliefs (whether we are consciously aware of them or not).

For example, someone might think he's not afraid to fly on an airplane, but in truth every time he's on a flight, during takeoff and much of the flight his knuckles are white from hanging on so tightly to his armrest. He may think he's free from fear of flying, but his actions show otherwise.

I (Dave) had a philosophy professor in graduate school who admitted that she was terrified of flying. As a rational person, she thought she could overcome her fear by reading up on all the various principles of physics that make flight possible. However, after reading extensively about Bernoulli's principle and the like, she found that she was more terrified than ever.

Or someone might pay lip service to the importance of helping the less fortunate without actually ever getting around to doing anything about it. He may like to believe it's a priority for himself, but his behaviors betray this to be self-deception. William James cites an example of a Russian woman weeping over the fictitious personages in a play while her coachman is freezing to death on his seat outside. She might like to think of herself as eminently empathetic, when in fact she may be in possession of precious little compassion.

This is why our actions are usually the better indicator of our truest beliefs than at least some of our "assent beliefs." We can call this action-based variant of belief our "dispositional beliefs," since they form our dispositions to behave in certain ways that reflect what we tend to really believe down deep.

Now try to identify a belief of yours that on reflection you'd say is likely false. Exploiting the "assent versus disposition" distinction explored above, perhaps a good place to look for a belief of yours that's likely false is where your "talk" and "walk" diverge. We mentioned self-deception as one source of such a dichotomy.

Another source is our common penchant to think more highly of ourselves than we ought. Ninety-four percent of college professors think their teaching skills are above average! Or consider this: a grade of C is supposed to mean "average," but most students go apoplectic in response to a C nowadays.[3]

Yet another possible source of misguided beliefs, we might suggest, comes from places down deep where we have been hurt and damaged,

---

[3]This has led to the suggestion of grade inflation using this rubric: A: Student has marginal to excellent understanding of the course material. B: Student is able to form a complete sentence, on the second or third try. C: Student can operate a writing instrument without harming self or others. D: Student has mastered many autonomic bodily functions. F: Student appears to be a multicellular organism.

perhaps in childhood. Take, for instance, someone who was abused as a child. Even if such a person—after years of healing and prayer and counseling—thinks he's largely over the damage incurred, remnants of it can remain. In fact, in the vicinity of those remaining vestiges of damage can crop up beliefs that are likely to be influenced by the damage. Such beliefs may not be assent beliefs, though, because they can often go unnoticed. They are instead dispositional beliefs skewed by past hurts and reflected in one's behavior.

The person, if asked, would likely deny that he believes the proposition in question. But his behavior may reveal something different. The abuse victim, for example, might subtly develop the idea, even as an adult, that he doesn't deserve a healthy romantic relationship. He habitually subverts and sabotages every relationship he's in, but not consciously. This is where counseling can be effective in getting at the root problem and seeking its amelioration. Becoming aware of such unhealthy dispositional beliefs doesn't fix them, but it does enable one to know where to focus one's intentional energies and prayers as one seeks healing.

So much for belief. What about *truth*? What makes a proposition true? Usually what we mean by truth is that the content of the proposition corresponds to the way the world is. There are some instances where this becomes problematic, but for now we can set those cases aside.[4] Correspondence with reality is the salient meaning of *truth* for present purposes. So, what makes the proposition that "the cat is on the mat" true? Well, how shall we put this? *That the cat is on the mat!* Not that one just believes it to be so or wishes it to be so. No. The cat is actually on the mat. Obviously, a proposition can't be known if it's false. We can know *that* a proposition is false, like twice two is five, but we can't know that twice two is five, because it is not.

Finally, what's meant by *justification*, the third ingredient for knowledge? It's unrelated to the theological notion that goes by the same name.[5] It is rather the idea of evidence. What is usually thought to distinguish merely true beliefs from knowledge is evidence. Suppose we

---

[4]Problematic cases include counterfactuals.
[5]Etymologically there is indeed a connection, but it needn't detain us here.

luck out and guess and then form the belief that there are extraterrestrials. We don't yet know there to be extraterrestrials. We might have a true belief, if extraterrestrials in fact exist, but not knowledge. Presumably such a belief, to qualify as knowledge, would require some amount of good evidence to take it as true. *How much* evidence is needed for knowledge can be hard to say.[6]

Scottish philosopher David Hume raised an objection to our belief in induction on the basis of lack of justification. Inductive inferences involve premises that somehow bolster their conclusions, but without guaranteeing them the way deductive arguments aim to do. Now, we might ask: What good reason is there to believe that induction is a reliable pattern of inference? Induction seems based on something like the idea that the future will resemble the past. But why believe *that*? Our best evidence seems to suggest that we believe it because *in the past* the future resembled the past. Now the problem becomes apparent: we can't assume the future to be like the past in our effort to show that the future will be like the past. What Hume saw is that there doesn't appear to be noncircular propositional evidence for the reliability of induction.

If induction lacks justification, then it would seem we can't rely on it for knowledge (since the JTB theory says justification is necessary for knowledge). Because so much of our knowledge comes from inductive inference, this raises a major challenge from skepticism. It gets even worse, because induction isn't alone among things that can't be noncircularly justified. Take memory, or the deliverances of testimony, or what our senses tell us. Or even that the world is more than five minutes old.

It turns out that in each of these cases no good noncircular argument can be cited for their reliability. If the world were created five minutes ago and made to look much older, including all of our memories implanted into us, there would be no way to show that the world is over five minutes old without assuming it. The evidence adduced would be

---

[6]It might be tempting to think the proposition in question has to be shown more likely true than false, but Richard Swinburne gives an example of an inductive argument that we take to provide good evidence for its conclusion despite not showing the conclusion to be more likely true than false: all the ravens we've seen are black, so all ravens are black.

consistent with both the old-world view and infant-world view. Likewise with memory, testimony, and our senses. This means that each of these lacks justification. So if justification is a needed ingredient for knowledge, what can we know? What would be left over?[7]

One fertile idea to get around these difficulties is that beliefs about our fundamental knowledge-gathering resources—memory, testimony, the senses, and so on—qualify as "properly basic" propositions. These are fundamental beliefs not based on other beliefs, but rather they are our proper starting points. They are beliefs on the basis of which we can legitimately infer other beliefs. *That our senses are generally reliable* might be an example of a properly basic belief; *that our memories are generally reliable,* another. Such starting points seem necessary, for a variety of reasons. One reason is to avoid an infinite regress. If every belief has to be based on a prior belief, then each belief would have to be justified by an infinite number of prior beliefs. How could such a process ever even get under way? Who has the time?

This goes, too, for moral knowledge. Consider a belief like this: *torturing children for the fun of it is wrong.* Suppose we get pressed to provide a justification for this proposition. What might one say? We could try to provide some more basic ethical principle on which this one is based, like the wrongness of imposing gratuitous suffering on sentient creatures, but then that principle could be questioned.

At some point there seems to be the need for something rock bottom, something fundamental, a legitimate starting point, which is just that obvious. If there are any moral truths at all, it would seem that at least some such axiomatic moral propositions hold. The wrongness of child torture for fun seems a pretty good candidate.[8]

Again, this isn't an argument that such propositions are true. We admit that we are largely assuming their truth to be the case. For readers convinced of moral truth, though, at least some moral propositions seem

---

[7]Certain tenacious evidentialists might say there may not be noncircular discursive evidence, but nonpropositional or nondiscursive evidence may still be available and must be available for knowledge to obtain. These thinkers deny that justification needs to be replaced with a different ingredient or condition in accounting for knowledge. We're obviously not settling this matter here.

[8]Or at least something in its close proximity.

likely to qualify as properly basic, axiomatic starting points: propositions from which we infer to other propositions, rather than propositions to which we argue on the basis of yet more obvious truths.

So-called particularists in ethics are those who tend to start with rock-bottom, eminently obvious moral truths, taken to be legitimate starting points. We have a great deal of sympathy with this approach. Frankly, if pressed to justify the most glaring instances of moral truths, we are hard pressed to know what to appeal to that could be even more obvious. Justification tends not to provide evidence on the basis of what's *less obvious*—such as some ambitious, controversial ethical theory. The wrongness of torturing children for fun is as obvious as can be. Even this doesn't capture Cartesian certainty, but it seems likely to provide knowledge.[9]

The approach to moral apologetics in this book primarily focuses on moral facts—like the wrongness of child torture for fun—that seem exceedingly obvious, facts that most everyone, believer and unbeliever alike, would readily acknowledge to be moral truths in need of explanation. Just today in the news was a heart-wrenching story about a mentally ill person being tortured by four young people who then live-streamed it on the Internet. There's little ambivalence we feel about such atrocious actions. It's obviously wrong—or at the very least we are altogether justified in believing it to be wrong. Particularists could embrace this approach, since they start with particular examples of obvious moral truths. Those who think that some moral facts are examples of properly basic beliefs could sanction our approach, too, since they take at least some moral facts as axiomatic and foundational.[10]

We would claim that we can know that it is wrong to torture children for the fun of it. Call it what you will: a veridical intuition, a particular moral proposition whose truth is obvious, a properly basic moral belief,

---

[9]The felt obviousness of the basic truths gives us a sort of impulse to believe them, which is a kind of justification, but perhaps the existence of this class of properly basic beliefs goes to show that there's something flawed about the analysis of knowledge as justified true belief. Again, with respect to properly basic beliefs, they seem to lack noncircular discursive justification, but without threatening their status as knowledge.

[10]Even if someone isn't an "intuitionist" per se, he may take at least certain moral intuitions as about as clear and obvious as anything at all. Such a person should resonate with our basic approach here.

a considered moral judgment innocent until proven guilty. Perhaps we're wrong to assume the reliability of the insight. But then again, if we're wrong about that, we're likely wrong about a whole lot more.

A good argument need not feature premises about which we can't possibly be wrong or premises that convince every thoughtful person. The wrongness of child torture for fun convinces us and strikes us as an altogether legitimate starting point, so on this basis we are happy to begin.

In class, I (Marybeth) often try to use humor to lighten things up a bit. I usually tend to make at least one person laugh. Often it's me. The point is, all we can do here is share what we find convincing. Readers are at liberty to draw their own conclusions. The next step is to account for this knowledge and to assess potential criticisms. We will argue that our secular ethics friends remain a bit vulnerable in this area.

## DARWIN AND DEBUNKING

Plenty of folks nowadays think that morality can be fully accounted for, one way or another, by evolution, a claim that we wish to submit to critical scrutiny. Note that our verdict doesn't concern whether evolution happened but that an evolutionary account of ethics is left wanting. Angus Menuge explains that a commonality across evolutionary ethics (EE) is the claim that the moral sense of human beings finds its origin in their natural history.[11] In other words, on EE, the shape of our moral sense could have looked quite different.

As Darwin puts it, "If . . . men were reared under precisely the same conditions as hive-bees, there can hardly be a doubt that our unmarried females would, like the worker-bees, think it a sacred duty to kill their brothers, and mothers would strive to kill their fertile daughters, and no one would think of interfering."[12] In such a scenario, (select) acts of fratricide or infanticide might have been thought of by humans as downright obligatory, rather than proscribed.

---

[11]The following four paragraphs draw heavily on Angus Menuge, "The Failure of Naturalism as a Foundation for Human Rights," *Moral Apologetics*, December 13, 2014, http://moralapologetics .com/the-failure-of-naturalism-as-a-foundation-for-human-rights/.

[12]Charles Darwin, *The Descent of Man* (Amherst, NY: Prometheus Books, 1998), 102.

Menuge has made a useful distinction here, which we noted earlier. He observes that Darwin can be taken in two different ways. "Weak evolutionary ethics," or "weak EE," says that, if we had been raised like hive bees, only moral psychology—our moral beliefs—would have changed. In other words, even if we didn't think so, fratricide and infanticide might still be prohibited. On the other hand, "strong EE" says that natural history dictates moral ontology (what actually *is* right and wrong). If "strong EE" is the case, our being raised like hive bees would make fratricide and infanticide right.

Strong EE's main problem is that it makes anything like human rights objectionably contingent. The notion of human rights and dignity disappears under these new hive-bee-like conditions. This presumably stands at radical variance with what's taken to be unquestionably true about ethics.

Whereas strong EE suffers from an ontological challenge, weak EE suffers from an epistemic one. Again, weak EE offers a theory of moral psychology. Although it's consistent with the existence of objective moral truth and human rights, it faces an impossible difficulty explaining knowledge of such realities. Remember: on weak EE, our belief in the rightness of fratricide and infanticide, not the nature of moral reality itself, is all that changes based on our being raised like hive bees. Even if the beliefs in question turn out to be true, weak EE provides no foundation for trusting our insights about moral reality. In fact, it gives us reason to think we couldn't.[13] In weak EE biological adaptedness (what is biologically good for the species or individual) and the moral good have no logical connection. If this is the case, Menuge concludes, it seems improbable—given the sweeping number of possible natural histories allowed by an evolutionary model—that the mechanism we have for forming belief would be likely to track moral truth.

Menuge is just one contemporary thinker who has used evolution to call moral knowledge into question. Alvin Plantinga is known for calling

---

[13]Earlier we saw that propositional justification might not be necessary for knowledge. Now we can see that it might not be sufficient, either, even when combined with true belief, for Menuge is laying out a case where a justified true moral belief wouldn't attain to knowledge.

all knowledge into question on the joint assumption of naturalism and evolution. For now our focus is just on moral knowledge. The challenge that concerns us here pertains to the dependence of moral beliefs on whatever is relevant in making morality true. Our task is to consider the way in which belief tracks reality. If such a dependence relation fails to obtain, then a tracking relation has not been established to show that our moral judgments depend on actual moral truth. There still be may be moral truths, but our justification for our moral beliefs will have been irremediably undermined. And an ethical system that fails to account for our moral beliefs faces serious challenges.

One reason for thinking that such a dependence relation obtains would emerge if the best explanation for a person's moral belief were to involve the truth of that belief. On evolutionary Darwinism, however, by Menuge's analysis it would seem that an exhaustive genealogy of our moral beliefs can be provided without addressing whether such beliefs are true. Unless there's a connection between moral truth and our moral judgments, the dependence thesis is undermined, justification for our moral beliefs is lost, and a "defeater" for moral knowledge has been identified.

Gilbert Harman, Guy Kahane, Sharon Street, Michael Ruse, and Richard Joyce are all examples of recent theorists who have launched a form of the (evolutionary) "debunking objection" against objective moral truth[14] or, more typically, moral knowledge. What all of these variants of the objection have in common is something like this: our moral belief-forming mechanisms are like darts thrown blindly. They are hardly likely to hit the small, distant target of moral truth an ocean away, if there even is such a thing. Evolution is about survival and reproduction, not moral truth.

Mark Linville deploys this sort of reasoning when he hammers an argument against evolutionary naturalism (EN) into this discursive format:

1. If EN is true, then human morality is a byproduct of natural selection.

2. If human morality is a byproduct of natural selection, then there is no moral knowledge.

---

[14]Or moral realism.

3. There is moral knowledge, so

4. EN is false.[15]

We are now going to look at one example of a Platonist trying to answer the challenge posed by Harman and others. Then, the final section of the chapter delves into some biblical teaching and theology to extend the discussion in a new direction.

## A PLATONIST

David Enoch, a contemporary Platonist, has defended moral realism in a recent book that has garnered much attention. Conceding that, on Platonism, our moral beliefs are unlikely to track moral truth directly, he tries to find a different way to account for the correlation.[16] His approach can be found in his *Taking Morality Seriously*, in which he attempts to show that his account of "robust realism" doesn't lose too many plausibility points in responding to the epistemic challenges of the debunkers.

To show a correlation between A and B, one might try to show that A is responsible for B or vice versa. This is a tracking account, but Enoch instead tries to show the correlation in terms of a third factor, C, that is (roughly speaking) responsible for both A-facts and B-facts.

His third-factor approach assumes that survival or reproductive success (or whatever else evolution aims at) is at least somewhat good—in the sense of better than the alternative. Not in every case, but at least generally. Moreover, selective forces (Enoch's C factor) have shaped *both our normative judgments and beliefs*, with the aim of survival or reproductive success in mind (so to speak). This accounts for the correlation

---

[15]Mark Linville, "The Moral Argument," in *The Blackwell Companion to Natural Theology*, ed. William Lane Craig and J. P. Moreland (Hoboken, NJ: Blackwell, 2009).

[16]In *God and Cosmos: Moral Truth and Human Meaning* (New York: Oxford University Press, 2016), Jerry Walls and I (Dave) discuss the tracking accounts, but we've decided not to discuss them here. It bears mention that John Hare, in *God's Command*, devotes a chapter to the challenge posed by evolutionary moral psychology. The last section of the chapter is on the topic of transcending our evolutionary situation with God. Among his insightful points is the way that evolution leaves us a mixture of tendencies to the good and the bad, so "we need something other than just an appeal to our nature to get us to follow the parts of the mixture that we should follow and not the parts we should not." He argues for a picture of divine command, mixed natural capacity, and divine assistance to make sense of this situation, a story he thinks can take adherents of the Abrahamic faiths toward a universal morality. Hare, *God's Command*, 304.

between moral truths and beliefs. In light of the fact that human survival and reproduction are by and large good aims—aims that normative truths recommend—our normative beliefs have developed to be at least somewhat in line with normative truths.[17]

In this way, Enoch argues that the fact that (roughly speaking) survival is good preestablishes the harmony between the normative truths and our normative beliefs. There is quite a bit more to Enoch's theory, but that's enough of a summary for present purposes. In the last section of this chapter, we wish to defend the thesis that Enoch's approach is actually not only deeply consistent with robust classical theism but arguably more so than with his own robust realism. Classical theists too would affirm that human beings have value, that (at least roughly speaking) their survival and flourishing is a moral good, and thus that the trajectory of evolution could certainly conduce to something morally good.

So now we wish to shift gears a bit and talk as Christians about what Scripture teaches about the value of persons and of life, and of God's intention to bring such life about to the full.

## CLASSICAL THEISM AND LIFE

Enoch denies that his thesis requires that human survival is of ultimate or even intrinsic value. But surely his case is made stronger if human survival and thriving—human life—*is* of intrinsic value, indeed, of infinite value. In an earlier chapter we discussed the issue of intrinsic human value at length, arguing that various secular accounts of morality face a formidable challenge accounting for such a reality well. Here we wish to argue that classical theism and, more specifically, Christianity can explain it better.

Indeed, we will argue that the theme of *life* is, most tellingly, perhaps the central integrating biblical motif. If so, and if we are right about what Christianity teaches and explains about the intrinsic worth of human

---

[17]"Given that the evolutionary 'aim' is good, the fact that our normative beliefs have been shaped by selective forces renders it far *less* mysterious that our normative beliefs are somewhat in line with the normative truths. This is so, then, neither because the normative truths are a function of our normative beliefs, nor because our normative beliefs have been shaped by selective pressures towards ends that are in fact—and quite independently—of value." David Enoch, *Taking Morality Seriously: A Defense of Robust Realism* (Oxford: Oxford University Press, 2011), 168.

persons, then we can deploy Enoch's approach ourselves. And we can do so even more effectively than can Enoch, predicating our analysis on a far more robust account of intrinsic human value than anything able to be generated by secular ethics.

Most will agree that life is clearly preferable to its opposite. At least *most* of the time. A husband and wife went to visit his doctor. After the physical, the physician asked to see the wife alone and confided to her: "Your husband is in critical condition. But if you are willing to fix him three nutritious meals a day, make love to him every night, and serve his every need, he will live to a healthy old age."

When she came out of the doctor's office, the husband asked, "Well, what did the doctor say?"

"He said you're going to die."

To this point, this book has largely featured philosophical argument, as we said we would do. We also promised a few departures from that, and now is one of those times. Here we intend to delve into a question of biblical theology because of the importance of this issue of life. Biblical theologians use a variety of lenses to forge unifying threads from the multiplicity of the Christian Scriptures. Such options include covenantal theology, kingship, and dispensationalism.

Another proposal suggests that behind all of these efforts is something even more fundamental: *life*.[18] Life can be argued to constitute the ultimate goal of all of these various efforts. At the root of it all is the very character of God, a character of love. Consider perhaps the most famous passage of all, John 3:16: "For God so loved the world that he gave his only Son, that whoever believes in him should not perish but have *eternal life*."[19]

All throughout Scripture we find recurring emphases in different notes and from disparate angles of the primacy assigned to life, human and nonhuman alike. To convey just a flavor of this rich theme, let's consider a smattering of relevant examples, which could easily be multiplied.

---

[18]This section is heavily indebted to the work of New Testament scholar Joseph Dongell.

[19]We could distinguish between biological life (*bios*) and spiritual life (*zoe*), arguing for the primacy of the latter. This is an important distinction indeed, but for present purposes we won't strongly differentiate these because we want to talk about life per se, what the two hold in common, and draw examples from a variety of places to make our central points.

Consider Genesis 1:20-22:

And God said, "Let the waters bring forth swarms of living creatures, and let birds fly above the earth across the firmament of the heavens." So God created the great sea monsters and every living creature that moves, with which the waters swarm, according to their kinds, and every winged bird according to its kind. And God saw that it was good. And God blessed them, saying, "Be fruitful and multiply and fill the waters in the seas, and let birds multiply on the earth."

References here, variously translated, to "teeming" and "swarming" speak to the volume of the life God generated—and notice that it's called "good"—an abundance of life. God is depicted not as one who metes out to us *just enough* but one who wishes to give us life abundant, *more than enough*. Christ proclaimed that he came not just to give us life but to give us life more abundantly (Jn 10:10). The word used there is transliterated *perisson*, bespeaking excessive, more than enough, beyond what's needed, overflowing. Not merely adequate or just to the full but well beyond that.

Again, consider Deuteronomy 8:7-9:

For the LORD your God is bringing you into a good land, a land of brooks of water, of fountains and springs, flowing forth in valleys and hills, a land of wheat and barley, of vines and fig trees and pomegranates, a land of olive trees and honey, a land in which you will eat bread without scarcity, in which you will lack nothing, a land whose stones are iron, and out of whose hills you can dig copper.

In 2 Kings 4 we find the story of an increase of a widow's oil—not just enough to meet her immediate needs but enough for her and her children to live on in perpetuity. This is a picture of the sort of God he is—a provider of abundant life. In Malachi 3, people who have robbed God are told to bring all their tithes into the storehouse, in anticipation of what God will do—to see "if I will not open the windows of heaven for you and pour down for you an overflowing blessing" (Mal 3:10). God is a gratuitous supplier, beyond our wildest imagination.

Some might be inclined to interpret such promises of life in purely eschatological terms, but notice this passage from Mark 10:29-30 in which Jesus is speaking to his disciples: "Jesus said, 'Truly, I say to you, there is no one who has left house or brothers or sisters or mother or father or children or lands, for my sake and for the gospel, who will not receive a hundredfold *now in this time*, houses and brothers and sisters and mothers and children and lands, with persecutions, and in the age to come eternal life.'"

What's obvious so far from this examination of biblical teachings on life is that primacy is assigned to more than life in a *quantitative* sense; it is assigned to life in a *qualitative* sense. It is not just about *surviving* but *thriving*. This is obviously relevant to ethics conceived of in a theistic sense, because morality, rightly understood, is not about weakness or missing out, about prohibitions and restrictions, but about living life fully, as it was meant to be lived.

Immorality—sin, to use biblical parlance—in contrast, tends toward death. We see from the start of the biblical revelation that it's God's intention that we thrive. Sin undermines that. This explains what otherwise might seem inexplicable to the casual Bible reader: that the priests in the Old Testament were explicitly forbidden from being around corpses.

In Genesis 3 we see the serpent's deception, hiding his real purpose of spreading death. Interesting to note is that the forbidden tree is the tree of the "knowledge of good and evil." The whole story of the Bible can be understood as a battle between life and death. Sin wishes to kill us and rob us of life. Christianity teaches that the great lie of the enemy of our souls is to reverse the polarities, to convince us that the most authentic life, the most fulfilling life, is one of immorality. On biblical terms, this is a hopeless contradiction, an impossibility.

We are deeply convinced that the reason many people resist the gospel message is that they have yet to come out from under this lie. They fail to see that God wants us to thrive and experience life to the full, probably because they don't grasp that God is a God of essential and perfect love.

Death is not depicted in Scripture as an old friend or an amiable uncle but a horrible foe, our final enemy. "But thanks be to God, who gives us the victory through our Lord Jesus Christ. Therefore, my beloved brethren, be steadfast, immovable, always abounding in the work of the

Lord, knowing that your labor is not in vain" (1 Cor 15:57-58). The resurrection of Jesus, the historical case for which we have explored elsewhere, effected the death of death, which is why Paul, as Gary Habermas puts it, can subject death to trash talking.[20] We don't merely have a truce with death. Because of the resurrection of Christ, we have confidence in God to overcome it and to overcome sin, the topic of chapter eight.

The Wisdom literature of Scripture, which initially stands in such stark contrast to the Sinai theology that comes before it, features observations over time about which behaviors lead to life and which lead to death. It promises that those who attend to wisdom will learn how to live life well. How does this general tendency to know about the good life by observing reality relate to listening to the words of God? Secularists galore appeal to such wisdom, thinking it captures the essence of morality, rendering God superfluous.

Notice, however, that the Israelites didn't believe wisdom was simply good sense that gave life. Wisdom, for them, started with faith in, reverence for, God. Proverbs 1:7 says, "The fear of the LORD is the beginning of knowledge; fools despise wisdom and instruction." And Proverbs 2:5-6 adds,

then you will understand the fear of the LORD
   and find the knowledge of God.
For the LORD gives wisdom;
   from his mouth come knowledge and understanding.

If Scripture is right on this point, there is a profound susceptibility to look at the data of life and make radically faulty inferences, seeing what we want to see rather than what we should see. We are like the parishioner who, after each week's sermon, said to the pastor, "You sure told *them* this week, Pastor!" By "them" he meant all the other church members, not himself. Until the week when there was a storm and the pastor and this parishioner were the only ones to show up at church. They held the service anyway, and afterwards he came up to the pastor and said, "Too bad they weren't here today; you really would have told them!"

---

[20]David Baggett, ed., *Did the Resurrection Happen? A Dialogue with Gary Habermas and Antony Flew* (Downers Grove, IL: InterVarsity Press, 2009).

The fear and reverential awe of God is the beginning of wisdom. We need a godly mind to make good sense of things. The wisdom writers knew that God created this world with discernible patterns, reliable causes and effects.

Too often the typical evangelical pattern in evangelism is to start at Genesis 3 with the fall. We talk up our guilt before God, our having fallen short. That's important, and embracing the cross requires recognition of our need of grace. But we should start even sooner, with Genesis 1–2, to create the fuller evangelistic picture. God made us all. Talking to people as if there's no connection between them and God is a mistake. Creation theology taken together with the Wisdom literature teaches us that in the very fabric of our being, we are made in such a way that our deepest longings are satisfied in God. Meeting God is not meeting a stranger. It's coming home. Conversion is not an alien invasion. It is a father's firm embrace and a mother's tender kiss.

This is why Wisdom literature is so concerned with *creation*. "The LORD by wisdom founded the earth; by understanding he established the heavens" (Prov 3:19). Wisdom looks back even further than Sinai, to the creation itself. The Christian message is to stop fighting the current of creation. This Christian life might be countercultural, against prevailing winds and currents in society, but a deeper current surges below. To experience intimacy with God is to be aligned with how, what, and who he made us to be. It is life as it was meant to be lived, going with God's great flow. The Christian message starts and ends with the resounding truth and gloriously good news of God's great love for absolutely everyone.

Consider one last thread in this biblical tapestry: Jesus as King. Israel longed for a king. The Gospels invest heavily in depicting Jesus as Son of David—the significance of which is that Jesus was king of Israel. Matthew 21 shows how the royal language proceeds. Jesus enters the capital city and goes straight to the temple. In the ancient Near East, the temple was associated even more with the king than with priests. Solomon built the first one, and it was named after him. Kings built temples. Later there was Herod's temple. Kings remodeled them and protected them. The king was almost a hyperhigh priest. So Jesus went to the temple to straighten things out—as king!

At the baptism of Jesus, he is anointed as king, baptized at the hands of a prophet. The Spirit falls on him, and then he's immediately tested— echoing David's pattern of anointing. In the ancient Near East, naming a king bespoke his rule. Naming a king pointed to the people's need to surrender to and obey him. But that's only just a part of its significance. It's wider than that.

When Jesus was arrested, what was the identity question pressed by Pilate? "Are you the king of Israel?" In John 18:36, Jesus says that his kingdom is not of this world. Jesus isn't punting to a purely spiritual kingdom but speaking to the source of authority per se. His kingdom is not *out of* this world. His authority isn't established through violence. Then, as Jesus is beaten, he is mocked as a king. The sign "King of the Jews" is put above his cross. He is crucified between two criminals, another instance of mocking the royal idea of who would be privileged to be at his right and left when he came into his kingdom.

The beautiful and dramatic irony of it all is that, though Pilate and the others thought they were mocking him, they were actually installing him as the real king of Israel. What they thought were empty gestures and mere mockery, going through vacuous motions, actually contained spiritual significance.[21] It is as if a wedding officiant, in rehearsal, had gone through all the motions of performing a wedding, including a declaration of marriage—and unwittingly married the couple a day early.

Psalm 2 and Psalm 110 showcase the real significance of the king of Israel, something of which Pilate had no idea. The king of Israel would be king over all the other kings. The king of Israel would be the cosmic ruler. It is precisely because Jesus is the king of the Jews that he is the king of the world. Who better, when teaching parables, to teach about the kingdom? The parables give us the inside scoop of God's kingdom from the king himself.

Kings were first of all warriors, and they governed. Chaos was thought of as the worst thing of all, featuring injustices running rampant. A king

---

[21]They also contained what philosophers of language, following J. L. Austin, would call perlocutionary force.

imbued society with order, embodied the right execution of rule and law, dispelled chaos, and promoted peace.

And to what end? *To enable life to thrive.* Not just because of the king's authority but because the king creates the order of what life should be. A recurring image of king in ancient Near Eastern culture was as shepherd. The king, too, was responsible for the health of his flock. "The LORD is my shepherd, I shall not want; he makes me lie down in green pastures. He leads me beside still waters" (Ps 23:1-2). Psalm 23 is a royal psalm. Jesus is the king who creates the environment in which life, our life, all life, can flourish.

We are convinced that perhaps the deepest difficulty people have is not yet seeing the shepherdly rule of God's kingship. What so often tragically hinders full surrender and a response of openness to God's overtures of love is that we haven't yet seen him as loving Father and protector. We remain unconvinced of safety in the arms and love of God. But we can trust him. He's a king who wants us to live and thrive.

Little wonder Paul prayed for those in Ephesus that they "may have power to comprehend with all the saints what is the breadth and length and height and depth, and to know the love of Christ which surpasses knowledge, that you may be filled with all the fullness of God" (Eph 3:18-19).

The source of the moral law is not an impersonal process that happens to conduce to biological life but doesn't require life to be particularly valuable. The ground, the source, the locus, the foundation of the moral law and the moral good is the one who superintends the process that made us from the dust, who wants to restore our soul, to lead us in the paths of righteousness for his name's sake, and who wants to reign and rule in our lives and give us abundant life and life everlasting.

## TALK BACK

1. Reflect a bit on the early discussion of this chapter on certainty and how difficult it is to obtain absolute certainty on anything. Is there an inherent tension between this philosophical discussion and the nature of principled faith? Can we have assurance of faith apart from clamoring for certainty?

2. Reflect a bit on how our actions are indicative of our most deeply held beliefs. Recalling the distinction made between "assent belief" and "dispositional belief," can you think of any instances from your own life where your "talk" doesn't match your "walk"?

3. In this chapter we describe morality as living life as it is meant to be lived. Is this how morality is understood today? If not, where does our contemporary understanding depart?

# CHAPTER 8

# MORAL TRANSFORMATION

*All human nature vigorously resists grace because
grace changes us and the change is painful.*

FLANNERY O'CONNOR, *THE HABIT OF BEING:
LETTERS OF FLANNERY O'CONNOR*

A July 9, 2016, piece on the satirical website *The Babylon Bee* puts a humorous twist on a serious subject. Titled "Woman Finally Accepts Doctrine of Total Depravity Now That Daughter Is Two," it reads:

NEW YORK, NY—Mary Eastwood, 29, says she struggled for years to accept the biblical teaching that human beings are innately corrupted by sin, preferring instead to think that people are basically good. However, now that her daughter Charlotte is right in the prime of her "terrible twos," Eastwood has changed her mind, fully embracing and even espousing the doctrine of total depravity.

"I had the hardest time coming to grips with the idea that all the people I see around me are marred by sin and without hope but for the grace of God," the young mother told reporters. "But now that Charlotte is two—hoo boy. That innate depravity is shining through with the brightness of a thousand suns."

Noting that her daughter, though small and cute, some days leaves her and her husband weeping in despair, Eastwood went on to say that no one in their right mind could handle a toddler for any amount of time and come out on the other end thinking human beings are "basically good."

"She's like a Category 5 hurricane with a cute face," Eastwood told reporters. "I love her to death, but wherever she is, darkness and destruction reign."

At publishing time, Eastwood was inviting an unbelieving friend to come to her house so Charlotte could convince her of mankind's radical corruption and desperate need for a savior.[1]

This chapter is about grace, forgiveness, and moral transformation, three closely related concepts. Up until now we have looked at foundational questions of moral metaphysics and epistemology. On that foundation, we are ready to turn to the two aspects of what's been called Kantian "moral faith," namely, (1) whether moral transformation, perhaps even moral perfection, is possible; and (2) whether morality is a fully rational enterprise. This chapter will feature an argument from grace and discuss the issues of forgiveness, moral change, and the acquisition of virtue. The next chapter will feature an argument from providence and deal with the issues of moral rationality, the correspondence of happiness and holiness, and moral motivation and hope.

## MORAL GUILT AND FORGIVENESS

A deep existential need of human beings is to be *forgiven* for their wrongdoings, not to be defined by them forever. Many people live in perpetual guilt because they think such forgiveness is impossible and that they are helpless to do anything about it. This chapter will make the case that a central aspect of moral apologetics is the power of the Christian hope to receive the divine grace to be forgiven and to be radically changed. This is the first aspect of Kantian moral faith, named for the work on it done by Immanuel Kant.

Kant was raised in the Lutheran pietistic tradition, a movement begun by Philipp Spener. What has come to be known as "Spener's problem" is the challenge of becoming not just *better* men and women but *new* men and women. We need more than a tweaking of our characters. Our whole moral disposition needs to be radically altered, for two reasons: the

---

[1]"Woman Finally Accepts Doctrine of Total Depravity Now That Daughter Is Two," *Babylon Bee*, July 9, 2016, http://babylonbee.com/news/woman-finally-accepts-doctrine-total-depravity-now -daughter-two/.

depth of our moral malady and the loftiness of the moral ideal. An honest assessment of our moral situations concludes there is a wide gap between where we are and where we should be.

We will arrive at this topic of transformation, but first we need to deal with the prior issue of forgiveness. By the end of our whole discussion, the close connection between forgiveness and transformation should become clear, not to mention how both of them underscore deficiencies in naturalistic ethics and the relative strengths of a theistic foundation for morality.

Robert Adams once wrote an article in which he summarized various moral arguments for God's existence, or at least rational belief in God. Along with several varieties of Kantian ethical arguments, he includes an argument based on his favored theory of divine command ethics that, if true, would entail God's existence. Near the end of the piece he writes the following suggestive sentences:

> I have focused, as most philosophical discussion of the moral arguments has, on the connections of theism with the nature of right and wrong and with the idea of a moral order of the universe. I am keenly aware that they form only part of the total moral case for theistic belief. *Theistic conceptions of guilt and forgiveness*, for example, or of God as a friend who witnesses, judges, appreciates, and can remember all of our actions, choices, and emotions, may well have theoretical and practical moral advantages at least as compelling as any that we have discussed.[2]

In a footnote at this juncture he adds that a theistic argument from the nature of guilt has been offered by A. E. Taylor and H. P. Owen.[3] We could add other names to the list of those who wrote about the evidential value of guilt, such as John Henry Newman. For present purposes, what we are intending to do, in the first half of this chapter, is to use such accounts as a springboard to highlight some of the important features of

---

[2]Robert Adams, "Moral Arguments for Theistic Belief," in *Rationality and Religious Belief*, ed. C. Delaney (Notre Dame, IN: University of Notre Dame Press, 1979), 116-40, emphasis added.
[3]See A. E. Taylor, *The Faith of a Moralist* (London: Macmillan, 1930), 1:206-10. See also H. P. Owen, *The Moral Argument for Christian Theism* (London: Allen & Unwin, 1965), 57-59.

guilt and the need it introduces for forgiveness. We will explore here the power of Christianity for explaining both the human problem of guilt and its necessary solution of forgiveness. The second half of the chapter will broach the issue of moral transformation.

Unless people remain in radical denial, most will acknowledge that there are all sorts of wrongs that they have committed, rendering them in some objective moral sense *guilty*. Sometimes people think they are guilty when they are not, and other times think they are not guilty when they are. But at least on some occasions our sense of guilt seems to track reality. In this era in which psychological categories reign supreme, many would argue that guilt is a useless and debilitating emotion, and it surely on occasion can be. Again, however, there are other times when it seems to be an honest and sober recognition of reality, of an objective state, something neglected to our peril.

It is fascinating that forgiveness possesses the capacity to address guilt. What likely explains this is that guilt is a social phenomenon featuring, among other things, rupture in relationships. This is why forgiveness has remarkable power to fix these ruptures and restore relationships to what they were before the damage took place. In fact, it can in many cases make those social ties stronger than before.

As Newman and others in the history of moral apologetics could see, though, there is a limit to how much human relationships can explain. Sometimes guilt doesn't seem to be connected to any particular human person. At other times the wronged person is no longer around to confer forgiveness. On yet other occasions the wrong seems to be so grievous that no human being likely has the authority to offer forgiveness. In all of these cases, it becomes more plausible to think that forgiveness by God himself is necessary.

Not only do we as human beings need forgiveness, we also have a need to offer it, rather than indulge bitterness and resentment. Contrary to Hannah Arendt's claim that it was exclusively the Judeo-Christian tradition that extolled forgiveness as a virtue, at least closely related notions can be found even among Greek philosophers such as Aristotle. Some have certainly thought that it was Christianity, in particular, that assigned such strong primacy to the virtue of forgiveness. Perhaps they are right that forgiveness took on greater urgency than it ever had before because of Christian teachings, eliciting accusations from Nietzsche of sublimating vengeance. But this is no argument that Christianity is wrong about the possibility and centrality of forgiveness.

Without something like forgiveness breaking the cycle of *lex talionis*, resentment, and retaliation, prospects for the future of social harmony would seem bleak indeed. Forgiveness for wrongdoing is at the heart of Christian thought and provides an excellent explanation of its possibility and importance. Christianity teaches that God is willing to forgive human beings for their sin against him, and that, in fact, wrongs done against us pale by significance to what each of us has done against God. God forgives us, and God enables us to forgive others. And if we're required by God to forgive others, he will also equip us with the power to do so. Even as Jesus was being nailed to the cross, he prayed to the Father for them to be forgiven. As fertile a topic for discussion as our forgiveness of others is, the current focus will remain on *God's forgiveness for us*.

We also need to distinguish between *guilt* and *feelings of guilt*.[4] The latter may be an indication of the former, but their distinctness is evident in cases where instances of the latter don't correspond to actual objective guilt. Feelings of guilt are like intuitions in this way: they may track reality, or they may not. Sometimes even commonsensical intuitions turn

---

[4]It's a perennially interesting question to ask how we can know there's such a thing as genuine guilt rather than mere feelings of guilt. Typically (though, as we'll see, not always), if guilt is real, we become aware of it by our feelings of guilt. In this way, there's something almost Kantian about recognizing the need to experience guilt affectively. Moral sentiments practically function the way Kant's categories of understanding do. But again, this isn't quite right because, as the discussion of psychopathy will illustrate, guilt can also be grasped more cognitively than emotionally. But such cases are relative exceptions, and more typically objective guilt, if it exists, is recognized affectively. This doesn't entail there's no objective referent, however, any more than the fact that experience of the empirical world has to be mediated through our senses precludes an objective referent. For many (though admittedly not all), the experience of at least some feelings of guilt carries a rich enough phenomenology that they're unwilling to think that the feelings aren't evidentially significant of genuine guilt on at least some occasions. For present purposes, it's to such persons that we're directing our argument, rather than trying to convince those skeptical about the existence of objective moral guilt that such a thing exists. That would perhaps be a worthwhile case to make, but it's not our present project.

out to be false—like the parallel postulate or the intuition that the shortest distance between two points is a straight line.[5]

On other occasions, though, intuitions can prove inexplicably accurate. Consider remarkable Indian mathematician Srinivasa Ramanujan, a prodigy who came to be known as the "prince of intuition."[6] For five years he collaborated with Cambridge mathematician G. H. Hardy, who recognized his genius. Ramanujan was able to churn out many incredibly complicated mathematical conclusions on the force of his amazing intuition for numbers, fractions, and infinite series.[7]

Similarly, feelings of guilt are plausibly thought to be veridical, even if they're not infallible. And surely they are susceptible to error. Some people have an inordinately sensitive conscience, internalizing feelings of guilt that are altogether inappropriate and unwarranted. We've mentioned poor Huckleberry Finn's situation on this score before. Others, through habitual practice, have seemed to acquire what the Bible refers to as a "seared conscience," not feeling bad even when they should. Others seem born with moral blind spots, afflicted with psychopathy and little to no empathy for the sufferings of others, grief at the loss of loved ones, or pangs of guilt for wrongdoing.

---

[5]It turns out that in non-Euclidean geometries neither is true. In the second, this is why it's the so-called geodesic that's said to be the shortest distance between two points. In Euclidean geometry the shortest distance between two points is a unique straight line, but in, say, Riemannian geometry it's not, as counterintuitive as that may initially seem.

[6]A piece I (David) wrote reviewing *The Man Who Knew Infinity*—the recent film on Ramanujan's life and work—explores other interesting connections to the moral argument; you can find that review here: "Intuiting the Beauty of the Infinite: Ramanujan and Hardy's Friendship and Collaboration," *Moral Apologetics*, November 5, 2016, http://moralapologetics.com/intuiting-the-beauty-of-the-infinite-ramanujan-and-hardys-friendship-and-collaboration/.

[7]What seemed to be his innate insights were often unaccompanied by formal proofs, or even coherent accounts, although some have suggested that this perception may have been partly a function of the shortage of paper when he put together his notebooks, and it was a practice of one of the books he'd read just to put down the conclusion. Even if Ramanujan was more discursive than some might suggest, the remarkable powers of his intuition were unparalleled and provide noteworthy evidence to show how penetrating intuitions can be, even if intuitions in general, and Ramanujan's mysterious intuitions in particular, were far from infallible. For a fascinating account of his life, see Robert Kanigel's *The Man Who Knew Infinity: A Life of the Genius Ramanujan* (New York: Scribner, 1991). Interestingly, Ramanujan often said, "An equation for me has no meaning unless it represents a thought of *God*." His theorems are still being plumbed for the light they shed on black holes, polymer chemistry, computers, and even cancer!

Incidentally, this raises an interesting challenge to a version of the moral argument that we can briefly address before we continue. Efforts to live up to the moral law inevitably fall short, C. S. Lewis noted, suggesting that this is true of everyone, most certainly himself. This suggested two realities for Lewis: the need for forgiveness to deal with the ensuing guilt for moral failures, and the need for help to meet the demand. Guilt, though not a particularly good thing in itself, does serve the useful purpose of making us aware of the need to be forgiven, which Lewis thought serves as a vital prolegomenon to the Christian gospel.

This is his methodology in book one of *Mere Christianity*, in which he gives his justly famous version of the moral argument. He begins with an unbending moral law and how we invariably fall short of it. In that book's last paragraph he explains his approach:

> My reason was that Christianity simply does not make sense until you have faced the sort of facts I have been describing. Christianity tells people to repent and promises them forgiveness. It therefore has nothing (as far as I know) to say to people who do not know they have done anything to repent of and who do not feel that they need any forgiveness. It is after you have realized that there is a real Moral Law, and a Power behind the law, and that you have broken that law and put yourself wrong with that Power—it is after all this, and not a moment sooner, that Christianity begins to talk. When you know you are sick, you will listen to the doctor. When you have realized that our position is nearly desperate you will begin to understand what the Christians are talking about. They offer an explanation of how we got into our present state of both hating goodness and loving it.[8]

A challenge to Lewis's moral argument is raised at just this point by Erik Wielenberg, because of the aforementioned category of psychopathy (or sociopathy).[9] Consider again Lewis's words that Christianity has nothing to offer "people who do not feel that they need any forgiveness."

---

[8]C. S. Lewis, *Mere Christianity*, Signature Classics ed. (New York: HarperOne, 2002), 35.

[9]Differences between these two psychological categories needn't detain us here, as the points to be made are generalizable enough and aren't parasitic on more fine-grained analyses. See Erik Wielenberg, *God and the Reach of Reason* (Cambridge: Cambridge University Press, 2007), 81.

Those afflicted with psychopathy generally *don't feel* as if they need forgiveness from anyone.

David Wood is an example. As a boy, he was emotionally unaffected first by the death of a pet, then later by the death of a friend. He is one of many (by some estimates up to a million people in the United States) who severely lack empathy, typical feelings associated with wrongdoing, tragedy, and the like. This is a real psychological reality and not meant as an indictment of any sort of those so afflicted. It seems to be an empirically verifiable phenomenon and not altogether uncommon at that. Wielenberg, with perfect legitimacy, raises this issue to underscore that, on Lewis's analysis, Christianity would have nothing to offer such people if, in fact, Christianity has nothing to offer those who don't feel they need forgiveness. On the assumption that Wielenberg is right, this would indeed detract from aspects of the moral apologetic case.

However, we would point to the rest of Wood's story.[10] If his story were unique, this reply to Wielenberg could be accused of being merely anecdotal, but it is one of many stories that could be cited. Let's flesh out more of his fascinating narrative.

Constructing his worldview to correspond with his flat and lifeless emotional perception of reality, Wood began to think that all of life was pointless. At the same time, he would try to hold his worldview together whenever occasional doubts crept in. He finally realized that if existence were pointless, so too was his effort to hold it all together. And then, he says, life offered him an alternative.

After a violent act Wood ended up in prison, where he ran into a Christian who was willing to defend his convictions rather than cower in silence or run for cover when Wood issued his usual barrage of insults and challenges. The believer, named Randy, challenged Wood in return, forcing him to articulate his convictions, at which point Wood recognized something for the first time: "Things that made perfect sense when

---

[10]This recounting of David Wood's story borrows from a piece by David Baggett, "On Psychopathy and Moral Apologetics," *Moral Apologetics*, December 11, 2014, http://moralapologetics.com /on-psychopathy-and-moral-apologetics/.

unquestioned seemed silly when questioned."[11] Questions of why the disciples would risk death to testify to the resurrection of Jesus or how life could emerge from lifelessness now began to plague Wood's mind.

In an effort to refute Randy's faith and consolidate his own convictions, Wood began reading the Bible. He was refraining from eating at the time—long story—and found in Scripture that Jesus was called "the bread of life." He wanted escape from his imprisonment and read that the Son of God can set us free. He was painfully sick at the time and read that Jesus was the resurrection and the life. Over and over again he was startled to find Christ to be the answer he was seeking.

He spent time reading the books on apologetics Randy had given him, and gradually his secular worldview began to crumble. The design argument and the argument for the historicity of the resurrection began to make more sense to him, and then (surprisingly) the moral argument began to speak to him as well. Heretofore he'd held two beliefs at the same time: (1) that humans are meaningless lumps of cells, *and* (2) that he was the best, most important person in all the world. The realization began to dawn on him how inconsistent these were. A *best person*, he began to see, required an objective standard of goodness. He went from thinking himself the best person in the world to the worst. He also realized that if his earlier assessment of morality was wrong and there really was an objective standard of goodness and rightness, he was in trouble.

At this point he recognized, without the aid of typical emotions, what John Hare calls the "moral gap": the gulf between where we are morally and where we should be. Either he was irremediably selfish and sick and there was no hope, or there was someone, or Someone, who could help. He knew that he, riddled with his psychological, spiritual, and moral maladies, couldn't help himself. But who could?

Gradually he came to think that only God could do it, and Jesus, the one God raised. Eventually, beaten down, desperate, barely able to know how, he prayed for forgiveness. His was a dramatic conversion, which happens on occasion. Instantaneously, no longer did he want to hurt

---

[11]His whole story can be found here: "Why I Am a Christian (David Wood, Former Atheist)," December 5, 2014, www.youtube.com/watch?v=DakEcY7Z5GU.

anyone, and, perhaps even more importantly, he had the strange sense that he had known the truth all along.

Wood's moral sense was damaged but not beyond repair. The grace of God and the use of his other faculties (such as that of reason) enabled him to understand that he did indeed have moral obligations after all. A psychopath is a person who doesn't feel appropriately about his actions, but as Wood's case shows, reason still leads to moral law. So psychopaths are not incapable of recognizing the moral law; they just lack the right emotional responses to it. Thus they are disadvantaged, but not in a way that precludes knowledge of the moral law. Perhaps we can conclude that having moral feelings is not a necessary condition for being morally accountable and that having these feelings is just a gift from God to aid in the moral life.

Wielenberg, therefore, may be treating conscience in an overly narrow sense. Perhaps he thinks of conscience as morally appropriate feelings that guide us to right action, but we could expand this understanding of conscience to include the deliverances of reason. In which case, if our feelings fail us, we are not left without a conscience, just without some of the faculties a healthy conscience has. The existence of people such as David Wood shows that the lack of empathy in some, rather than *hurting* the case for moral apologetics, might actually *help* it!

Today Wood runs an apologetics ministry: Acts 17 Apologetics. He realizes now that true freedom is deliverance from his earlier desire to turn against his Creator. Echoing C. S. Lewis, he says he now believes in Christianity as he believes in the sun—because by it he can see everything else.[12] Wood perhaps didn't have the advantage of most: a well-functioning conscience and active capacity for empathy, which God can indeed and often does use to draw people to himself. Lewis was right about that but perhaps overstated the case, because God has other resources besides.

People don't fall through the cracks if God is a God of love. In an important sense, we are all morally sick to the core and in need of healing

---

[12]C. S. Lewis, "Is Theology Poetry?," in *The Weight of Glory*, rev. and exp. ed. (New York: Macmillan, 1980), 92.

that only God can provide. We all need to become not just *better* people but *new* people. Contra Wielenberg, despite Wood's deficiency he was still able to apprehend the truth, recognize the possibility he was wrong, throw himself on God's mercy, and emerge from darkness into the light. And for a person who underwent such radical transformation, these words from Ezekiel 36:26 seem poignantly apt: "A new heart I will give you, and a new spirit I will put within you; and I will take out of your flesh the heart of stone and give you a heart of flesh."

## BY GRACE THROUGH FAITH

For those who sense or otherwise recognize their need for more than just the forgiveness that fellow human beings provide, Christianity has the ready prescription. Rather than seeing guilt as an unfortunate psychological impediment in need of ignoring or replacing, Christianity suggests it can reflect an objective moral condition, one in need of addressing, and by the grace of God real guilt—not just feelings of guilt—can be taken away. People can be forgiven.

Keep in mind that one of the functions of falling short of the moral ideal is to make us cognizant of guilt in need of forgiveness. Another, Lewis suggests, is to remind us of our moral weakness, our need for moral change, indeed for radical moral transformation. Christianity has something remarkable to offer on this score: not only are *forgiveness* and reconciliation with a holy and loving God made possible by God's grace, but so is profound moral *transformation*. Recall Augustine's claim that God bids us to do what we can't, in order to reveal to us our dependence on him.

To reiterate, this is the first aspect of Kantian moral faith—the conviction that the moral life is possible. Whether we can really change and become radically better people is a crucial moral question, and one of the real tests of a worldview is how effectively it holds out the rational hope for such transformation. Just about any worldview can offer some prospect for a modicum of ethical change, a tweaking of character, a nominal improvement in morals, a modest acquisition of virtue. Many people, however, whether devout or secular, testify to a frustration when it comes to their deeper ethical longings and aspirations. We repeatedly find ourselves subject to the same nagging moral failures and stubborn character flaws. Sometimes the harder we try to effect moral improvement to take strides forward, the more our efforts seem futile.

It often seems that our best moral efforts at improvement only scratch the surface. It's like pulling weeds from the garden without getting at the roots. The inevitable result is that they creep back time and again. How can we get at the roots of our moral maladies? Are we destined only ever to skate the surface, never to plumb the depths? How can we do more than ameliorate our behavior and deal with what really ails us? We would submit that this is an existentially central question for all of us as moral agents and human persons, believers and nonbelievers alike. This is a quest common to the human condition.

Many would eschew the concern for moral improvement and the dream of moral transformation, or even perfection, as wishful and Pollyannaish thinking. But many others from a broad sweep of worldview perspectives would admit to recognizing this as at least a very human and natural sort of desire. They may lament there's no way in which we can retain such a realistic hope. They may insist the best we can do is settle for small improvements and modest incremental moral victories on the personal level, or improved social conditions on a cultural level. But sadly, they think, the hope for much more is an idle pipe dream.

We, however, are not so sure that such an aspiration is insignificant or easily dismissed. Indeed, we remain open to the possibility that this longing for more, cognizance of our need for radical moral improvement, is a rather telling indicator about larger realities, a useful clue about the human condition.

We have seen moral apologists of the past recognize the reality of this longing and call to purity and holiness as evidentially significant. A. E. Taylor, C. S. Lewis, John Henry Newman, Immanuel Kant, John Hare, and others have identified a gaping chasm between the best we can do as human beings and the exacting standard of morality. Lewis was ambitious enough on the point to argue that recognition of the moral demand, and the way each one of so habitually falls short of it, is perhaps our best clue as to the meaning of life.

Kant's argument from grace, what we are calling the argument of this chapter, was likely the first major attempt to use this dimension of morality to argue for rational belief in God's existence.[13] If Kant's argument works, the conclusion will be along these lines: if classical theism and historical Christian teaching provide the best explanation both of the diagnosis of the moral maladies of people and the prescription for its healing, then this aspect of morality provides us at least some good reason to infer to its truth.

For help structuring the argument and making it accessible, let's use insights and categories gleaned from Kant's argument. This is not the only way to do it, but it's at least one effective way in which to make the case. The argument from grace stems from recognizing both a very high moral demand and the human inability to meet that demand without some sort of outside assistance. Although Kant will be used to structure the discussion, we will depart from a strict Kantian analysis at a few junctures when there is need to do so.

## THE DEAR SELF AND CONSCIOUSNESS OF THE MORAL LAW

Kant is famous for writing, in the conclusion of his *Critique of Practical Reason*, "Two things fill the mind with ever new and increasing admiration and awe . . . the starry heavens above me and the moral law within me."[14] Kant took moral deliverances seriously. One of the features of the Lutheran Pietism in which he was raised was the assignment of primacy to conscience, which arguably was strongly related to the way the mature Kant never seriously doubted the veracity of his moral consciousness.

---

[13]Since this book favors an abductive argument for God's existence, the Kantian use of the distinction between theoretical and practical reasoning need not detain us. Theoretical reasoning might yield a conclusion such as "God exists," or, equivalently, "It's true that God exists," or "We can know that God exists." Practical reasoning in a Kantian spirit is more likely to yield a conclusion such as "It's rational to believe in God," or "It's necessary to postulate God's existence for practical reasons," or "It's rational to have faith or hope in God's existence." In light of the fact that even Kantian practical arguments almost inevitably carry implicit theoretical components (as C. Stephen Evans and many others have argued), it will suffice for our practical purposes to conceive of the argument from grace along abductive lines that blend aspects of the theoretical and practical.

[14]Immanuel Kant, *Critique of Practical Reason*, trans. Lewis White Beck (Indianapolis: Bobbs-Merrill, 1956 [1788]), 166.

What did Kant think the moral conscience and moral consciousness reveal? He believed they show, among other things, a strict moral demand. Ultimately, morality demands nothing less than the effort of seeking perfection, doing the right things for the right reason—respect for the moral law. It is an eminently demanding requirement, yet the standard is unrelenting, neither indulgent nor compromised. Since perfection obviously can't be attained in this life, and because *ought implies can* (once a few qualifications are added), death must not be the end. We must be able to continue the quest for perfection subsequent to death. This is an argument for immortality, since the quest is never completed; rather, the "holy will" is approached only asymptotically.

Kant's insight here may well apply to aspects of the moral experience. For example, we may grow into ever greater relations of love with others and with God himself throughout eternity, a process that will never end. Perhaps if Kant's argument were explicated in that way, it would have potential for an argument for immortality. But the way he worded the argument seems to go contrary to Christian thought. This, then, is one of those promised points of departure we have with Kant, as Christian theology clearly teaches that moral perfection, something like Kant's holy will, is indeed achievable for human beings. We will, as believers, ultimately be entirely conformed to the image of Christ. Every last vestige of sin will indeed be removed. We will be holy as God is holy. Christianity also teaches immortality, no doubt, but Kant's argument for it based on the unreachability of the holy will seems fatally flawed.

Immortality, of course, is not enough. Without God, the head of the kingdom of ends, to provide the needed help, immortality alone would leave us with the same devotion to the "dear self" (that stubborn bent toward self-consumption), the same taint of the race—for it is not just the high moral demand that generates the moral gap between where we are and where we need to go. The culprit is also our entrenched, intractable, recalcitrant moral corruption. Human beings have a serious moral problem, a deeply flawed moral disposition in need of a revolution of the will. No mere tweaking of the paradigm will do. Radical change is needed.

We are all, Kant thinks, born under the evil maxim. On Kant's ethical system, concerning the plethora of subjective maxims (the principles on which we base our actions), they all boil down either to the good maxim, which subordinates desire to duty, or the evil maxim, which subordinates duty to desire. It is not that we are as evil as we could be, but the human race is surely tainted. Our "dear self" tends to reign supreme. Commentators on Kant such as John Hare attribute Kant's recognition of human moral frailty and self-consumption to his Lutheran upbringing, which depicted the essence of our sinful condition as *homo incurvatus in se,* being curved in on oneself.

Kant saw clearly that the moral demand is very high, while also recognizing that we have a natural propensity not to follow it, privileging Scotus's so-called affection for advantage (over the "affection for justice"). We have a natural tendency, when forced to rank these, to privilege evil over good, self over others, desires over duty.

This needs to change, but how can we do it on our own? We seem unable to. As A. E. Taylor later put it, we can't pull ourselves up by our own hair. Kant likewise saw that we find ourselves in a dilemma: we need to privilege the good maxim, but our natural tendencies are too strong in the other direction of privileging the self and our own desires. Born under the evil maxim, we can't reverse the ranking by our own devices.

On a Kantian picture, we all ought to behave in a certain way, in accord with the moral law, but at the same time we encounter intractable obstacles. Our natural capacities are not up to the task. Yet the moral demand remains pressing on us—a demand whose deliverances we lack the sensitivity or sympathy to figure out and abide by, but whose content could be both figured out and actualized by the perfect moral thinker and paradigm. The moral gap then generates its consequent sense of moral failure and the conceptual difficulty that we labor under a demand that is too prohibitive, well beyond our capacities.

If morality is beyond our capacities, but ought implies can, how can morality be authoritative for us? The problem can be resolved if there are additional resources outside ourselves we can tap into. Then the operative principle is "ought implies can *with the help available.*"

But this means we *ought* to seek that help, and we are culpable if we don't. Hare, sensitive to clues in Kant, identifies three possibilities for closing the gap without appeal to divine assistance: (1) to exaggerate our capacities to be moral, (2) to lower the moral demand, or (3) to identify some set of secular substitutes for divine assistance in meeting the demand.

Kant anticipated the first strategy, inflating our moral capabilities, but rejected it when he referred to "man's self-conceit and the exaggeration of his powers."[15] Kant also anticipated the second effort, lowering the demand, when he said that "we may imagine that the moral law is indulgent as far as we are concerned," but it's an approach he rejected.[16] The last effort to answer the challenge of the moral gap tries neither to exaggerate human capacities nor to lower the moral demand, but rather to recognize the gap but then locate some nontheological substitute for God's assistance to close it. Kant usually seemed skeptical at the prospect that such secular standards would suffice. John Hare lays out a performative variant of the moral argument based on this Kantian structure in his excellent book *The Moral Gap*.

## SAVED TO THE UTTERMOST AND SOCIAL TRANSFORMATION

Let's wrap up this chapter by extending it in a few directions. First, notice that on a Christian understanding, hope for moral transformation is at the center of its soteriology (doctrine of salvation). Contra Kant, a holy will, something like impeccability, is a living hope. Total transformation, complete conformity to the image of Christ, is finally within our grasp. The yearning for perfection isn't wishful thinking but a veridical intimation of reality. If such a thing is possible, isn't it worth pursuing? Isn't it something all of us should care about, particularly if the realization of such a possibility depends on our doing so?

Such theological luminaries as Calvin and Luther were best known for emphasizing justification by faith, which has to do with forgiveness of

---

[15]Immanuel Kant, *Lectures in Ethics*, trans. Louis Infield (Indianapolis: Hackett, 1930), 126.
[16]Ibid.

sin and reconciliation with God. Of course they also had something to say about sanctification. But it's John Wesley who is better known for emphasizing sanctification by grace through faith, which pertains to the moral transformation that transpires especially after justification. Wesleyan theology dovetails entirely with this extension of the argument from grace to encompass not just forgiveness but radical change. God doesn't just forgive us our sins. He can deliver us from sin itself—freeing us from not only its consequences but its grip.[17]

Beginning with the disciples and early church leaders, Christianity has spoken of the possibility of radical transformation not merely in words but in example. What but supernatural intervention explains Saul of Tarsus, zealous persecutor of Christians, embracing their faith and becoming the apostle Paul, its major advocate? Or Peter, who once denied even knowledge of Christ, boldly proclaiming the gospel without fear of recrimination? Story after story like these fills the pages of church history: Augustine's turn from his profligate lifestyle, Saint Patrick's escape from slavery only to return to minister to the very people who once enslaved him, John Wesley's Aldersgate experience.

V. Raymond Edman collects twenty such stories of modern Christians in *They Found the Secret*, including figures like Salvation Army commissioner Samuel Brengle, author of *Pilgrim's Progress* John Bunyan, missionary to South India Amy Carmichael, and devotional writer Andrew Murray. These stories demonstrate the transforming work of the Holy Spirit, as Edman explains:

---

[17]Old Testament scholar Dennis Kinlaw puts it even more strongly: "I was a student at Princeton sitting in a class with Emile Caillier, a philosopher. He was giving some lectures on holiness in the Reformed tradition, and I wondered what a good Reformed philosopher would have to say on that subject. As you might expect, he dealt with Luther and Calvin and their predecessors, and then with the development of the Reformation. But after he had done that, he said that if you want to find the classically stated Reformed doctrine on holiness, you do not look to the Reformers. Their concern was how to be justified; how a person could be accepted before God, be justified before God. But the human mind does not learn two lessons at the same time. The lesson that needed to be learned in the Reformation was justification. So, he said, if you want to find the classical statement of the Reformed doctrine of holiness, you cannot look at Luther or Calvin. Rather, you must look to John Wesley, and when the Methodist movement calcified, to the Salvation Army and its doctrinal statement on entire sanctification. There is the classical statement of the Reformed doctrine of holiness." Dennis F. Kinlaw, *Lectures in Old Testament Theology* (Anderson, IN: Francis Asbury Press, 2010), 413.

Out of discouragement and defeat they have come into victory. Out of weakness and weariness they have been made strong. Out of ineffectiveness and apparent uselessness they have become efficient and enthusiastic. The pattern seems to be self-centeredness, self-effort, increasing inner dissatisfaction and outer discouragement, a temptation to give it all up because there is no better way, and then finding the Spirit of God to be their strength, their guide, their confidence and companion—in a word, their life.[18]

If Christianity is true, what is possible for them is possible for all.

Second, and last, the argument from grace has implications not only for individuals. It also bears on larger social structures and dynamics, which themselves can harden into systemic injustices, promote dysfunction, and perpetrate evils of various sorts, on the one hand, or, more positively, advance social justice, lift up the downtrodden, and give hope to the marginalized. An important truth test of a worldview is its fruit.

Here it is relevant to adduce what Paul Copan has dubbed a historical aspect of moral apologetics: the role played by Christ and his devoted followers. Copan cites specific cultural developments that can be shown to have flowed from the Jewish-Christian worldview, leading to societies that are "progress-prone rather than progress-resistant," including such signs of progress as the founding of modern science, poverty-diminishing free markets, equal rights for all before the law, religious liberty, women's suffrage, human rights initiatives, and the abolition of slavery, widow burning, and foot binding.[19]

Even outspoken atheist Jürgen Habermas, in his later work, acknowledges this inescapable and profound debt human rights discourse today owes to the biblical worldview:

Christianity has functioned for the normative self-understanding of modernity as more than just a precursor or a catalyst. Egalitarian universalism,

---

[18]V. Raymond Edman, *They Found the Secret* (Grand Rapids: Zondervan, 1984), 11.

[19]See Paul Copan, "Reinforcing the Moral Argument: Appealing to the Historical Impact of the Christian Faith," paper presented at the Evangelical Theological Society, November 19-21, 2014, San Diego.

from which sprang the ideas of freedom and a social solidarity, of an autonomous conduct of life and emancipation, the individual morality of conscience, human rights, and democracy, is the direct heir to the Judaic ethic of justice and the Christian ethic of love. This legacy, substantially unchanged, has been the object of continual critical appropriation and reinterpretation. To this day, there is no alternative to it. And in light of current challenges of a postnational constellation, we continue to draw on the substance of this heritage. Everything else is just idle postmodern talk.[20]

This chapter has advanced an argument from grace: that by God's grace we can make sense of and provide a prescription to both the ubiquitous existential experience of what seems like real and objective moral guilt and the yearning for radical moral improvement, perhaps even moral perfection—certainly an inspiring and animating aspiration.

## TALK BACK

1. What is the connection between forgiveness and transformation? What is the relationship between our obligation to forgive and God's forgiveness of us? How does Christian theology explain the mechanism by which we can perform this otherwise impossible task?

2. In wrapping up David Wood's story, we borrow an analogy from C. S. Lewis: Christianity is like the sun—by it we can see everything else. What does Christian belief allow us to see about reality that is otherwise easily missed?

3. This chapter offered a few biblical and historical examples of lives transformed through faith and the grace of God. Can you think of others? Do you have any personal experience or firsthand knowledge of others in this regard?

---

[20]Jürgen Habermas, *Time of Transitions*, ed. and trans. Ciaran Cronin and Max Pensky (Cambridge: Polity, 2006), 150-51.

# CHAPTER 9

# MORAL PROVIDENCE

*How little people know who think that holiness is dull.*
*When one meets the real thing . . . it is irresistible. If even*
*10% of the world's population had it, would not the whole*
*world be converted and happy before a year's end?*

C. S. LEWIS, *LETTERS TO AN AMERICAN LADY*

ABOUT FOUR YEARS AGO, my (Dave's) mother was in the last stages of terminal cancer. She had been admitted to the hospice wing of the hospital, and as her final breath drew near, I prayed to see an angel when she died. I had heard of such stories, in which the dying or their family members had a glimpse of the divine in this hour of need, and I asked God for one myself.

The night came, and nearing midnight, with Marybeth and me there, my mother breathed her last. I saw no angel. Instead, I cried like a baby—a hungry, angry baby—for a few minutes, recovered, then went to tell the nurse my mom was gone. The nurse came down to the room and confirmed it. I thanked her, along with the rest of the staff, for all their help. Then I asked her what her name was.

"Angel," she said.

And I had to laugh to myself. Sometimes we have not because we ask not, and sometimes we have not because we don't ask specifically enough.

You may not have asked for it, but this chapter will give you an argument from providence. The argument is directly related to a Kantian account of the greatest good for human beings. Readers may know that Kant distinguished between what he called the "phenomenal" and "noumenal" realms. To put it succinctly, the phenomenal is the realm of what we directly experience, whereas the noumenal is what remains beyond our experience. Look at a table, for example. What you experience directly, he thought, was a perception of the table mediated through various lenses. The table as it is in itself, unmediated, remains beyond our direct experience.

Kant thought that human beings are members of both the noumenal and phenomenal realms. We are put in touch with transcendent realities through morality. On those terms, a life of virtue alone would be for us the highest good. But we are more than noumenal creatures. We are also phenomenal creatures, inhabitants of this world of sense. As such, this introduces a further need and legitimate goal, namely, happiness. So our highest good combines the two: to be both virtuous and happy. Rationality, it seems, demands we pursue both, which prompts consideration of how they square with each other.

By the end of this chapter we will make clear what we think would be missing from the moral life without an integral connection between virtue and joy, and ultimately between holiness and a world set right. Without the hope for such integration, holiness is found to be at irreconcilable odds with happiness. In that case, morality would seem to lack something important.

This chapter will present an argument from providence, which is centered on this double sense of our highest good: the combination of happiness and holiness, of virtue and joy. Theism, so the argument will conclude, holds out the promise of such an ultimate correspondence and perfect synthesis of the two. We will also argue that, though our happiness is important, it is not properly thought to be our highest goal.

## HOLINESS AND HAPPINESS

The argument of this chapter moves our discussion to the second aspect of Kantian moral faith, namely, the question of whether happiness and holiness cohere, of whether the just and virtuous are also ultimately those filled with joy and satisfaction. For morality to make sense, to avoid being an absurdity (with holiness and happiness at intractable odds), it would seem that morality and happiness must perfectly converge. Something of an airtight relationship between them is needed. But more specificity is called for, because the Stoics and the Epicureans both assumed, in their own way, such an airtight connection.[1]

Kant disagreed with both of their formulations, insisting that happiness can't be reduced to virtue or vice versa. Happiness and virtue remain distinct. Our experiences, in fact, give us little reason or hope to think that they will perfectly correspond in this life. Each one of us can easily recall times when what we wanted to do was a far cry from—or even an outright rejection of—what we ought to have done. As far as we can tell from our lived experience, nature is indifferent to our moral purposes. Unless such a perfect correspondence ultimately obtains, however, morality becomes *rationally unstable*. We must find a way to assure ourselves that morality and happiness are consistent, indeed that they perfectly correspond.[2]

Kant's solution is that we need belief in God to give us this assurance.[3] And such assurance is needed for morality to make full rational sense. The fundamental issue here pertains to whether there's a rational fit between happiness and virtue. Since rationality dictates our obligation to pursue both happiness and virtue, the rationality of the moral enterprise demands that such a goal be obtainable. Ensuring such a correspondence, however, is not within our powers.[4] Since morality and rationality give us this end (the union of virtue and happiness), if we are to pursue the morally good life in a way that is rationally stable, we must believe that this highest good is really possible.

---

[1]For Stoics, virtue was enough for happiness. Epicureans, instead, privileged happiness, believing that virtue has no value in itself. It was only to be sought as a means to happiness.

[2]So that we can know, minimally, we do not have to do what is morally wrong in order to be happy.

[3]Kant gives this argument in the dialectic of the *Critique of Practical Reason* but also at the beginning of *Religion Within the Boundaries of Mere Reason* and at the end of the first and third *Critiques*.

[4]Two interpretations of the (conjunctive) highest good are possible: (1) The less ambitious is a world in which virtue results in happiness, and (2) the more ambitious is a world in which everyone is happy and virtuous. Hare argues that rational stability, the full rational authority for morality, requires the actuality of the first and the possibility of the second.

In order to sustain our belief in the real possibility of the highest good, Kant would argue, we therefore have to assume the existence of a transcendent author of nature who can bring about the conjunction of happiness and virtue. Hence morality inevitably leads to religion. In this context Kant says we need to recognize our duties as God's commands. We have to do this because by so doing we can rationally believe in the real possibility of the highest good, the end that morality itself gives us. When Kant defines religion as recognizing our duties as God's commands, the notion of religion is of a moral faith in the governance of the universe: that how things *ought to be* is sustained by how things *fundamentally are.*

Something like this conviction seems to be at the heart of Martin Luther King Jr.'s philosophy of nonviolent resistance. Despite the terrible injustices perpetrated against himself and his colaborers in the civil rights movement, in the face of brutal opposition, King insisted on not responding in kind, entrusting to God his cause and the outcome of the movement he inspired. Only through resolute trust in this transcendent reality that shoots through the material world and imbues it with significance could King proclaim that the arc of the moral universe is long but bends toward justice.[5]

## WHAT'S AT STAKE?

Why do we need to believe in the possibility of the highest good, understood in the sense of happiness and virtue coming together? We have been speaking in terms of rational stability, which is a legitimate category of its own, but this can be cashed out or augmented in several ways. We wish

---

[5]Nineteenth-century abolitionist Theodore Parker said, "I do not pretend to understand the moral universe; the arc is a long one, my eye reaches but little ways; I cannot calculate the curve and complete the figure by the experience of sight; I can divine it by conscience. And from what I see I am sure it bends towards justice." A century later, King paraphrased these words in a prepared statement he read in 1956 following the conclusion of the Montgomery bus boycott. He later used a similar paraphrasing to great effect in two famous speeches and his final sermon: "How Long, Not Long," delivered in March 1965 on the steps of the Alabama State Capitol; "Where Do We Go From Here?," delivered in August 1967 to the Southern Christian Leadership Conference; and his "Remaining Awake Through a Great Revolution" sermon, delivered in March 1968 at the National Cathedral. In each instance, King's paraphrase included the words, "The arc of the moral universe is long, but it bends toward justice."

to consider two such ways. Then we will offer our own take on how best to identify what's at stake here, which strikes us as something important.

The issue of *rational stability* primarily raises the question of whether morality is a fully rational endeavor. This seems to be an important question in its own right. If morality is less than fully rational, is it something we should remain committed to, especially when doing so is painful or costly? Many share the intuition that morality is nonnegotiably important and indispensable. Note that such a view seems to be assuming that morality is fully rational. But, as with the foundational moral truths of human value and moral obligations, this assumption is a starting point. What, we must ask, lies behind this reality? The fully rational nature of morality requires explanation.

What is it about morality that ensures its rationality if it, among other things, doesn't ultimately cohere with happiness? What if morality, as it sometimes seems to, even militates against or otherwise precludes happiness? Consider putting your life on the line to rescue someone from drowning, or remaining sexually faithful to a spouse whose disease or accident inhibits or precludes marital relations. Moral faith on this score is a laudable reaction, we think, but only if such faith is rational and not fideistic (blind).

This, however, calls for an explanation of where the full rational authority of morality derives. Kant, we think, was right to locate its source in God. His was not the most direct route from morality to God, but it is a significant and thoughtful attempt at forging such a connection that, in our estimation, carries considerable evidential and existential weight.

A second way to talk about what's at stake and explicate the meaning of rational stability is in terms of *moral motivation*. John Hare offers a nuanced motivational interpretation of Kant on this point. On his reading, Kant maintains that we are capable of acting morally without doing so *because* it will lead to our happiness. According to Hare, Kant thinks we cannot sustain our commitment to the moral life unless we can have confidence that acting morally is compatible with our happiness, at least in the long run. So Hare has Kant claiming that we make compatibility with our happiness a condition of, *though not our reason for*, doing what morality demands.

Kyla Ebels-Duggan, however, offers a critique. Hare's approach, she argues, is implausible as a reading of Kant. In fact the moral psychology that Hare articulates more or less exactly describes the structure of the "evil will" to which Kant refers in the *Religion Within the Bounds of Bare Reason*. Instead of making morality (permissibility) the condition for acting to secure her happiness, the evil will reverses the order. She makes her happiness the condition on which she is willing to act morally.

> Kant thinks that human beings *are* like this, but also that we *ought not be*. This last thought goes missing on Hare's approach. The empirical world may be much less hospitable to morality than it looks from the comfort and safety of the lives that most of us live. Those who act well may indeed make themselves vulnerable to those who do not. Kant holds that *even so* the moral demand is uncompromising.[6]

Ebels-Duggan seems right about Kant's stance, and if so, this is another juncture at which we find ourselves parting company with Kant. More than Kant, we are comfortable with staking morality's claim on full moral motivation on the airtight case between morality and happiness in the long term. Without this assurance, which we think theism is eminently qualified to provide, moral agents would, we think, be justified to find their moral motivation wane.

For moral apologetic purposes, we can put the case as follows: a less-than-airtight case between morality and happiness detracts from moral rationality and/or from moral motivation. Either option detracts from the moral enterprise. Classical theism can, without reducing virtue to happiness or happiness to virtue (allowing the two to remain distinct), ensure the airtight connection between virtue and happiness, thereby contributing to the rational stability and authority of morality.

A third way to articulate what's at stake here is in terms of *moral hope*. Arguably, this is more deeply consistent with Kant's own approach than the motivational point. Ebels-Duggan makes this case in

---

[6]Kyla Ebels-Duggan, "The Right, the Good, and the Threat of Despair: (Kantian) Hope and the Need for Hope in God," available at www.academia.edu/9803513/The_Right_the_Good_and_the_Threat_of_Despair_Kantian_Ethics_and_the_Need_for_Hope_in_God (accessed August 22, 2016).

her excellent article. We think is a fitting way to draw our discussion of Kant and moral apologetics to a close, because several interesting threads will converge.

Ebels-Duggan discusses the tension that arises in ethics between deplorable actions and deplorable consequences. It doesn't always follow that they are linked. Such a tension often operates at the heart of excruciating dilemma cases where the choice is between choosing an abhorrent action or allowing an abhorrent consequence. Kant would consistently assign primacy to avoiding the abhorrent action, even if such a choice results in awful consequences.

For example, say that torturing a terrorist's child will force him to reveal the location of a bomb set to explode, a revelation that will prevent the deaths of many. The abhorrent action—torturing the child—must still be avoided, no matter that avoiding doing so might—and likely will—result in many more deaths. So, on Kant's view, not only are we incapable of ensuring an ultimate correspondence between virtue and good states of affairs (happiness writ large), but sometimes our actions will actually work against those states of affairs, at least in the short term. Kant knew that we are also obligated to pursue those good results, though not at the expense of neglecting our duty.

In light of this, moral agents can on occasion be tempted to despair. In fact, some have succumbed to the temptation, thinking that our ethical dreams will inevitably come to ruin. Kant's answer, instead, was one of hope. Owing to his theism, he retained hope that ultimate reality is good, that the good will win, that tragedies will be redeemed, that injustices will eventually be fixed and the world set right. Theoretical reason can't ensure or guarantee such hopes are founded, but neither can it preclude the possibility. It is at least feasible, and morality itself requires such hope. So Kant thought this hope was well grounded for powerful practical reasons. Its very possibility ensures that it's no mere wishful thinking for something we know can't happen.

Hope, rather than moral motivation, is an answer about what's at stake that requires little departure from Kantian principles. And hope is needed by everyone, not just the weak-willed, those of us who might all too easily lose moral motivation in circumstances of ethical diffi-culty. Indeed, hope is needed for the strongest-willed and most consis-tently virtuous, for they are often the ones most acutely aware of the tension between virtue and good temporal consequences, either for oneself or others.

Even if doing the right thing doesn't make the world worse, there's no guarantee it will make the world better. William Wilberforce's decades-long mission to end the slave trade in Great Britain powerfully exem-plifies the need for hope in pursuing a moral life. His conversion to Christianity marked a change of Wilberforce's heart and instilled in him a deep desire for social reform. He is lauded today, and rightly so, for this work. But behind the ultimate triumph of his cause lie years of perse-verance in the face of overwhelming odds.

Wilberforce saw more defeats than victories, but his steadfast com-mitment to the abolitionist goal, despite these setbacks, testifies to the sustaining force of faith in the moral order, as he himself articulates: "Accustom yourself to look first to the dreadful consequences of failure; then fix your eye on the glorious prize which is before you; and when your strength begins to fail, and your spirits are well-nigh exhausted, let the animating view rekindle your resolution, and call forth in renewed vigour the fainting energies of your soul."[7]

Adducing an example such as Wilberforce—or King earlier—risks tying the primacy of virtue to significant and noteworthy results. We may wonder how our moral convictions and actions could even begin to compare to the achievements of such great people. Remembering the stories behind the historical legends can help a bit with that, for both men were committed to right action for its own sake, to human dignity and upholding human value as worthy in their own right, despite the setbacks and temptations to give up. The same courage is often needed when the moral victories and opportunities for faithfulness are less public and more likely unsung, or even unnoticed altogether.

---

[7]William Wilberforce, *A Practical View of the Prevailing Religious System of Professed Christians, in the Higher and Middle Classes in This Country, Contrasted with Real Christianity* (London: Cadell, 1830), 66.

Fixing this in our mind, we can say with William James: "I am done with great things and big plans, great institutions and big success. I am for those tiny, invisible loving human forces that work from individual to individual, creeping through the crannies of the world like so many rootlets, or like the capillary oozing of water, which, if given time, will rend the hardest monuments of pride."[8]

## THREE IMPORTANT POINTS

This leads to our final three points, all of them directly relevant to moral apologetics. First, most typical moral arguments start with clear ethical deliverances on which most everyone would agree, like that the torture of children for fun is bad. Its obvious wrongness requires explanation, and the argument proceeds from there. Far less common is starting with hard dilemma cases. But this discussion has yielded an interesting result, namely, that starting with dilemma cases can be useful for moral apologetics, too.

All of us, strict Kantians or not, will find ourselves in situations where we have no reason at all to think that doing what our conscience declares is right will produce good consequences, much less the best ones. Yet we still feel like the virtuous action is morally required. Robust faith in a good God in these situations can provide the needed assurance that those temporally bad consequences aren't the end of the story. Such hope means that even the most difficult moral dilemma cases won't prove intractable after all, at least on classical theism, and that hope rather than moral despair is the rational response.

Second, hope for a world redeemed and restored certainly speaks to the social dimensions of the argument from providence. Earlier we went from the individual to the social. This time, let's take the discussion in the opposite direction. Rational hope for a world set right isn't merely hope for the aggregate but for the individual. On various consequentialist readings, hope for the aggregate might suffice. Robust hope demands more. It demands hope for every individual, with no one falling

---

[8]William James, "To Mrs. Henry Whitman—Chocorua, June 7, 1899," in *The Letters of William James*, ed. Henry James (repr. Kessinger, 1926), 2:90.

through the cracks. This point resonates well with the discussion from an earlier chapter about God's concern and offer of hope for each individual person. This is good news indeed, made possible by a good God.

On Kant's view, every person is of inestimable value. Each and every one is precious, with infinite dignity and worth. Redemption is available for all. And in light of some of the unspeakable tragedies persons have endured in this life, hope would require something incommensurably awesome posthumously to make those lives worth living. Kant, on this interpretation, foreshadows Marilyn McCord Adams saying that God himself will be that incommensurably great good who can redeem every life. She writes, "If Divine Goodness is infinite, if intimate relation to It is thus incommensurably good for created persons, then we have identified a good big enough to defeat horrors in every case."[9]

The moral orderer must be powerful enough to bring about the highest good, loving enough to will it, and involved with the world in such a way as to enact it. Thus the being that Kant thinks that we must rationally hope for is an omnipotent, benevolent, and providential agent, very like the God of the religious tradition on which he draws. So Kant argues that, though we cannot know that there is such a God, in a very strict sense of "knowing," the person committed to morality is rationally committed to the hope that there is. The commitment to morality entails a commitment to hope in God, construed very much along Judeo-Christian lines. So the virtuous person hopes that there is such a being, one who can and will bring moral order out of apparent chaos.

And third, again in a Kantian spirit, perhaps we have an obligation to hope. If we care about the tragedies of this world, if we have cultivated a life of virtue, holiness, and love, might it be altogether rational to insist that hope is much more than a luxury or eliminable prerogative? Instead, might it be our binding rational duty? To hope for a world redeemed, for gratuitous evils to be defeated, for the loveless to be embraced, for injustices to be healed? For life to turn out a comedy, not a tragedy?

---

[9]Marilyn McCord Adams, *Horrendous Evils and the Goodness of God* (Ithaca, NY: Cornell University Press, 1999), 82-83.

Here is how Richard Creel makes just such a case:

> As long as it is logically possible that evil be defeated, that innocent suffering is not meaningless and final, it seems to me that we have a moral obligation to hope that that possibility is actual. Therefore we have a moral obligation to hope that there is a God because, if there is a God, then innocent suffering is not meaningless or final. . . . The seeming meaninglessness, absurdity, and waste of innocent suffering and tragic loss are overcome only in the existence of God. To be sure, the Holocaust was enormously tragic—but without God it is even more tragic. Indeed, a far greater evil than the evils of history would be that the evils of history will not be defeated because there is no God. This seems to me a terribly important point that Dostoyevsky's Ivan failed to consider.[10]

Once more, on our reading, we take the import of the argument from providence to suggest rational warrant for believing in God for the sake of (1) rendering the moral enterprise *rationally stable*, (2) providing the sort of *moral motivation* able to sustain us in any and all circumstances in which we might find ourselves, and (3) undergirding *moral hope* rather than despair in light of our inability to ensure a world set right.

We rationally can and morally must hope that, though setting the world entirely right and making justice and peace embrace isn't *our* job, it is the solemn, sacred undertaking of *Someone*, who will be faithful to do it.

## WHY HAPPINESS SHOULD NOT BE OUR HIGHEST GOAL

Although we disagree with Kant on the issue of whether considerations of happiness *can* play a legitimate part in moral motivation, we now wish to conclude this chapter by arguing that such considerations shouldn't function as our *deepest* motivation or *highest* goal. To make our case, we wish to start by acknowledging that happiness is a perfectly legitimate goal. Full rational authority of morality requires that there's an airtight connection between happiness and holiness. Additionally, the pursuit of joy is a legitimate moral motivation.

---

[10]Richard E. Creel, *Divine Impassibility: An Essay in Philosophical Theology* (Cambridge: Cambridge University Press, 1986), 149-50.

Nevertheless, *happiness should not be our highest goal or deepest motivation.* To be clear, we are not arguing that there's anything necessarily illegitimate about having happiness for a goal or even a motivation. Of course there *could* be something awry in certain instances, such as when someone is motivated by entirely egoistic reasons. Or if my happiness includes or results in, even indirectly, the suffering of others, then it would seem that I shouldn't pursue that. Not all self-interest is selfish, though, and we're inclined to think that self-interest is a legitimate moral motivation. Our highest moral motivation or goal, however, shouldn't be happiness. What then should be our ultimate moral lodestar, our fundamental guiding moral principle? Not self-interest but a relationship with God, in whom there's room for everyone's fulfillment and joy.

In light of the airtight connection we argue exists between happiness and holiness, though, some might think that this is a distinction without a difference. We disagree. With Kant we would insist that happiness and holiness, though inextricably tied together, remain two different things. And even if in practice there are ways they can't be separated, their distinction still obtains. In fact, both their distinction and their organic connection can shed light on some otherwise puzzling and poignant scriptural passages, as we will explore shortly.

One of the strongest advantages of robust theistic ethics, and a Christian understanding of ethics in particular, is that it provides an account of how it is that morality and godly virtue ultimately correspond with joy and fulfillment.[11] Sidgwick saw that theism could potentially effect a rapprochement between self-interested and altruistic motivations. Because he was unwilling to embrace theism, however, he concluded that ethics is left saddled with this insoluble dilemma. It is indeed a powerful philosophical advantage of theistic ethics to integrate these disparate human inclinations and thus make morality a fully rational enterprise. The genuine difficulty of secular ethics to admit of such a solution is one of its most obvious deficiencies.

---

[11]In light of the "dualism of the practical reason," there seem otherwise to be disconnects between rationality and morality. See Henry Sidgwick's *Methods of Ethics* (Indianapolis: Hackett, 1981).

As we have seen, that Kant thought that self-interest cannot play any part in legitimate moral motivation didn't mean that he was indifferent to questions of ultimate happiness. Nor was he unconcerned with whether the world itself is a fully moral place. As several insightful commentators on Kant have pointed out—thinkers ranging from Reformed philosopher John Hare to Oxford dons Keith Ward and Terrence Irwin—there are ample resources in Kant to suggest that morality and moral motivation are considerably more connected to theism than is generally noticed.[12]

George Mavrodes once wrote that Kant had clearly recognized that, for morality to retain its full authority, reality itself must in some sense be committed to morality.[13] As noted before, we depart from Kant in suggesting that considerations of happiness can play a perfectly legitimate role in moral motivation. But we resonate with his claim that the pursuit of happiness in principle is trumped by something else. Happiness shouldn't be our highest goal. There's something yet more important we should aim at, and the beauty of it is that, by so doing, we'll find the happiness we desire.

The point has been succinctly put in Scripture: "But seek first his kingdom and his righteousness, and all these things shall be yours as well" (Mt 6:33). That there's ultimate correspondence between holiness and happiness is a glorious truth, but it doesn't vitiate the urgent need to be forgiven and transformed, for the dear self to be dethroned.

Scotus took a double account of motivation from Anselm (1033–1109), who first made the aforementioned distinction between two affections of the will, the *affection for advantage*—an inclination toward one's own

---

[12]At a 2013 conference at Oxford both Ward and Irwin argued persuasively to this effect. See John Hare's *The Moral Gap: Kantian Ethics, Human Limits, and God's Assistance* (Oxford: Oxford University Press, 1996).

[13]See George Mavrodes, "Religion and the Queerness of Morality," in *Ethical Theory: Classical and Contemporary Readings*, 2nd ed., ed. Louis P. Pojman (New York: Wadsworth, 1995). Kant's argument that moral demands need to be understood as divine commands, and his conviction that morality provides good practical reasons to believe in God's existence, would suggest the idea that Kant tried to erect a law without a lawgiver to be inaccurate. Kant was not indifferent to the issue of human happiness but was fastidiously deliberate to emphasize that it is important that such happiness be the happiness *that comes from virtue*.

happiness and perfection—and the *affection for justice*—an inclination toward what is good in itself independent of advantage.[14] Scotus, echoing Anselm, says that we are born with a ranking of advantage over justice, which needs to be reversed by God's assistance before we can be pleasing to God.[15]

We should be willing to sacrifice our own happiness for God if that were to be necessary, which it is not (by God's grace). The paradox is palpable here, but it should be faced squarely. We are called to do something that seems altogether counterintuitive, but it is only this sort of attitude of self-renunciation that, on God's scheme, gets us to the true path of joy. The self must be dethroned. To find life, we must be willing to give it up, entrusting ourselves to the God who resurrects.[16]

As we grow to be like Christ, we should be conformed to his image, and part of what this involves is coming to love what God loves. Love is essentially other-regarding. We see this most clearly in the *perichoretic* relationship of the Trinity,[17] in which the Father loves the Son, the Son the Father, and so on.[18] So at a moment of generosity or compassion, if someone expresses love in the purest way, the focus is not on himself at all. Rather, it's on the person to whom he is showing the generosity or compassion. Love is for the other's benefit. His love for the other person is for the other's interest, not his own—even though it ultimately corresponds with his own.

---

[14]Anselm, *De Concordia* 3.11; *De Casu Diaboli* 12. Reformed ethicist John Hare makes much of this in his *God and Morality: A Philosophical History* (Oxford: Wiley Blackwell, 2009), esp. 92.

[15]John Duns Scotus, *Reportatio* II, d. 6, q. 2, n. 10, trans. Thomas Williams, in "From Metaethics to Action Theory," in *The Cambridge Companion to Duns Scotus*, ed. Thomas Williams (Cambridge: Cambridge University Press, 2003), 346.

[16]Old Testament scholar Dennis Kinlaw writes, "Self-interest is the supreme characteristic of a sinful person. It has been said that sinfulness is to be 'curved inward upon oneself.' Conversely, the purpose of the redemption offered by Christ is to undo our distorted orientation—to turn us outward, so that we are not interested in ourselves but in the well-being of others. . . . Self-interest is well demonstrated by the question, 'What's in it for me?' Jesus never strived to get something for himself. The Gospels relate no instance in which Jesus' self-interest was his first consideration." Dennis Kinlaw, *The Mind of Christ* (Anderson, IN: Francis Asbury Press, 1998), 101.

[17]*Perichoresis* is the Greek term often used to describe the relationship between the persons of the Godhead. It translates literally to "rotation" in English and is also defined as co-indwelling, co-inhering, and mutual interpenetration.

[18]David Baggett and Ronnie Campbell, "Omnibenevolence, Moral Apologetics, and Doubly Ramified Natural Theology," *Philosophia Christi* 15, no. 2 (Spring 2014): 337-52, explores this theme in greater detail.

Such a consideration helps make sense of Romans 9:3. There Paul, in the grip of genuine and profound grief over the state of apostasy many of his fellow Jews have fallen into, plays a remarkable role as an intercessor: "For I could wish that I myself were accursed and cut off from Christ for the sake of my brethren, my kinsmen by race." What is often cast in English translations as Paul's "wish" or "desire" is likely better interpreted as his *prayer*, the common New Testament rendering of the particular Greek word used here.

In Romans 10:1 Paul reiterates prayer language regarding his wish for his fellow Jews. Perhaps most importantly of all, Paul is almost certainly making an allusion to the paradigmatic scriptural example of Israel's apostasy in Exodus 32–34 that has as its focal point Moses' famous intercessory prayer in Exodus 32:32. After the idolatry and apostasy of his people during the exodus, Moses prays, "But now, if thou wilt forgive their sin—and if not, blot me, I pray thee, out of thy book which thou hast written." Most Bible commentators think the allusion to Moses in Paul is clear, despite the lack of verbal similarity between Romans 9:3 and Exodus 32:32. The parallels between Exodus 32–34 and Romans 9–11, their thematic coherence, amount, and the recurrence of the allusion are strong enough to persuade most commentators to affirm it.[19]

Moses pleads for mercy for his people, asking to be included among them if they are not forgiven. The *book* to which Moses is likely referring is the book of the covenant, which is the last book mentioned prior to this passage. To be removed from the book would entail exclusion from the benefits and blessings of the covenant people. In a similar vein, Paul, rather than asking for his sacrifice to serve in lieu of the punishment his fellow Jews deserve because they are rejecting Christ, echoes the same spirit as Moses by identifying with them. Clearly Paul is not writing them off. The parallel with Moses may well reveal that Paul's prayer, though undoubtedly sincere in a very deep sense, is already shown to be a prayer that God will not answer (by removing Paul from among the covenant people and relegating Paul to hell).

---

[19]Gordon-Conwell Theological Seminary professor Brian Abasciano makes this case in his exegesis of Romans 9. For example, see Brian J. Abasciano, *Paul's Use of the Old Testament in Romans 9.1-9: An Intertextual and Theological Exegesis* (Edinburgh: Bloomsbury, 2006).

Nevertheless, that perdition in Paul's case would have been, *per impossibile*, the potential result of his prayer infinitely intensifies the seriousness of the intercession. Moses may have had little conception of an afterlife at that stage in salvation history, whereas Paul had a quite fleshed-out account. The hypothetical, however remote, does not diminish its value in conveying a truly self-sacrificial spirit of intercession.

Much could be discussed when it comes to the parallel between Moses and Paul here, but the present point is confined to their shared self-sacrificial spirit of intercession. Both were operating within a framework of covenantal promises. Both were contending with watching their people reject God's chosen mediator, and both were willing to throw in their lots with the rebellious among their brothers and sisters.

For present purposes, what both powerfully illustrate is a spirit of putting others before themselves, of self-sacrificial love and intercession. Arguably, this is at the heart of the Christian message. Heavenly hope is a glorious hope indeed. But the essence of the Christian message is intimacy with God that has among its effects our growing in conformity with Christ and learning to love as he loves.

To see what such love looks like, we must look to the cross, which is about radical self-denial and self-renunciation. This is the thought behind the words of Jonathan Edwards, repeated at the close of Presbyterian ordination services for generations: "I would be willing to be damned for the sake of the glory of God."[20] Such a profound sentiment—even if in principle never fully able to be attained but only approached, and by God's grace never in practice actually required—comports with the spirit of Paul's and Moses' intercession.

In Philippians 2:4-8 we find this:

> Let each of you look not only to his own interests, but also to the interests of others. Have this mind among yourselves, which is yours in Christ Jesus, who, though he was in the form of God, did not count equality with God a thing to be grasped, but emptied himself, taking the form of a servant, being born in the likeness of men. And being found

---

[20]Jonathan Edwards, *Religious Affections*, ed. John E. Smith (New Haven, CT: Yale University Press, 1959), chap. x.

in human form he humbled himself and became obedient unto death, even death on a cross.

Often Philippians 2:4 is translated to say not to look *alone* to one's own interests, or *only* to one's own interests (as in the RSV), or to look to the interests of others *also*, which is not the right translation, so why is it there? Dennis Kinlaw conjectures that it is because we twenty-first-century Christians don't believe the Lord can deliver us from self-interest, so we insert our assumptions.[21]

We are told by Jesus in the New Testament to "love one another as I have loved you. Greater love has no man than this, that a man lay down his life for his friends" (Jn 15:12-13). Jesus came to serve and be expended and sacrificed. He knew God would exalt him, it is true, which doubtless served as great solace as he endured unspeakable suffering for us. But to say that this is the reason he did it—more so than out of his love for us—is to foist a reading on Scripture that seems at variance with the consistent biblical motif that other-regarding holy love is God's central quality and guiding motivation, which combined best exemplify God's glory.

Before there was ever a world over which to be sovereign, God was love, so the pages of Scripture and the doctrine of the Trinity tell us. When the Bible speaks of our sharing in God's glory, it means first and foremost to share in God's holy other-regarding love—not a desire for self-aggrandizement or self-exaltation. Falling short of God's glory is due to sin—the essentially self-regarding orientation of carnality. Being conformed to the image of Christ turns self-interested motivations upside down and inside out.

We are called to love God with all of our hearts and souls and minds, and our neighbor as ourselves (Mt 22:37-40). The most important command makes no mention of pursuing pleasure or happiness as a necessary motivation for virtue or worship. Self-love is presupposed in the second-most-important command—and one vitally connected to the first. In a sense we cannot help but love ourselves. It is the way we're hardwired.

---

[21]Dennis Kinlaw, *The Mind of Christ* (Anderson, IN: Francis Asbury Press, 1998), 101.

Making the choice to privilege the pursuit of one's fulfillment, one's happiness, as the most exalted motivation of all, though, goes beyond what's in evidence. In fact it goes contrary to many of the explicit teachings of the Bible, which privilege an other-regarding orientation of love.

At the heart of the Christian message are powerful truths about self-sacrifice. Indeed, there's something profoundly right about the "disinterested benevolence" of which Edwards spoke—the radical commitment to God no matter what, even if it means the loss of our joy. Similarly, the Pauline passage of self-sacrifice shouldn't be dismissed too soon—as if the whole reason it's there is for us to say that it couldn't happen. Indeed, it couldn't happen, but there's something else important to see here: in principle, at some level, that's the sort of commitment God deserves, and that's the sort of fate we should be willing to endure.

We should love God and others that much. Of course, psychologically, this is all entirely beyond our own powers, but we still recognize in these examples something of a decisive moral end: to love others so much that we're willing to make the ultimate sacrifice of ourselves. Happiness shouldn't be our greatest and deepest goal.

Christianity goes a step further, for part of the gloriously good news of the Christian gospel is that there's also something profoundly *wrong* about the "disinterested benevolence" of which Edwards spoke, because God is not that kind of God. *In principle* the standard remains, putting to the lie that Christianity is at its heart a mercenary exercise. But *in reality*, because of who God is, it will never have to be met by us because the world will ultimately be shown to make perfect moral sense. God would never send a redeemed and faithful child to hell forever, demanding his worship anyway. He is not that kind of God. The gospel really is *good news!*

Likewise, in Paul's case, the passage is there for good reasons, among them to show that there's a more powerful goal, a more ennobling motivation, than simply one's own happiness. Primacy is not to be assigned to pleasure or happiness alone but to something even greater, something very much like self-giving love, the very sort of love operative in and characteristic of the Trinity itself.

To live such love, by God's grace, is to know God himself most deeply, where fullness of joy can be found, the only source of the deepest satisfactions for which we were made. He is a God of unspeakable love, infinitely deserving of our deepest devotion, worthy to be trusted with our profoundest needs and most passionate desires. Entrusting ourselves to him in love, obedience, and service yields a hope that will not disappoint and a joy that will endure forever.

Near the end of *Till We Have Faces*, Orual hears some disconcerting words. After much of the book has dwelt on her indictment of the gods, she's told, "He is coming. The god is coming into his house. The god comes to judge Orual." A reckoning is coming, and now Orual is on trial. But she has come to know who she is and to grasp the sense in which philosophy taught her how to die, before it was too late. She has realized the ravenous darkness within, the clamor and rancor of selfishness, that what she'd thought was her best was actually her worst. She has also come to see the grace available to be transformed, the divine surgery that can excise the malady within. She has stopped fighting, which will make the imminent reckoning not something dreadful but something beyond wonderful.

"The earth and stars and sun, all that was or will be, existed for his sake. And he was coming. The most dreadful, the most beautiful, the only dread and beauty there is, was coming. The pillars on the far side of the pool flushed with his approach." Orual casts down her eyes. And there, reflected in water, are two figures, two reflections, her beautiful sister Psyche's and her own.

But there are two Psyches, both beautiful beyond all imagining, yet not exactly the same. "You also are Psyche," she hears. She has been transformed and made into a thing of ineffable beauty, her individuality intact. Her reckoning, transformation, distinctive loveliness, capacity for selfless love, and joy unspeakable are all summoned, convened together, and happily reconciled in that glorious moment—in the presence of the one who, all along, was the answer she sought, before whose face "questions die away."[22]

---

[22]C. S. Lewis, *Till We Have Faces: A Myth Retold* (New York: Harcourt Brace Jovanovich, 1956).

And with that, Act Two comes to a close. We have now seen the fourfold moral case for God. Moral ontology and epistemology, and the two dimensions of moral faith, collectively constitute the full moral case for the existence of God it was this book's intention to offer. In each case, theism (and in some cases, only distinctively Christian theism) has been argued to possess superior resources to provide their explanation and grounds, their possibility and plausibility.

## TALK BACK

1. Why is it important to subordinate a desire for happiness to a desire for holiness? In what ways might moral hope enable moral motivation?

2. How might the prevalence of evil in this world mandate a moral obligation to hope? How can the resources of the moral argument bolster such hope?

3. Do you believe that self-sacrificial love is possible? What evidence do we have from Scripture of such love?

ACT III

# ENACTING
# THE COMEDY

Now that we've introduced the main players, what story about the world we live in do they tell? As we've seen, moral goodness, moral obligations, moral knowledge, transformation, and providence are compelling indeed and intimate, rich features of reality. Although we've examined them in isolation to this point, they are not dry, dusty, lifeless things. Instead, they participate in a beautiful performance, together enacting an alluring dance that tells of life and love and joy. Act Three takes the various arguments that constitute Act Two of this book to reveal the cumulative strength of the whole case, arguing that theism and Christianity explain this assortment of moral realities in a powerful and coherent way.

Step by step we've gone, showcasing along the way the moral demand and our inability to reach it, the attractiveness of goodness and how far our world is from it. But as we'll see, the gospel steps into this reality, turning what seemed a tragedy on its head—for the tale morality truly tells, on a Christian view, what these players bring to life, is an unsurpassable comedy.

# CHAPTER 10

# A GALA PERFORMANCE

*He has showed you, O man, what is good;*
*and what does the* LORD *require of you*
*but to do justice, and to love kindness,*
*and to walk humbly with your God?*

MICAH 6:8

AT LONG LAST THE TIME HAS COME to assemble all the pieces and put the whole moral case together. The case is cumulative, abductive, and teleological. It is cumulative in the sense that it contains four main parts: moral facts, moral knowledge, moral transformation, and moral rationality. It is abductive in that it argues that theism and Christianity provide the *best* (not necessarily the *only*) explanation of moral phenomena. The case is consistently teleological because all of morality is suffused with a divine purpose or goal: God's kingdom and his righteousness, and the abundant life for which we were created.

The colorful actors in the play we have arranged, or characters in the narrative, have ranged from values and obligations, and from evil and agency, to moral knowledge and Kantian moral faith. Together they pack quite a punch. To reveal why, let's review the evidence, tie up some loose ends, and try to feel the force of the whole case.

Once more, allow us to reiterate that we realize that we haven't answered every question or provided anything like a slam-dunk argument. Resistance at numerous junctures is natural, expected, and healthy.

Philosophy is hard. What we endeavored to do here is give readers enough food for thought so they can savor what we have to say, whether or not they come to agree. It's the start of a discussion, not the end.

## MORAL VALUES AND OBLIGATIONS

We began with moral values, the topic of moral goodness in particular, and zeroed in on something of great intrinsic value: human beings themselves.[1] C. Stephen Evans refers to a few moral "natural signs," which, he argues, point not just to God's existence but to God's nature. The God to which such signs point is a God who is essentially good and desires a relationship with human persons. A natural sign functions to make people aware of God's reality but does not entail God's existence. The evidence, though real, is resistible and subject to various interpretations.

The two moral natural signs are the sense of moral obligations and a special sense of worth and dignity. Similarly, William Lane Craig's moral argument references objective values and duties. This book took for its test case of objective moral values the specific issue of distinctive human value—distinguished from a mere "price." Examining various substantive ethical theories, we saw that, divorced from a theistic framework, they are prone to fail to undergird intrinsic human dignity and the sort of basic human rights that such dignity entails.

John Hare writes that when we look at the great movements toward the recognition of *human* value over the last sixty years, we will often find a religious motivation: "I am thinking of Martin Luther King and the civil rights movement, and the Lutherans in East Germany and the fall of the totalitarian state. Why is this? It is because of the nature of the God they worship." Hare admits it is true that belonging to a community is very important, but the God of Abraham not only includes us in community but pushes us out beyond community, to meet the needs of the

---

[1]David Bentley Hart writes, "Among the mind's transcendental aspirations, it is the longing for moral goodness that is probably the most difficult to contain within the confines of a naturalist metaphysics." David Bentley Hart, *The Experience of God: Being, Consciousness, Bliss* (New Haven, CT: Yale University Press, 2013), 251.

poor and the marginalized who are the objects of God's care just as much as we are. "God commands both the inclusion and the moving out."[2]

On the specific issue of human dignity—intrinsic human worth—we are inclined to think that most everyone can apprehend such a reality. The question we must face, though, is what best accounts for such value?[3] A naturalist may have a deep appreciation for intrinsic human value, but that doesn't mean that he has an adequate or the best explanation for what makes it the case that human persons have this dignity.

A quick example is late secular philosopher Philippa Foot, whose book *Natural Goodness* attempted to provide a purely naturalistic understanding of moral goodness by appeal to what she called "natural normativities." The thirty-two teeth humans have or the reproductive patterns of rabbits are examples of such species-specific natural normativities, which came about as a result of evolution. Particular natural normativities—such as, say, the enjoyment of friendships among humans—conduce to our survival and flourishing, and, for that reason, take on distinctively *moral* significance.

Interestingly, however, Foot denied being a consequentialist, so she would not have said that friendship is good because it promotes human welfare. In fact, she would deny this, just as she would deny that what promotes the life of cancer cells is a good thing. Hers is a nonconsequentialist analysis. But notice that what she has not provided is reason to think, on her view, that human survival is *an intrinsically good thing*.[4]

Or take Christina Korsgaard's effort to articulate a Kantian sort of account of morality in her *Sources of Normativity*. She thinks what separates humans from other animals is their ability to act on the basis of a self-conception, what she calls a "practical identity," such as "mother" or "economist." She thinks practical identities create unconditional obligations. But surely we don't want to say the Mafioso has an obligation to perform some horrible misdeed to retain his self-chosen identity.

---

[2]John E. Hare, *God's Command* (Oxford: Oxford University Press, 2015), 307-8.

[3]Or at least a question in its vicinity, such as what is the only explanation of such value? Or is such value more likely on theism or on atheism? And so on.

[4]See Philippa Foot, *Natural Goodness* (Oxford: Clarendon, 2001).

Korsgaard responds to the challenge by saying the Mafioso has a deeper obligation to give up his immoral role. She says that our identity as moral beings—as people who value themselves as human beings—stands behind our more particular practical identities. But her attempt to do justice to the Kantian principle of respect for others seems to be a tacit recognition of moral realism—that others are in fact worthy of being shown such respect and accorded such dignity. She is altogether right to affirm that people have intrinsic value grounded simply in the *kinds of beings that they are*, but this reflects a sort of moral realism to which she claims to be offering an alternative.[5]

Or take a social contractarian analysis, according to which we, as a society, might agree, tacitly or explicitly, to accord and respect the rights of others. This would be tantamount to denying that there are such things as basic human rights, because until they come into existence through the social contract, they didn't exist. Basic human rights on this account are thus altogether contingent. Time and again, secular efforts seem able to go only so far to account for basic human rights and inherent human dignity.

In contrast, on a Christian understanding, the value of human persons is found in the personhood of God. "The value of human persons is found in the fact that, as bearers of the *imago dei*, they retain a significant resemblance to God in their very personhood. God and human persons share an overlap of kind membership in personhood itself, and human dignity is found precisely in membership in that kind."[6]

Moreover, persons aren't valuable only in the aggregate, but each and every person is of inestimable worth and dignity. To be loved by God, the very locus of goodness itself—each of us differently, but all of us infinitely—to have been created by God for a purpose, to have been imbued with inalienable rights, to be invited into a relationship of perfect and perfecting love, to be created for good works and a specific calling:

---

[5]See Christine M. Korsgaard, *The Sources of Normativity* (Cambridge: Cambridge University Press, 1998).
[6]Mark Linville, "The Moral Argument," in *The Blackwell Companion to Natural Theology*, ed. William Lane Craig and J. P. Moreland (Hoboken, NJ: Blackwell, 2009), 443.

this is the sort of robust and significant account needed to do justice to our deep-seated intuitions and apprehensions concerning the dignity and value of persons.

What about moral obligations? As we discussed earlier, moral obligations, robustly and classically construed, are authoritative and an odd fit in a naturalistic world. A number of naturalists are giving up on the whole idea of moral obligations, recognizing their incongruity in the world as they conceive it. Many of them are unwilling to water the concept of moral obligations down to something more domesticated. Furthermore, they are willing to bite the proverbial bullet, embrace the implications of their worldview, and eschew objective moral obligations.

This is by no means to suggest that most naturalists are willing to jettison the category of moral obligation. Many of them retain it and insist they can continue making good sense of it. Even if they can make sense of a kind of moral obligation, though, we've been arguing that their explanation won't be as good an explanation as theism and Christianity can provide. We don't consider our case an ace, just a serve. Returns are expected and welcomed.

As moral skeptics rightly recognize, the authority of moral obligations needs an account. The Anscombe intuition requires explanation. We submit that Christian theism—entailing a loving, perfect God who commands, who knows us better than we know ourselves, who knows truly what is in our ultimate best interest, and who desires the best for us—can most effectively provide it. Little wonder that Alvin Plantinga thinks a moral argument on the basis of objective moral obligations is the best piece of natural theology on offer, and that Craig reports that this is the most persuasive argument he presents on college campuses.

## EVIL AND AGENCY

Before moving on to the issue of moral knowledge, we thought it would be worthwhile to touch on a relevant issue, namely, the problem of evil and moral agency. Paul Copan writes,

> The fact that people can recognize evil in the world suggests a moral compass that is not arbitrary. Kant spoke not only of the starry heavens

above but also of "the moral law within." If real evils exist in the world—
evils we associate with Stalin, Hitler, Pol Pot, and Mao Tse-Tung—then
we are assuming an objective design plan of sorts: there is a way things
ought to be, and evil is a departure from that.

But if there is no design plan and nature is all there is, then why think
things should be any different from the way they are? And maybe the evils
in the world, especially when they directly affect us, can serve as something of a wake-up call for us. The familiar cry for justice—as old as humanity itself—suggests a transcendent moral standard above national
laws and social contracts. Not only does evil remind us that things ought
to be different from the way that they are; it also reminds us of the need
for outside assistance to address profound evils both outside of us and
within our own hearts. We all have a deep longing that evil will not have
the last word.[7]

Evil is often touted as excellent evidence against God's existence, but we
remain deeply unconvinced. Evil is horrible indeed, but its very horribleness
is little accounted for by a naturalistic perspective. On that sort of worldview,
why expect anything different? Take for now only the example of moral
evils—the evils perpetrated by people on other people. On a naturalistic
perspective, the likely scenario is that we are complicated organic machines
whose every behavior is an inevitable result of the causal laws at work in the
world combined with the preexisting conditions. How, on that sort of view,
is there any room for moral guilt, moral regret, moral condemnation? How
could there be genuine moral agency, or ability to do otherwise?

We are not suggesting naturalists don't care about evil but that naturalism itself has a hard time taking it with the seriousness it deserves. It's
exactly because so many of them do take evil seriously that we'd suggest
they should subject their worldview to critical scrutiny on this score.

Regarding the previous topic of moral obligations, how could there
be such things in a world in which everything that happens is determined to take place just as it does? Plenty of secularists and naturalists

---

[7]Paul Copan and Kenneth D. Litwak, *The Gospel in the Marketplace of Ideas* (Downers Grove, IL:
InterVarsity Press, 2014), 148. (Pretty good, Paul. Just remember: every time the coffee machine
at work breaks down, there's no need to ask what the grounds are for believing it. Just say no.
We're rooting for you.)

themselves are coming to this very conclusion, and for good reason. In truth, much of the perceived force of the problem of evil is parasitic on aspects of a transcendent understanding of good and evil that is hard if not impossible to make sense of in a naturalistic world.

What does make excellent sense of the real existence of moral goodness and its opposite, moral evil, is theism generally and Christianity particularly. The entirety of the biblical revelation is the story of what God is doing to bring healing to this world, banishing all suffering and evil and corruption altogether.

Sin and death are indeed our enemies, enemies that Christ will defeat completely. As Trappist monk Thomas Merton puts it, "It is of the very essence of Christianity to face suffering and death not because they are good, not because they have meaning, but because the resurrection of Jesus has robbed them of their meaning."[8] Evil is a distortion of the good. Christianity teaches that the world is being set to rights, and evil subverted and defeated.

Great missionary to India E. Stanley Jones once gave an address on evil and suffering in which he offered the Christian response to suffering:

> That you can take hold of suffering and sorrow and frustration and injustice and not bear it, but use it. Almost everything beautiful in the pages of the New Testament has come out of something ugly. Almost everything glorious has come out of something shameful. [Christians] don't ask to be exempt. They don't ask to be taken out of suffering. All they ask is inner soundness of spirit so they can take hold of the raw materials of human life as it comes to them—justice and injustice, pleasure and pain, compliment and criticism. And they can take it up into the purpose of their lives and transmute it and make it into something else. That is an open possibility of living—in spite of.[9]

In that same address, Jones tells of the conversion of twentieth-century Chinese political and military leader General Chiang Kai-shek.

---

[8]Thomas Merton, "To Know the Cross," in *Bread and Wine: Readings for Lent and Easter* (Walden, NY: Plough, 2003), 45.

[9]David Baggett and Marybeth Baggett, *At the Bend of the River Grand: One Hundred Thirty Years of the Passionate Pursuit of Holiness at Eaton Rapids Camp Meeting (1885–2015)* (Lexington, KY: Emeth, 2016), 92-93.

His wife attributes his embrace of Christianity to the witness of a Christian medical worker whose lived-out response to evil testified to the gospel's truth:

> When Chiang Kai-shek's army swept across that country, in the early days, . . . and they looted a hospital belonging to a missionary . . . his life work went to pieces. But he followed after the army and tended to their sick and their wounded. When Chiang Kai-shek heard about it, he said, "What makes that man follow after and tend to the sick and wounded of the very people who looted his hospital? What makes him do it?" And they said, "He's a Christian. That's why he does it." Then said Chiang Kai-shek, "If that's what it means to be a Christian, I'm going to be a Christian." Then, in the midst of an anti-Christian movement that was sweeping that country, to the astonishment of everybody, Chiang Kai-shek announced that he was a Christian. That doctor had calamity come upon him, but through that calamity, he showed his spirit. And through the revelation of that spirit, he won one of the greatest men of this age. And through him, it may win a great nation. You see, he took hold of injustice and turned it into something else. He had mastered a way to live. And it may be that through your suffering and frustration and defeat, you can show a spirit, and that spirit will do far more work than all your years of work. They'll look through that little revelation, and they'll see something eternal abiding in that moment. That's the Christian answer. The Christian answer is to take hold of everything and make it into something else. That is victory.[10]

A naturalistic understanding of reality has little to offer by way of hope in the face of evil, or resources to suggest that the world should be anything different. Neither can naturalism make much sense of meaningful agency, certainly not the sort of free will required for ascriptions of genuine moral responsibility. Without such freedom, however, how can we make sense of a category such as *regret*?[11]

---

[10]Ibid.

[11]William James once described a hideous scene of a man killing his wife, which stirred powerful revulsion in the hearts of his readers. With a masterful stroke of understatement, he then added, "We feel that, although a perfect mechanical fit to the rest of the universe, it is a bad moral fit, and that something else would really have been better in its place." He then soberly adds, "But for the deterministic philosophy the murder, the sentence, and the prisoner's optimism were all necessary from eternity; and nothing else for a moment had a ghost of a chance of being put

On a robust theistic vision of reality, the human condition is something very different. We have been conferred meaningful free will, the sort of agency to make morally significant decisions. Without such freedom, ascriptions of moral responsibility simply don't make sense, any more than holding an ATM responsible for malfunctioning. If we are the product of nature and nurture alone, and all our decisions are determined, then we are not the relevant source of our actions. It's hard to see how, on naturalism, we can rightly be held deeply responsible for our choices.[12]

## MORAL KNOWLEDGE

How well does naturalism fare in comparison to theism in explaining the category of moral knowledge? Prospects for a tracking account are brighter on a theistic account. Theism can provide a better explanation of the reliability of our moral cognitive processes, a more direct tracking account.

It is a deeply teleological account of moral knowledge, based on an intentional explanation of our belief-generating and belief-evaluating capacities that track objective moral truth. Angus Ritchie writes, "All that the theist needs to add to the account given by evolutionary biology is the claim that the world is providentially ordered so that the interaction of the quasi-teleological process of natural selection and of the spandrel-like features it generates yield an outcome which enables human beings to apprehend that which is of objective value."[13]

---

into their place." William James, "The Dilemma of Determinism," in *The Will to Believe and Other Essays in Popular Philosophy* (New York: Dover, 1956), 147.

[12]It's notoriously difficult to convince those who claim to be skeptical about free will that we're actually free—but such persons insisting we should be doing anything different right now lacks much sense. Kant initially tried to construct an argument for freedom but later thought better of it, realizing his argument was circular. What he saw, though, and we're inclined to agree, is that something like genuine free will in more than a compatibilist sense is needed if the deliverances of morality are to be taken with great seriousness. This, though, requires human persons to be more than what naturalists say they are. We must be more than collocations of atoms if we are to be significantly free moral agents, able to be held deeply responsible for our choices. Ascriptions of either moral praise or blame make little if any sense if naturalism is true, but such ascriptions, we have good reason to think, *do* make excellent sense, which gives us reason to look for a better worldview.

[13]Angus Ritchie, *From Morality to Metaphysics: The Theistic Implications of Our Ethical Commitments* (Oxford: Oxford University Press, 2012), 174.

In terms of a nontracking account, recall that David Enoch's attempt to explain correlation without tracking also seems more workable on theism than atheism. This is because Enoch himself doesn't, and likely can't, predicate his view on the intrinsic value of human persons or their survival. Christian theism, in contrast and in particular, identifies for the human telos not mere biological survival but rich and abundant *life*—thriving, flourishing, *eudaimonia*, *shalom*, all packed into one. We saw this in our earlier foray into biblical theology that yielded the theme of *life* as perhaps the central biblical motif.

What the Bible makes clear is that God wants to live among his people, to indwell them. Forgiveness of sins is not enough. We must be healed of sin itself, and we are to move on toward indwelling—perhaps even transfiguration. Time and again in the biblical narrative, what impedes God's presence in the lives of his people is sin and unfaithfulness. Why is it so important for God to live in his people? Why is such immediate presence necessary? Ezekiel 47:1-12, among other passages, shows that one of the major benefits of the presence of the living God is that it gives life in abundance. Life bursts forth; even fertility breaks loose. Who will live in God's tent?, Psalm 15 asks. He who walks blamelessly, who doesn't slander.

What such passages show is that God wants to *impart* his holiness. Not through some sort of rigid legalism, rule upon rule, but by a conversion of the heart. God wants to give us a heart of love, by which all sorts of rules will automatically be followed. Love is central to God's purposes, because God is love. This is why loving God with all of our heart, soul, mind, and strength, and our neighbor as ourselves, fulfills the whole law. By becoming people of love, we can fulfill God's law. Love is the pathway of holiness. Love has for its deepest passion bringing the other to the fullness of life. To seek God and his highest is to seek abundant life.

Our earlier exploration of biblical theology arose in our discussion of propositional knowledge, which is altogether fitting, because its culmination in a life of perfect love is possible as we come to know God personally. We need to do more than *know about* God. We are privileged to *know God*. Such knowledge bespeaks intimacy, experience with, relationship, love. God is not a proposition to assent to in sanguine fashion.

He is a personal God of perfect love who invites us into vital communion with him. Such a relationship, moreover, is altogether transformative, the next issue to consider.

## MORAL FAITH

Intimacy with God holds out the prospect for transformation—indeed, the hope of complete transformation. This is the first aspect of Kantian moral faith: the moral transformation that can take place with God's help. Even prior to the issue of transformation is the need for forgiveness. But what Christianity teaches is that by God's grace we can be both forgiven and changed to the uttermost.

Here's how John Oswalt, a Wesleyan and distinguished Old Testament scholar, puts it: the Wesleyan movement generally (and the Wesleyan camp meeting tradition specifically) exists

> to proclaim to the world and the church the full message of salvation, that not only is Christ's power sufficient to save a person from the guilt and condemnation of sin, but also from its power. How desperately the Church and the world need to know that God can deliver us from self-serving and self-centeredness, that he can enable us to live lives that are truly an expression of the holiness of God, in moral purity, in spiritual power, and in self-giving love.[14]

Without the life-imparting resources of Christian theism, prospects for moral improvement seem destined to be nominal at most, and finally futile and doomed to failure. At death any incremental moral improvement is the end of the story, and aspirations for more are wishful thinking.

Christianity, in contrast, teaches that our highest ethical yearning can be satisfied. God can replace our heart of stone with a heart of flesh. He can effect a revolution of the will and solve Spener's problem by making us not just *better* people but *new* people. He can allow Anselm's affection for justice to assume primacy over the affection for advantage. He can heal the "dear self" and can replace the evil maxim with the good one.

---

[14]Baggett and Baggett, *At the Bend of the River Grand*, 276.

He can save us to the uttermost and make all things new. He can transform us into the people he intended us to be, holy as he is holy.

Not only that, he can solve the dualism of practical reason—reconciling happiness and holiness. What seems an irremediable tension on naturalism can be entirely reconciled on Christian theism. Not only is radical transformation available in a robust, vibrant, saving relationship with God, there we also find our deepest joy, the profoundest satisfactions for which we were made. They go intimately hand in hand.

Even still, though, there is something higher than our own happiness that gets priority, which can help resolve an otherwise befuddling biblical conundrum. Why, we might wonder, in the unfolding progression of God's revelation, is God slow to make teaching explicit about the afterlife? For Abraham, for example—whose faith is the paradigm for us—there was little to no awareness or expectation of life after death.[15]

C. S. Lewis, in his *Reflections on the Psalms*, offers at least one attempt at an account:

> It is surely . . . very possible that when God began to reveal himself to men, to show them that He and nothing else is their true goal and the satisfaction of their needs, and that He has a claim upon them simply by being what He is, quite apart from anything He can bestow or deny, it may have been absolutely necessary that his revelation should not begin with any hint of future Beatitude or Perdition. Those are not the right point to begin at. An effective belief in them, coming too soon, may even render almost impossible the development of (so to call it) the appetite for God; personal hopes and fears, too obviously exciting, have got in first.[16]

God wanted our love and fidelity, with nothing at first except this-worldly benefits in return. Then, in the fullness of time, he let the proverbial

---

[15]See Dennis Kinlaw, *Lectures in Old Testament Theology* (Anderson, IN: Francis Asbury Press, 2011), 125, where Kinlaw writes, "There is no indication that Abraham was expecting God to do something in the other world. Abraham was expecting Him to do it in the here and now."

[16]C. S. Lewis, *Reflections on the Psalms* (New York: Houghton Mifflin Harcourt, 1964), 40.

cat out of the bag and revealed that not only *can* our appetite for God be satisfied, but it *can and will be eternally satisfied.* For those who love and obey God, who come to know him and experience the abundant life of intimacy with him, there isn't the slightest possibility of anything less than the eternal fullness of joy for which he made us.

If trinitarian love is primordial reality, we can never advance our true self-interest by selfish behavior, but when we selflessly return love to the God of perfect love, we thereby inevitably promote our own ultimate well-being and highest happiness. Christian theism explains how morality can be a fully rational enterprise and consistent with a hope that won't disappoint and that liberates us from moral despair.

## ALL TOGETHER NOW

Put all the pieces together, and the result is momentous: a cumulative, abductive, teleological moral argument for God's existence. It ranges metaphysical and epistemic matters and speaks powerfully about the problem of evil and moral agency. It accounts for moral knowledge and canvasses both aspects of Kantian moral faith.

The divine loom weaves together the warp of moral facts with the weft of moral knowledge and, by turns, the taut threads of moral faith.[17] To vary the metaphor, in the same way that a labyrinthine maze of jumbled metal filings suddenly stands in symmetrical formation in response to the pull of a magnet, likewise, the right organizing story—classical theism and orthodox Christianity—pulls all the moral pieces of evidence into alignment and allows a striking pattern to emerge.

As a result, our case for theism features not only the explanatory advantages of each individual part but also the added epistemic merit of a package that deeply coheres and together constitutes a compelling organic whole. Christian theism provides the necessary explanations, and, in our estimation, does so better than its alternatives. This is evidentially significant, as well as intuitively, intellectually, and aesthetically satisfying.

---

[17]The following two paragraphs draw on material from David Baggett and Jerry Walls included in *God and Cosmos: Moral Truth and Human Meaning* (New York: Oxford University Press, 2016), 300.

**TALK BACK**

1. Do you conceive of God as all-good, all-loving, all-knowing, all-powerful? If not, what resistance do you have to this conception? If you think of him in this way, how does that conception influence your life and faith?

2. What is the Christian conception of personhood?

3. We quote E. Stanley Jones as saying that almost everything in the New Testament came out of something ugly. Can you think of any examples? What does it say about God that he can and does bring beauty out of ashes?

# A PLAY AT MARS HILL

*Those who practice philosophy in the
right way are in training for dying.*

SOCRATES, IN PLATO'S *PHAEDO*

IT WAS A BRILLIANT DAY IN JUNE, oppressively hot in the sun but surprisingly comfortable in the ample shade. Pitch-white cumulus clouds floated in a vivid blue sky, and the idyllic and picturesque scene, bordering the surreal, made belief in the gods tempting and altogether understandable. The scene was Athens, at Mars Hill, with the Areopagus off to our left and the formidable Parthenon looming, nearly hovering in its elevation, to our distant right. The year was 2013.

In front of my wife and other onlookers, I grabbed the fellow by his arm and ushered him before the crowd, demanding an explanation. He and I were role-playing a reenactment of Paul at Mars Hill. In reply to my demand for an account of his behavior and mysterious words, he launched into a meticulous and animated rendition of the famous Pauline passage from Acts 17, the topic of this book's spotlight. Antony Flew once said of Paul that he had a first-rate philosophical mind. My fellow thespian has such a mind as well, not to mention an infectious flair for the dramatic. His name is William Lane Craig.

I first spent serious time with Craig when he, Paul Copan, Jerry Walls, and I held a book panel discussion on *Good God* in San Francisco, organized by my friend Mark Foreman. Knowing Craig and I were going to lock horns on a few issues, I was of course petrified beyond words. Christopher Hitchens said Craig was the one theist who could strike fear in the hearts of atheists. With the prospect of facing off with Craig on a few points, I became existentially acquainted with such fear myself, and I'm a theist! It turned out to be a memorable occasion, and I've been grateful ever since that Craig didn't melt me with his brain. In truth the warmth of both Craig and Copan that day made the event nothing less than a delight for me and Jerry.

What made the panel discussion in California especially gratifying was that Copan had been Craig's student, and I had been Walls's student. The protégés relished time with their mentors that day. One of Jerry Walls's teachers at Notre Dame was Alvin Plantinga, incidentally, whom we've had occasion to mention several times in this book. One of my favorite stories about Jerry is the time he cropped a page from an article in which Plantinga, appropriately edited, wrote, "I'm inclined to agree with Walls." Then he proceeded to blow it up, got Plantinga to sign it, framed it, and hung it on his office wall.

Anyway, a few years after the panel discussion, on the Reasonable Faith cruise that stopped at Athens, my wife and I were privileged to get to know Bill and Jan Craig quite a bit better. In addition to being one of the kindest and most distinguished fellows we have ever met, Craig is, in our estimation, the greatest living Christian apologist. So it was quite a moment to be able to play out the famous Mars Hill scene with, of all people, one of our heroes. Near where Plato and Euthyphro had their famous exchange, in the environs of the storied birthplace of Western philosophy, William Lane Craig, a few other players, and I performed our little play—him Paul, me Dionysius the Areopagite, one of Paul's famed converts.

Craig is excellent at articulating a variety of arguments for God's existence, perhaps none more so than the cosmological argument. In fact, one of our motivations in working on the moral argument is to contribute to its articulation with the same energy and rigor with which Craig has advanced the cosmological argument, or Gary Habermas the argument for the historicity of the resurrection, or Richard Swinburne the design argument, or Alvin Plantinga the modal ontological argument.

Of course we personally fall short in numerous respects, but it remains our aim. The resurgence of interest in the moral argument over the past few decades bodes well for the community of Christian philosophers to attain to the goal eventually.

Craig himself has done brilliant work on the moral argument, and his favored version pertains to objective moral values and duties—together making up the first dimension of this book's fourfold argument for God's existence. His approach features a deductive argument that goes like this:

1. If God doesn't exist, then objective moral values and duties don't exist.

2. But objective moral values and duties do exist.

3. So, God exists.

The argument of this book has been abductive rather than deductive. In a deductive argument, the premises logically guarantee the conclusion.[1] Craig has used this argument to good effect in a great many venues, and we celebrate his success. Our preferred approach, however, is to argue not that God is the *only* explanation of moral truth, but rather that God is the *best* explanation of various moral truths. Depending on the context, and how much time can be invested, both approaches—a deductive argument and an abductive argument—have their own advantages.

Stipulating the reasons for our preference enables us to construct an acrostic as pithy as it is cheesy, so of course we can't resist. To begin, the first premise of Craig's argument is based on a particularly troubling Counteressential: a world in which God, the very ground of being, doesn't exist. To speak of features of such a world is akin, to our thinking, to speculation about features of impossible worlds, which, outside analytic truths, seems problematic.

Second, Acknowledging the rich features of a world like our own, if it could exist without God, should weaken one's confidence that secular

---

[1] Again, in Craig's argument, the logical form is called *modus tollens*, and it's a logically valid argument form. This means that the relationship between the evidence and conclusion is airtight. If someone wishes to resist the argument, she has to call into question the truth of at least one of its premises. The logical form is impeccable.

ethics can explain nothing about morality. Of course, if classical Christianity is true, there couldn't be a world like this apart from God.

Third, Craig's opponents may be tempted to **R**eject moral realism rather than naturalism, as Joel Marks did, whom we discussed in an earlier chapter.

Fourth, ignoring legitimate insights from secular ethicists severs the **B**ridge it's helpful to build in dialogue with them, whereas a more abductive approach is freer to look for common ground.

Finally, **S**aying uncomfortable (and needless) things such as "Rape is morally okay if God doesn't exist," even if correct in some real sense, is off-putting and shuts down discussion rather than facilitating it. The abductive approach instead takes as axiomatic the wrongness of rape and invites a conversation about what best explains it, conducing to a dialogical approach.

Put them all together for the result: **C**ounteressential, **A**cknowledging, **R**eject, **B**ridge, and **S**aying: **CARBS**. Which aren't good for anybody! Of course we jest; as we said, his argument has a lot going for it and can be used to powerful effect.

Still, we think an abductive variant of the moral argument avoids the problem by asking what best explains various moral phenomena. This book has, in brief compass, offered a sustained abductive case that a theistic and Christian explanation trumps secular ethics. The latter is not without its resources, but if we're right, that's largely because, in truth, if God exists and is the Creator and sustainer of this world, not a square inch of it is really secular after all. God and the world, we are convinced, provide the better explanation of moral realities than the world alone.

Once more, we celebrate the good success of Craig's approach to the moral argument, from which we have learned a great deal. Our disagreement, if it even qualifies as such, is a small and friendly one, and far eclipsed by the many and deep agreements we share with him. And in this light, with the warmest regards and deepest respect, we dedicate this small volume to him and his wife, Jan, dear friends and colaborers.

Far from an extraneous hypothesis, God completes the moral mosaic otherwise left undone. He is the great cornerstone of a mighty edifice, without which the building doesn't really come together. We have endeavored to make this case not as a mere intellectual exercise—but rather so that readers, if they haven't already, would consider opening their hearts and minds to the joy and hope on offer from the heart and hand of a perfectly loving God.

We had a lot of fun writing this book, and we hope that you enjoyed reading it. We're all in this together, and if it's the true, the good, and the beautiful you seek, we consider you a kindred spirit. Many blessings in your quest.

## TALK BACK

1. Compare and contrast Craig's deductive moral argument with our abductive argument. What do you find compelling about each?

2. Faith today is often dismissed as either intellectually dishonest or naive. In what ways might the various examples of the moral argument challenge that depiction?

3. Can you think of ways that you could draw from the resources of this book in talking with people from other faith traditions?

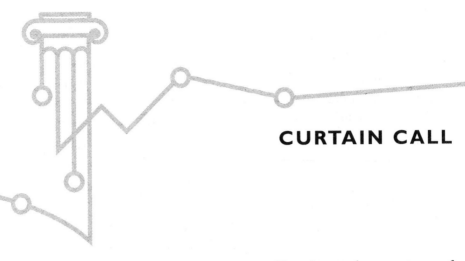

# CURTAIN CALL

THIS BOOK IS ONE OF SEVERAL of late that mark a resurgence of interest in theistic ethics and moral arguments for God's existence. Exciting new work is being done in this area, and we believe the best is yet to come. An evidential consideration in favor of a worldview is its ability to provide explanations of important phenomena with the resources at its ready disposal. Christian theism can explain a wide range of moral phenomena exquisitely well, we have argued, which counts as evidence in favor of its truth.

This book has been about faith, hope, and love. It's been about truth, goodness, and beauty. What has emerged is, in our estimation, a compelling set of considerations that merit the reader's closest attention and best energies of analysis.

The Christian gospel is glorious news, but in a number of contemporary circles it suffers a publicity nightmare. A message of hope and liberation, it frequently invokes specters of bondage. What promises forgiveness sounds instead like condemnation. Good news is heard as bad.

A variety of factors have contributed to this lamentable state of affairs—from the derision of religion by vocal opponents, the daily reminders of religious conviction gone awry, the off-putting sanctimony of some outspoken religious adherents. This book has been less concerned with exploring those reasons than in countering their results, by emphasizing again the radically glorious nature of the gospel using moral truth as a springboard.

We are convinced the most important mistake fueling (and stemming from) the current publicity crisis is a failure to understand the goodness and love of God. Even some who might profess belief in a God of perfect goodness harbor doubts God really loves them. Few questions are larger or more existentially central than *what God is like*. This book has been as much about *who God is* as about God's *existence*. The question of *whether* God exists is obviously an important one. And it's a question to which much of our professional work has been dedicated. But it is just as important, if not more, to know *what* God is like.

Unlike most other arguments for God's existence, the moral argument is particularly effective at speaking to both the mind and heart, and giving evidence not just that God exists but that he is good and loving, indeed perfectly so. And if that's who God is, as we've argued we have good evidence to suggest, it is splendid news indeed. Perhaps the best of all possible news!

We appreciate the time you took to read this book. We believe strongly in its message, and we hope it inspires readers to think more deeply about these important topics. If this was your introduction to the moral argument, we hope this book helped capture your imagination, spark your curiosity, and whet your appetite for more—and that it is just the first step of a long and fruitful journey of exploration to come.

We have provided an argument in these pages that we think worthy of your most serious and sober consideration. The morals of the story are nothing less than a message of hope and offer of salvation from the God of resplendent grace and goodness and glory.

None of this was intended purely as an intellectual game. Rather, we wanted to come alongside and help you ponder morality and its implications, to think about thinking, and glean insight into ultimate reality. As Christians we wish to encourage you, in all earnestness, to take this occasion to pursue the truth and, finding it, to abandon yourself to it, with all of your being.

The overtures of the God of all goodness constitute good news indeed. A gift of inestimable value awaits your acceptance.

## TALK BACK

1. What lingering questions do you have? Where might you look for answers or more information?

2. We have talked about the gospel throughout this book as good news. How is it good news for you?

3. What barriers do you personally have in receiving this message? How might you proceed in thinking about it some more?

# ADDITIONAL RESOURCES

MORALAPOLOGETICS.COM IS OUR ONLINE SITE where you can glean all sorts of additional resources relevant to the moral argument. As it continues to expand, we will be including more material both from the history of moral apologetics and on issues related to the overlap of moral apologetics and spiritual formation. We also hope to forge fresh connections between moral apologetics and explicit biblical teaching. Readers are encouraged to avail themselves of its various materials. The site features work by philosophers, theologians, Bible scholars, historians, and experts in literature. There's something for everyone (except vampires).

# GENERAL INDEX

virtue ethics. *See* virtue
   theory
virtue theory, 89, 126-28, 135
Volf, Miroslav, 24-25
Wallace, David Foster, 49
Walls, Jerry L.
   in book panel discussion
      with author, 233-34
   *God and Cosmos,* 38, 88,
      134, 152, 167
   *Good God,* 38, 88, 101, 148,
      233
   *Heaven,* 87-88

on naturalism, 87-88,
   152-53
prior obligations
   objection, 148-49
trinitarian love, 98
work of, 87
Ward, Keith, 209
weak evolutionary ethics, 165
Webb, Clement, 32
Welcker, Friedrich, 41
Welty, Eudora, 138
Wesley, John, 193
Whitehead, Alfred North, 62

Wielenberg, Erik, 77, 183-84,
   186
Wilberforce, William, 204
Williams, Rowan, 78
wisdom literature, in
   scripture, 172-73
Wittgenstein, Ludwig, 77
Wood, David, 184-87
worldview differences,
   significance of, 27
"Worn Path, A" (Welty), 138
Zagzebski, Linda, 82-83

# SCRIPTURE INDEX

# Finding the Textbook You Need

The IVP Academic Textbook Selector
is an online tool for instantly finding the IVP books
suitable for over 250 courses across 24 disciplines.

**ivpacademic.com**